'Juliet Mitchell's astonishingly rich contributions to psychoanalysis and its social meanings, from *Psychoanalysis and Feminism* onward, culminate in *Fratriarchy* with a stunningly new conception of siblingship and what she tellingly calls "the Law of the Mother." This is a great and convincing work, taking us through psychoanalytic theory, and literature—finding its most eloquent enactments in Shakespeare. A major book by one of the leading thinkers of our time'.

**Peter Brooks**, Sterling Emeritus Professor of
Comparative Literature, Yale University, USA

'In her riveting new book, *Fratriachy: The Sibling Trauma and the Law of the Mother*, Juliet Mitchell makes a persuasive case for a psychoanalytic examination of sibling relations. Omitted from psychoanalytic discourse – until now – is what Mitchell characterises as "The Law of the Mother": the force that tempers a child's homicidal impulses against their perceived usurper. In casting a light on horizontal relations and exploring their interactions with vertical control, Mitchell provides a fantastically entertaining and important feminist analysis of the functions of patriarchy and fraternity in a social world'.

**Inbali Iserles**, award-winning author of children's
books and fellow of the Royal Literary Fund (2020–
2022), University of Cambridge, UK

'The contention of the existence of a horizontal axis along which siblings interact is the starting point of *Fratriarchy*. With her characteristic theoretical consistence and exquisite clinical sensitivity Juliet Mitchell proposes that the intersection of this horizontal axis with the hierarchical vertical patriarchal axis set the coordinates needed for an understanding of the universality of the prohibitions of incest and murder. The consequences of these prohibitions are different when operating on the horizontal and the vertical axes as they correspond to different Law-givers and different recipients. Mitchell's Law of the Mother rules during the pre- social infancy prohibiting incest and murder between siblings along the horizontal axis. It is the necessary complement of the Law of the Father -to use the Lacanian translation of Freud's formulation- that prohibits incest and murder in the vertical axis of filiation'.

**Max Hernandez Camarero**, former Vice-President of
the International Psychoanalytical Association and
Founding Member of the Peruvian Psychoanalytic
Society. He has been honoured with the Mary
Sigourney Award

'In the face of war, and gender, racial, and colonial oppression, it is crucial to define new frameworks of analysis that have the potential to end violence. Mitchell's fascinating account of the Law of the Mother, sibling trauma, and the fratriarchy offers a route to deliverance articulated through new narratives about the self and the others, and a call to sisterhood'.

**Laura López Paniagua**, Bard College Berlin

'In Juliet Mitchell's *Fratriarchy* the author drives her argument with free-wheeling and exhilarating force, into the prevailing foundations of psychoanalytic thinking—the Law of the father, the paternal function of the Oedipus, and its antecedent, the earliest relationship with the mother, "good enough" or not. What is left out, she asserts, is the separation and loss of infancy specifically through the replacement of the toddler by the baby he/she is no longer. This trauma is a product of "The Law of the Mother," and its consequences are death of the toddler, who dare not risk, by fulfilling the wish to murder the baby, his or her own death by maternal abandonment. Mitchell puts this dilemma powerfully, starting with the psychoanalytic writing of Winnicott and Klein, the British pillars of early infantile experience. Their early cases all start with the trauma of the birth of the sibling, but their theoretical focus backs away from this trauma, looking for antecedents in the first months of life. Juliet Mitchell says look again, at the trauma which is equal for boys and girls, and which marks the entry into all the relationships outside the family, those relations which will eventually find expression in love and war. Confusions of love, sex and gender, the ubiquity of war, are the discontents we live with and Juliet Mitchell has much to say to illuminate the world in which we find ourselves. And she offers more than she explores in relation to adolescence. It is a riveting read'.

**Sara Flanders**, British Psychoanalytic Society, UK

'Juliet Mitchell is a field-defining thinker. In the long awaited *Fratriarchy*, Mitchell brings her world-renowned work as a feminist psychoanalytical and political scholar together with her personal observations on child development and sibling relations as a practitioner over the past twenty-five years. Central to Mitchell's distinctive argument is the misdiagnosis of 'sibling trauma' and the far-reaching social and political consequences. Theoretically radical as well as autobiographical, this is an extraordinary book and a 'must read' for all those with a curiosity for understanding human society through familial dynamics'.

**Jude Browne**, The Jessica and Peter Frankopan
Director of the University of Cambridge Centre for
Gender Studies

'In this engaging new book which is very much a continuation of her earlier work, Mitchell elaborates the Law of the Mother: the danger of murder or incest on the part of the usurped toddler when the new sibling is born, is mediated by the mother. Throughout Mitchell's writing there has been a deft weaving of sex, violence and death. Mitchell has never been fearful to challenge psychoanalytic shibboleths. This is exemplified many times in her new book. For example she considers how the usurped sibling's brush with murderousness and death challenges the Freudian assertion that death is unrepresentable and can only be known through the idea of castration. In a characteristic intellectually and clinically informed discourse, she cites Pontalis' challenge to this Freudian notion that death is unrepresentable through a thesis that Freud himself knew death only too well with his child-hood losses, his half-brother aged eighteen months and through his own somatic preoccupation with his sick and ailing body: his own dying. This example highlights the call to read and engage with the continuing work of one of contemporary psychoanalysis's most thoughtful and challenging of writers'.

**Rosemary Davies**, Institute of Psychoanalysis, UK

# Fratriarchy

In *Fratriarchy*, Juliet Mitchell expands her ground-breaking theories on the sibling trauma and the Law of the Mother. Writing as a psychoanalytic practitioner, she shows what happens from the ground up when we use feminist questions to probe the psycho-social world and its lateral relations.

In this pivotal text, Mitchell argues that the mother's prohibition of her toddler attacking a new or expected sibling is a rite of passage from infancy to childhood: this is a foundational force structuring our later lateral relationships and social practices. Throughout the volume, Mitchell chooses the term 'Fratriarchy' to show that, as well as the up-down axis of fathers and sons, there is also the side-to-side interaction of sisters and brothers and their social heirs. Making use both critically and affirmatively of Freud, Klein, Winnicott, Bion, Pontalis and others, *Fratriarchy* indicates how the collective social world matches the individual family world examined by established psychoanalysis. Decades on from Mitchell's work on psychoanalysis and feminism which argued that feminism needed psychoanalysis to understand the position of women, *Fratriarchy* now asks psychoanalysis to take on board the developing practices and theories of global feminism.

This volume will be essential reading for analysts, psychotherapists, psychologists and anyone who wants to re-think the ubiquity of unconscious processes. It will also interest students and teachers of social theory, psychoanalysis, group analysis, gender studies and feminism.

**Juliet Mitchell** FBA is a psychoanalyst, socialist feminist, emeritus professor and author.

# Fratriarchy

## The Sibling Trauma and the Law of the Mother

Juliet Mitchell

Routledge
Taylor & Francis Group

LONDON AND NEW YORK

Cover image credit: Vertical-Horizontal Composition (1916), Sophie Taeuber-Arp

First published 2023
by Routledge
4 Park Square, Milton Park, Abingdon, Oxon OX14 4RN

and by Routledge
605 Third Avenue, New York, NY 10158

*Routledge is an imprint of the Taylor & Francis Group, an informa business*

© 2023 Juliet Mitchell

The right of Juliet Mitchell to be identified as author of this work has been asserted in accordance with sections 77 and 78 of the Copyright, Designs and Patents Act 1988.

*British Library Cataloguing-in-Publication Data*
A catalogue record for this book is available from the British Library

*Library of Congress Cataloging-in-Publication Data*
Names: Mitchell, Juliet, 1940– author.
Title: Fratriarchy : the sibling trauma and the law of the mother / Juliet Mitchell.
Description: 1 Edition. | New York, NY : Routledge, 2023. | Includes bibliographical references and index.
Identifiers: LCCN 2022037696 (print) | LCCN 2022037697 (ebook) | ISBN 9781032364407 (paperback) | ISBN 9781032388533 (hardback) | ISBN 9781003347125 (ebook)
Subjects: LCSH: Siblings—Psychological aspects. | Psychoanalysis and feminism. | Mothers—Psychology.
Classification: LCC BF723.S43 M56 2023 (print) | LCC BF723.S43 (ebook) | DDC 155.44/3—dc23/eng/20221017
LC record available at https://lccn.loc.gov/2022037696
LC ebook record available at https://lccn.loc.gov/2022037697

ISBN: 978-1-032-38853-3 (hbk)
ISBN: 978-1-032-36440-7 (pbk)
ISBN: 978-1-003-34712-5 (ebk)

DOI: 10.4324/9781003347125

Typeset in Times New Roman
by codeMantra

For Romy who helped me so much — with all my love.

# Contents

# Preface

Two-year-old girls as well as boys have tantrums; both are reacting to the arrival or prospect of a sibling; the responses of both are subject to the mother's law. How do girls come to be unviolent and to receive violence as a definition of their womanhood and boys to perpetrate it as a defining descriptor of their manhood? This is just one of the questions, certainly a major one, about our social world. An 'answer' does not have to do primarily with the usual suspects, children and their parents (patriarchy) but, instead, with sisters and brothers (fratriarchy).

Some fifty years ago, I asked this question of world-wide and world-long 'sexual difference' as a primal social construct under patriarchy. *Psychoanalysis and Feminism* (1974) turned out to be the culmination of what I had found to be missing in my 'Women: the Longest Revolution' (1966).[1] That essay had hit the ground running, as the same year had set a marker for second-wave feminism with the foundation of NOW (the National Organization of Women) in New York. I was working in both the UK and the USA and was struck, indeed staggered, by American feminists' pillorying of Freud and psychoanalysis.

In the mid to late sixties, psychoanalysis did not feature in the emergent women's movement in England. But in the US, a popular calendar presented a dart's board of Freud's head with a dart through his eye; how vaginal frigidity had been made to trounce clitoral sexuality was a focus of the assault on psychoanalytic theories of sexuality. *De rigueur*, the forthcoming bigselling books had a chapter blaming psychoanalysis for patriarchy.[2] Back home I went to the library to read a few essays by Freud and read twenty-three volumes, his collected works. The effect was that after a few try-outs[3] *Psychoanalysis and Feminism* was published, and at the same time I started

---

1 'Women: The Longest Revolution', *New Left Review*, 41 (Nov/Dec 1966). Widely reproduced as a booklet and translated into twenty languages.
2 Part 2: 'Feminism and Freud' *Psychoanalysis and Feminism* 1974.
3 'Shrew' 1969, *Modern Occasions* 1971 and 1972, *Woman's Estate* 1971–72.

to train as a psychoanalyst. *Fratriarchy: The Sibling Trauma and the Law of the Mother* is the result of that training and that clinical practice. Nearly fifty years later, this book on death and fratriarchy is the sequel to that earlier analysis of sexuality and patriarchy.

In fact, this is both a sequel to the argument – moving from patriarchy to fratriarchy – and a reversal of the method – from that of an academic, a university lecturer, to that of a practitioner, a psychoanalyst. Author and audience are reversed. *Psychoanalysis and Feminism* hoped to convince feminists of the need to use psychoanalysis to examine the unique place where an oppressive *patriarchal* division of the sexes is embedded in all our unconscious processes. Here, *Fratriarchy* hopes to convince psychoanalysts of feminism's understanding of the universal taboo against the desired *murder* of a sibling, which is both an unconscious determinant and an aspect of a primal process of socialization, underlying the *fratriarchal* dimension of the oppression of women.

The child has to take on board the prohibitions of incest and murder as these universally subtend the psyche of sociality. The prohibitions have different effects on the vertical (parental) and horizontal (sibling) axes.

# Introduction

## What This Book Is About

This book is about the long-term effects of what happens between siblings and those that follow on from them socially. My perspective is that of a psychoanalytic practitioner on surveying the yawning gap in our understanding of the psyche of the social world. My argument is that psychoanalytical thinking needs to reflect anew on theses and observations from the social political world – in particular, that of the world-wide position of women as understood by feminism. Bringing in the pre-Oedipal and the mother, first-wave feminism between the wars transformed psychoanalysis. In reverse direction, current feminism with its demand to 'politicize the personal world' has greatly benefitted from psychoanalytic understanding of private experience. However, although it has gained important new insights and foci, contemporary psychoanalysis is largely still awaiting its full transformation by second, third wave and now global feminism – this study is a modest proposal arising from the twenty-five years during which I have been working on siblings and their social heirs.

The 'terrible twos' of infancy have been underestimated – the notorious tantrums at this age are a trauma because the toddler is no longer allowed to be 'itself': the one and only baby of the family. The mother prohibits both its hating and loving reactions to the new baby. If there is no baby, then the violent response is to the thought of one, at the expected time. At some point in its third year the toddler survives this trauma – and so do the parents! This recovery probably facilitates our failure to take what has happened seriously. The trauma is turned into a simple rite of passage from infancy to childhood. However, the whole constellation of sibling trauma and the prohibitions of the mother which operate between her children impacts in a foundational manner on later life.

At their core, families consist of various permutations of parents and children. In their childhood, the children change from pre-social babies and infants to becoming socialized children and future adolescents and adults. However, these children, as well as being daughters and sons in a

DOI: 10.4324/9781003347125-1

hierarchical 'vertical' family structure, are also siblings, sisters and brothers interacting laterally among themselves on a horizontal social axis.[1] What proceeds concerns these siblings at the point where they both join in the existent psycho-social life and originate their own. But neither the trauma nor the threats with which the mother prohibits the reactions to it ever quite vanish. Instead, in updated form they emerge, in particular, in later life-changing or traumatic circumstances such as marriage or war.

My concern with the psycho-social or 'social unconscious' comes as much from my feminism as from my psychoanalytic practice. As feminists, my generation, in recognizing women's collective oppression, demanded that the world as we put it 'politicize the personal' – that private life and the private family be opened up to public and political scrutiny and struggle. Any other group that also recognizes its oppression has a stake here. Much of both the practice of oppressing and the experience of being oppressed can be deeply unconscious. In its unique task of making what is unconscious become conscious, psychoanalysis can greatly aid how we think about that struggle. Why then does it avoid the crucial sibling dimension of the social? The question is asked of psychoanalysis but trying to remedy the neglect that is so prominent within its bounds concerns any taker.

Unconscious and conscious processes are simply different ways of thinking. When describing an unconscious way of thinking as a system, Freud called it a 'primary process' as distinct from the 'secondary process' of consciousness. When we dream, we are thinking unconsciously, associating one image with another, one wish with another. We condense several of these into the same place or displace them from one to another without a sense of time or place. Unconscious thinking works by symbolization, association, condensation and displacement, avoids unpleasure while constantly seeking pleasure, however compromised. Conscious thinking, on the other hand, works linguistically, with logic, reasoning and in recognition of reality. This is the case the world over: *as modes of thinking*, unconscious and conscious are everywhere the same. This is a central and critical contention throughout the book. The mother has a key role in establishing a consciousness of reality along with a simultaneous establishment in her child of unconscious processes in dealing with her absolute prohibitions of sibling murder and incest – prohibitions that set up the social – her contribution to the psycho-social aspect of the world's law – the Law of the Mother.

Planned some years ago, this book's original title was *The Sibling Trauma and The Law of the Mother*, which continues throughout as a unifying theme. We need a new theory to address the presence of clinical and permanent social material latent in scattered psychoanalytical work; this entails pertinent

---

1   Andrew Solomon, one of my doctoral students, used the vertical/horizontal distinction that I was deploying, to great effect in his *Far From the Tree*.

points being reiterated in different and new ways in the various contexts. I start with the suggestion of a *sibling trauma*, which takes place when we are toddlers and when the first sister or brother may, or may not, come along. At this age, last or only children or those whose sibling arrives before or after toddlerdom, experience the very same trauma. Younger children will be confused; older, only or last children may be more controlled. The trauma has happened when it was actually a toddler and therefore it emerges in the psychic toddler still present in every child. The toddler's personage as baby has been bestowed on another. Where previously babyhood was the highly significant being and status of the toddler, now the actual new or expected arrival is claimed by everyone as the one-and-only baby.

Traditionally weaning occurred at around the eighteenth month of the child's life and parents would have been engaged with negative or positive thoughts about a further child. Clinical evidence suggests that the toddler becomes cognizant of this possibility and feels threatened. All our lives, alone or together as a group or a larger mass, crowd or 'mob', we can all feel and act like these toddlers with their trauma, their delights and their difficulties, their charm and their tantrums. Above all in a crisis we ask again, as individuals in a group: '*who am I?*'.

As daughters and sons, children grow up and eventually, in some way or other as their needs become attenuated, partially or entirely leave their family of origin. To the contrary, siblings very early on extend their relationships to social versions of biological sisters and brothers. They open up laterally into 'childhood' with girlhood and boyhood, sisterhoods and brotherhoods. These are friends and enemies and a host of in-between lateral relationships. Variations of these social relationships grow stronger not weaker with age and whether good or bad, and whether in sisterhoods or brotherhoods, are in some way available lifelong.

If we re-position siblings where they belong on the horizontal axis, their social contribution favours the construction of positive communities as much as the pathologies commonly associated with psychotic behaviour in social groups. The peer group which they start to form at around three years old and partially leave the family to the new baby (even if it does not arrive) is a medley of disparate siblings, each with their own particular individual sibling trauma recently behind them; this is generic to all of them. Each comes together as a new group of older siblings, who become both friends and enemies. And it works in reverse – the social takes its characteristics not, as is usually argued, from the massification of people, but from the good and the bad of the toddler.

It is only and always as children that we have the original hard task of becoming social human beings. It is for this reason that childhood and the child, who is always a part of ourselves, is the focus of psychoanalytic practice and theory. We are conceived and born both into biological families and into a penumbra of social relations which near and far constitute 'society'.

Studies of the family and of society are legion, but what we need to elicit is the same child who is always, differently, in both. As we investigate the social the family has also to be in the back of our minds.

Becoming members of human society is initially achieved through the interaction of siblings yet the fundamental rules come from parents in the family. Most of the world today operates upon patriarchal and patrilineal vertical family lines through what has been called the 'Law of the Father'.[2] When he is four or five years old this Law is instilled in the father's son and in his daughter in so far as she is the same as her brother. This is the world-renowned but much contested 'Oedipus complex'. Incest with the mother is universally prohibited by the patriarch who threatens his son with castration – which although in the main symbolic may seem potentially actual to a small child. Instead, or rather as well as, I argue in this book that prior to this stage, the mother insists on the same prohibitions, but with different effects – she insists that there must be no incest or murder *between* her children, that is between the siblings. On the social, horizontal axis, this prohibition between siblings applies equally to sisters and to brothers as they reach two to three years old – and it is this prohibition that I claim as the *Law of the Mother*.

As far as we know, and however diversely, all societies regard some excesses of both killing and sexuality as inherently asocial. Generically we call these excesses 'murder' and 'incest'. Their *prohibition* becomes the essential, always demanded, barrier between what humans can and cannot do. But what I am proposing here is that the same prohibitions, the same Laws, have different Law-givers – mother or father – and different recipients in importantly different relationships – siblings or offspring. The toddler's wish to eradicate the new baby and the Oedipal child's desire for a sexual relation with the mother would seem to have nothing in common. Yet both desires are totally prohibited. The identical nature of the law against murder and incest, the one uttered by the mother and the other by the father, make the prohibitions equally *foundational* of the psycho-social in both the family and society. Thus, it is because they are foundational that the illicit desires together with their forbiddance will appear repeated beneath future trauma of any sort and major transitions (such as puberty) in human life.

The physical and psychological onset of reproductive potential at puberty is recognized as necessitating a repetition and renewal of the Oedipal prohibition of incest with the mother. As this prohibition is achieved, adolescents will envisage the possibility of their own future parenting. Yet sisters and brothers must update their own lateral experience into whom they may or may not be in love with and marry, and whom they may or may not hate and kill. What happens to the equally foundational Law of the Mother which is

2   Jacques Lacan.

missing from the record? This failure to recognize her Law and its effects means that the contribution of social, lateral relations to the triumphs and maladies of adolescence is dangerously absent. For example, the prevalence of eating disorders should recall the food faddism of toddlers; the murderousness of the earlier desires is present in the knife crimes of later gang-warfare; the transformation of the death-experience of the sibling trauma is present in the psychosomatic illnesses, the worrying self-harm and in the endemic suicidality of the teenager. At puberty there is a crucial repetition of both the sibling trauma and the implications of the 'Law of the Mother', although this time around there is also a future gender division of marriage (girls) and fighting (boys).

Although both sets of prohibitions against murder and incest – the vertical set and the horizontal one – are mostly internalized so that they feel natural and instinctive, the pre-social desires to offend persist: the Laws remain in place through an always present threatened punishment. The father symbolically threatens his son with castration which represents a symbolic 'death' in the child's mind. The mother says she will desert her utterly dependent toddler if it does not obey, and this abandonment would be a further experience of 'death', such as it encountered in the sibling trauma when the new sibling became the one and only baby which the sibling had believed itself to be. Symbolizing, or representing, death and surviving an experience of death are psychically different – one you survive, the other you avoid. The toddler more-or-less survives.

The prohibitions fall on the recipients at developmentally different times in their childhood. The Law of the Mother which I am proposing is established when the infant's psychic stage is described by psychoanalysts as 'narcissistic-psychotic', indicating that it considers there is mainly itself in the world and its grasp of reality is at best fluid. The infant is toddling rather than walking, and usually it is speaking *but is as yet without metaphor*. These requirements of walking and an awareness of metaphoric language have been fulfilled at the stage of the Oedipus complex and the inauguration of the Father's Law. But both stages underlie social life.

The original sibling trauma has no precedent. This makes it what is called an 'actual' trauma. This is a technical term to describe an occurrence of great significance in the toddler's history; a concept with which as we will see, we can break new ground. However, the sibling trauma becomes a precedent itself when the mother prevents the toddler's wish both to assimilate the new sibling (prospective incest), and to eliminate it (attempted murder). The mother has all along been introducing reality to her child but now her prohibitions against incest and murder constitute an absolute 'law'. In response, the child develops defences such as denial, dissociation, foreclosure, projection, or splitting into the only good or the only bad. Subsequently, it is these defences which will be socialized or become pathological. The social and the pathological are on a continuum.

The toddler's world is one where, following the new sibling's birth, the task is to develop an understanding of self and other – an uneven process of identifications, mirroring, feeling empty and alternatively full of itself, mixing fantasy and actuality. The pre-social child forms a social group, and both leaves the family and yet stays within it, where its pre-Oedipal individual self as son or daughter heads straight for the Oedipus complex in the forlorn hope of monopolizing the mother. The mother as always urges reality wherever she is placed, and on the horizontal axis she oversees the transformation of the sibling trauma and of her own threat to desert if her prohibitions are not obeyed. The trauma of annihilation becomes *a rite of passage* in which we witness the success – or otherwise – of the whole extraordinarily difficult transition from pre-social infancy to social childhood.

What holds it all together, actually for the child and intellectually for us? A crucial thread runs throughout the investigations recounted in this book. Where the father's Law, expressed through the threat of symbolically castrating the boy for his desire for maternal incest, opens the door to the presence of *Symbolization* at large, I propose that the Law of the Mother offers *Narrative* to the world – stories about the self and others. She embeds this in a wide network of narrators: grandparents, for example, will tell grandchildren how their parents were like or unlike them, and vertical history is 'lateralized' as in the imagination of the toddler, its parents turn into the children they once were. The history of 'before' becomes the 'present' and the 'future'. The mother's narrative helps her toddler to see that its trauma is like that of other people or other animals – the toddler itself is like these others. *They have all survived.* The toddler is urgently set on grasping its newly gained awareness of metaphor and consumes and contributes to the mother's stories. A central question arises: does the story's 'all's well that ends well' help to contain the experience of death in the sibling trauma? Small babies like rhythm repeated and repetitious patterns feature from earliest infancy, but the toddler becoming a social child wants a story, usually the same story, read or told to it over and over again as though its life depended on it. Perhaps because, in a sense, it does; here there is a 'compulsion to repeat' and the story helps to manage a trauma.

The individual and the social are one and the same person – yet in psychoanalysis our entire focus is the individual in the family. The individual is always a social person in lateral relations ranging from wives and husbands, enemies and friends and sisters and brothers acting on a horizontal axis which is always present. It is this socio-individual who is untheorized. Group Analysis works with small, medium or large therapeutic cohorts and usefully sees the sibling basis of the lateral participants in its practice and hence includes it in its theories. However, these group-analytical sisters and brothers are a feature of the group practice rather than uniquely significant actors. It thus misses the implication of the fact that the individual sibling is the first subjectively experienced lateral relationship, and the first sibling that 'replaces' the older one produces a general 'generic' response with permanent although variously expressed effects.

By focussing on siblings as they move into the place where they belong, my aim is to provide the context in which we can further understand the construction of the social and of death, of bisexuality, of gender and gender inequity, of the implications of both marriage and the world-long ubiquity of war which found society. Freud's highly controversial concept of a 'death drive' takes on a new significance with the horizontal axis. Furthermore, we can consider how the fratriarchal, structural division between sisters and brothers impacts on the position of women and feminism. This is the horizontal axis in contradistinction to the vertical axis – both are crucial, but the horizontal has been strikingly neglected.

Three theorists – Donald Winnicott, Wilfred Bion and J.-B. Pontalis – can be used to fill this gap. In this order, they offer an understanding of the early narcissistic psyche, the distinction of social from individual unconscious–conscious processes and the centrality of death in fraternities – all three are indispensable for my perspective on the social world. Effectively all Winnicott's child case references highlight the sibling trauma, although his thinking relegates it to insignificance; Bion developed and then abandoned his major contribution to establishing that the psyche of the social was utterly distinct from that of the family; Pontalis claimed that death was more crucial than sexuality for psychoanalytic theory and went on to dissect the nightmare of fratriarchy. I found that using these thinkers on these topics was a two-way process – what do they contribute to a picture of the horizontal and what does introducing siblings and the mother's law contribute to their work?

Donald Winnicott's clinical work abounds with the central importance of the sibling trauma, but his approach is restricted to the interaction of mothers and babies. His important notions of transitional and potential space suggest the 'othering' of the mother which opens up the world of other people – this engages in sensitive and illuminating ways with the empirical situation of mothers and babies, but omits that of the all-present siblings who, as he repeatedly insists in his practice, trigger the child's psychological breakdown. What he writes of the psychotic-narcissistic stance of the baby, still active in the adult patient, and the concepts he develop from this apply equally to the toddler. If we highlight Winnicott's own clinical practice with its omnipresent sibling trauma then we can shift his uniquely developmental perspective to one that is also structural. His developmental perspective refers to a particular moment or period of time whereas the sibling trauma is foundational at all times. Structure and development are always mixed together experientially but need to be conceptually separated if we are to appreciate the social as well as the family provenance of the psycho-social.

I was initially drawn to Bion's work for this study because of his insistence on a complete distinction between the family and social group. The theory he expounds in *Experiences in Groups* was developed above all from assemblages of psychically invalided soldiers who had to be returned to fight in World War II. His work offers not just a unique analysis of his practice but also of his attempt to provide myths thought of as 'models' as a distinctive way of theorizing psychoanalysis – the myths he suggested were not the incestuous Oedipus but the suicidal Sphinx and the Tower of Babel. From within his account, these can be made to find an interesting place for the omitted sibling. Thus, Bion's unique portrait of the social can be used to show how the empty world is filled for social siblings and in turn inserting siblings enriches and further explains the aspects of Bion's account.

Unsurprisingly, the mother is more insistent on prohibiting the potential murder of her new baby than forbidding incest with it. Murder is death. Jean-Bertrand Pontalis, famous for his indispensable co-authored *The Language of Psychoanalysis*,[3] argued that death and the 'death drive' were as, if not more, important for psychoanalytic enquiry than sexuality: 'I even believe', he wrote in the 1970s, 'that [the theme of sexuality] was largely accorded a more prominent role in order to conceal [the theme of death]'.[4] We have a dense chapter, 'On Death-work', in his book *Frontiers of Analysis* on how Freud had found ways around the subject of death until the formulation of the highly controversial concept of a 'death drive'; then, much later, Pontalis moved to an agonizing self-analysis of his relationship with his – by then dead – older brother and of fratriarchy – 'frère-ocity' – as an abomination – with one or two redeeming features!

The topics which I have elicited from these three very different famous authors – the sibling trauma, the distinctive psycho-social psyche, death and fratriarchy – intermesh with each other; this produces a unity from what would otherwise be their disparity. The unity helps fill the absence I am addressing. This is augmented by the other well-established psychoanalytic authors with whom I engage. These too are deployed in a double way. What does their work offer to an understanding of the horizontal axis? Conversely, what do their own accounts gain from having added to them the socializing position of siblings? The absence of the *social unconscious*

---

3   J. Laplanche and J.-B. Pontalis, *The Language of Psycho-Analysis*, London: Hogarth Press, 1973. I owe a great deal to warm exchanges with Jean Laplanche but J.-B. Pontalis whom I met publicly but did not know personally has ended up receiving my appreciation for his 'pairing' relationship with Freud (Chapter 5). In fact, their book's depth of knowledge makes this true for either and both of them. I always consult them. Their knowledge of Freud is superb. However, because I am going against their own highly independent Freud–Lacanian approach what I write is my understanding as a practising psychoanalyst above all indebted to Freud but trained as an 'Independent' in the mixed perspectives (Anna Freud, Melanie Klein, Independent British) of the British Psychoanalytical Society.

4   J-B Pontalis, *Frontiers in Psychoanalysis. Between the Dream and Psychic Pain*. London: Hogarth Press, 1981, p. 184.

in the psychoanalytic discipline feels almost an absurdity. That this is the situation, however, is confirmed from two directions. We find it is potentially present in the work of these very representative and well-known authors and simultaneously if we add siblings to their theses, then their work is enhanced.

In the final section I argue that the concept of 'gender' should be used exclusively for the horizontal axis. Its crucial unconscious determinants can only be understood when they are juxtaposed with the standard psychoanalytical concept of vertical 'sexual difference'. Sexual difference between girls and boys comes about when the girl is no longer psychically a boy and instead has her own female Oedipus complex. Horizontally, gender is something else altogether. For Gender, psychoanalysis must take its cue from the feminist development of the concept in the 1970s. Gender is a social sexual differentiation from biological sex, from female/male; it can be same sex or other sex. Originally it was consciously borrowed by UK feminism from a branch of American psychoanalysis! My own use differs, emphasizing that it is based on a foundational postulate of 'psychic bisexuality'. Bisexuality is commonly taken as choosing a partner of either sex. However, if that occurs, it is only secondary. Bisexuality is subjective – the presence of the other psychological sex in all of us. It underlies transgender and other intersex possibilities. It is not Gender but the aforementioned 'sexual difference' that is commonly referred to in psychoanalytic thinking. The concept is famously deployed in Freud's notorious lecture 'Femininity' (1932/33). As I show, the lecture can be read to account for what feminism has specified as the 'oppression' of women.

In puberty the teenager has to negotiate in new conditions what she or he can make of their desire for sex and death in the face of what is still allowed by the original law of the mother prohibiting incest and murder between them. I briefly examine this before concluding with a focus on the sister. A brief reference to Shakespeare's portrait of Isabella, the *sister* in *Measure for Measure*, joins the equally brief evocation of subjective 'bisexuality' in *Twelfth Night*, and this book comes to a conclusion, which is also a beginning, with the under-explored biological sister as founding the institution of sisterhood in conjunction and disunity with her social sisters.[5]

## Why Psychoanalysis?

This book makes use of a psychoanalytic perspective for the interested general reader. A large element of our personal and social interaction is achieved unconsciously – and unconscious processes are the one and only

---

5 This book is forthcoming as *Siblings and Sisters in some plays of Shakespeare*. Many thanks to Leverhulme for their patience with this long overdue book.

subject-matter and practical task of psychoanalytic work. Introducing the fact of a horizontal axis has forced the meeting point of the unconscious and consciousness into the foreground. Thinking about being just two years old engenders an easy and attractive flow between these two different ways of thinking – consciousness for grasping reality and unconscious processes for hiding effectively one's forbidden desires. Insisting on reality as the mother incessantly does is not a part of the Law of the Mother – that is reserved for her absolute prohibition of murder and incest.

As well as the focus in Part 2 on Winnicott, Bion and Pontalis, I make use of major psychoanalytic classics which form the continuing basis for contemporary work, and which provide easily available theories as well as clinical case-histories. Within the field, Freud himself is a *lingua franca* and thus examinable and usable. Other practitioners have been selected insofar as I felt that they address priorities in mapping the territory of the social from a psychological perspective. Such priorities include the theme of death, the construction of the social world, narcissistic–psychotic modes of operating in this world, psychological defences and subjective bisexuality. Present-day contemporary and substantial, much-discussed clinical work both emanate from and often leads to these earlier, original discoveries. By re-engaging with these past authoritative endeavours, psychoanalysis as a tried and tested 'knowledge' can be re-considered and re-used differently, and in such a way as to save the past from the enormous condescension of posterity, as the historian Edward Thompson has put it.

The unconscious, uncensored desiring of the infant and small child, although apparently tamed and left behind, persists most obviously in an untrammelled form in the dreaming and psychologically disturbed symptomatology of the adult. We can describe the thinking process we bring with us at birth as mixed unconscious–conscious – neither the one nor the other is organized into separable distinct modes of thinking. The distinction between the two modes comes about both gradually and abruptly – gradually a 'pre-conscious' type of thinking develops into a conscious mode with the increasing acquisition of reality. But the shift from a descriptively unconscious condition to an actively dynamic one is a more abrupt transition. It results from what has to be done psychically to accommodate the prohibitions against incest and murder so that they become persistent but '*unknown*' parts of our being – in their 'feel' they are not unlike innate instincts. Classically (and indubitably), this is achieved with the *repression* of the incestuous Oedipal desire for the mother – it becomes as though the wish had never been experienced. Freud described this 'repression' in these terms:

> We have learnt from psychoanalysis that the essence of the process of repression lies, not in putting an end to, in annihilating, the idea which represents a drive but in preventing it becoming conscious ... when it is

unconscious it can produce effects, even including some which finally reach consciousness.[6]

However other dynamically unconscious ways of forgetting pre-exist the repression of Oedipal desire. Thus, as well as forgetting, we usefully 'displace' and 'sublimate'. But also both normatively and pathologically we can 'split', 'deny', 'project', 'foreclose' and 'dissociate'. We then socialize these pre-conscious or descriptively unconscious processes and it becomes necessary to discover if they become dynamically unconscious on a horizontal axis – bound up with an utter refusal to be aware of one's illicit desires. What happens first to the sibling trauma, and then to the prohibition of the toddler's desire to murder and have incestual relations with its new sibling? The toddler's defences – such as its constant 'no' which can more than equal its mother's reiterations – are in fact weaker than Oedipal repression.

Although we can remember its effects, it seems we do not recall the experience of being annihilated in the original sibling trauma itself. Instead, it can return as the same experience in comparably traumatic moments. To try to understand how this works psychically I have attempted to develop an under-used notion of 'primary repression', which is not only quite distinct from secondary repression but also different from the toddler's other modes of defence. This matters because it opens the door to understanding trauma as a social experience – as in, for instance, war.

In the unconscious primary process, in general, a free psychic energy attaches itself wherever it wants in a wild and wanton way; it is indifferent to reality. Its driven avoidance of unpleasure means that pleasure entails a satisfaction that is identical to the condition or object that provides it – a chocolate *is* the pleasure rather than its cause. Defences against the forbidden desires are established in the unconscious when the child enters for itself the society of which it has always been a part and accepts its demands. In this extraordinarily brief and condensed period of childhood, from roughly two until about five years old, the social and the civilized must become established within us as an unconscious process but also as a conscious one. It is not surprising that this can go wrong. This is why psychoanalysis is about the small child who persists within us all our life.

The psychoanalytic claim is that this past can be transferred into the petri dish of a present-day clinical setting: here patients (or 'analysands') live out key thoughts and feelings about their world and the parents on whom in their

---

6  S. Freud, 'The Unconscious' (1915), *The Standard Edition of the Complete Psychological Works of Freud, Vol. XIV*, trans. James Strachey, London: Hogarth Press, 1957, p. 166. (References to the Standard Edition will hereafter be given as *SE* with volume number.) Winnicott describes a psychic obliteration in his notion of 'A Fear of Breakdown'. See also his mention of Hannah (p. X).

infantile dependence they utterly relied. The analysts listen as though they stand in the role of these historical figures, but their listening also depends on the fact of their own 'counter-transference', their own thoughts and feelings which are a means of learning what patients themselves unconsciously know. In this endeavour, first and foremost psychoanalysts are intensively and extensively patients themselves; in this practice they develop patient-experience and clinical training so that both continue thereafter as an ever-ongoing 'self-analysis', to which all the analysts mentioned here subscribe, and to which the work of J.-B. Pontalis (Chapter 7) and Rachel Chaplin (Chapter 8) bear full and most explicit witness. There is thus an undertow of mutuality within the clinical exchange and an interlocking communication of unconscious thinking. Being both alike and unalike is the basic condition of the sibling situation – the possibility of mutuality for better or worse. It is the explicit condition of their unconscious interaction and of the lateral relations.

If, as becomes clear, siblings autonomously contribute to the unconscious processes which are the only focus of psychoanalysis, then how does this play out in the social world – for instance in such psycho-social maladies as stealing and self-harm? The interest in the psychology of siblings that precedes and succeeds my own concern has focussed, by and large, on their interactive relationship – i.e., almost invariably and their rivalry.[7] Differently here, the fact that siblings initiate anew the sociality of the ever-present horizontal axis again gives them a structural rather than an exclusively relational significance. Rivalry, an interpersonal dynamic, is replaced by a conscious and unconscious preoccupation with the sameness and difference between people. Again, this entails prioritizing structure over development. In a future–past movement, the horizontal axis always goes back to start with siblings and their trauma and forwards into where we are going next.

**Part 1: The Toddler's World** describes the constitution of a horizontal axis of social relations emanating with the toddlers' awareness of siblings and proceeding through their social heirs to adult marriage and warfare. The toddler loses its being and place as baby of the family which had defined who the world and itself had thought it to be. An account of the sibling trauma and the law of the mother follows. Someone else now is, or could be, the baby that the toddler thought it was – and everyone thoughtlessly agrees to this usurpation. The toddler wants the baby to be more of itself and simultaneously to get rid of it for good. The mother prohibits her older child's desires for what would become incest and murder. Around three years of

---

7   Psychoanalysts also use 'rivalry' as a sort of short-hand observation for a distinguishing feature which does not invite analysis! For the most interesting instance of this, see John Rickman in his work with Wilfred Bion during World War II (Chapter 4). This is before Rosemary Davies wrote her important article on the subject.

age, no longer a baby or even a toddler, the infant becomes a small child and more-or-less forgets the problems of its past. 'Infantile amnesia' – forgetting our pre-child years – commonly associated with the later Oedipus complex, commences at this earlier point.

The original sibling trauma is an 'actual' trauma. This was a concept widely re-visited with the vast killing in World War I which seemed not to have any childhood precedent. Although there are plenty of traumas in babyhood it is argued that the sibling trauma is different: it is its actuality which is 'foundational' with no historical precedent. After this, on the absolute prohibition of the mother, the sibling trauma itself becomes the precedent to be repeated in the traumatic vagaries of future life.

The mother has all along been introducing reality to her offspring. Differently, her prohibitions against incest and murder constitute an absolute 'law' – the Law of the Mother. The child develops psychic defences such as 'splitting' which will be socialized – friend or enemy – and/or become pathological – schizoid tendencies or schizophrenia – psychotic pathologies which are widely acknowledged to be the flipside of social normality.

The toddler's world is one where following the new sibling's birth the task is to develop an understanding of self and other – an uneven process through identifications, mirroring, feeling empty and alternatively full of itself, mixing fantasy and actuality. Part 1 concludes with a description of the toddler's crucial transition from the pre-social to social group within the framework of the always social world into which we are born – the horizontal axis.

**Part 2: Three Theories.** There are three distinctive features of the proposed horizontal axis: clinical descriptions of a sibling trauma lie in the narcissistic–psychotic stage of social relations; the social is distinct from the familial; the prohibition on murder between siblings is stronger than that on incest and therefore death takes precedence over sexuality in the unconscious, and this leads finally to a full thesis on fraternity which we need to examine for the horizontal axis.

Part 2 discusses three central constituents of the social horizontal axis through the work of Donald Winnicott, Wilfred Bion, and J.-B. Pontalis. D.W. Winnicott's vivid and pertinent case-histories displaying the sibling trauma and his depiction of the narcissistic stage of development is the setting which we need to use for the crisis of the toddler confronting the new baby. Bion's *Experiences in Groups* is used to demonstrate that the social is entirely different from the family; J.-B. Pontalis' 'On death-work' that death and the difficult concept of a 'death drive' must be foregrounded over sexuality. And in 'Brother of the Above', a booklet written some thirty years later Pontalis describes 'frerocity' among pairs of brothers in literature, psychoanalytic instances and his own personal history – a hugely resisted but compulsory self-analysis. Is fraternity a hope or a disaster?

The clinical offerings of **Donald Winnicott** are rich in siblings and thus an excellent and irreplaceable resource. There is no place for a 'sibling trauma' in Winnicott's mother-and-babies two-year-old 'separation trauma' of which it is so essentially a part. Introducing siblings enables their presence in the case-histories to be added to Winnicott's outstanding accounts of the narcissistic–psychotic developmental context.

**Wilfred Bion** made a radical separation of the social and the family. With the exception of his younger sister in his autobiographical writings and references, he did not mention siblings. It might therefore seem perverse to select *Experiences in Groups* – from which siblings are missing – as the body of work most useful for arguing for their importance. But the task is: can Bion's propositions about social dynamics be cannibalized for siblings and/or can adding siblings amplify Bion's argument?[8]

Bion explores the dynamics of the social group – the milieu of the toddler becoming a small child. The child persisting in the malingering or traumatized adult is at stake. Bion calls the group's psychological corner-stone its 'basic assumptions'. These are the social versions of what would be seen as psychotic in individual analysis – but they are not; they are *sui generis* for group thinking. The neurotic of the Oedipus complex is also social; this he designates a 'work-group'. For children (whom he does not consider) it would be the positive child–child interaction from playing to studying away from the family in what from the social viewpoint is mis-named 'latency'. This is a veritable 'anti-latency' of children vibrant amongst themselves between three years old and puberty. What can Bion's work offer siblings and can they offer something to it? In both directions, the exchange is partial, not total. However, both aspects are claimed as foundational, so using Bion's theses of the social and the group within it becomes mandatory. In turn, reading siblings into Bion's groups puts the feet of a part of its important and provocative theory on simpler ground.

Siblings are nowhere in J.-B. Pontalis' 'On Death-work', written in the 1970s as the penultimate chapter of *Frontiers of Psychoanalysis: Between Dream and Psychic Pain* (1981). But thirty years later his feelings exploded in a short cutting-edge booklet grounded in his dire relationship with his deceased older – and only – brother: *Brother of the Above* (2006). His reconfiguring of death and of Freud's proposal of a 'death drive' can be read alongside this later work to reveal a space where death, the unconscious and brothers appear to be inextricably linked. For Pontalis, 'death' must be realized as dominant in the how and why of our psyches in such a way that it is no longer overshadowed by the pre-eminence of sexuality but joins or

---

8   An earlier version of part of this chapter was given as "Siblings and the Other", the first of the Wolfson Lectures, Oxford University, February 2005; and also for the Annual Lecture of the Northern California Society of Psychoanalytic Psychology, San Francisco, CA, April 2005. At the time of writing, it reads pertinently when our sociability is being so stressed under lockdown for the pandemic of Covid 19.

transcends it in psychoanalytic thinking – a large undertaking for a ten-page essay. *Brother of the Above* and 'On Death-work' can be seen as connected through the sibling trauma and the mother's law. It is as though one theme – death – had unconsciously led him to the other – to siblings, or rather, to brothers. Or was 'On Death-work', written when Pontalis was in his fifties, already unwittingly impregnated with the nightmare of his relationship with his older brother? Lying behind this chapter is the argument that a primarily repressed sibling trauma and the subsequent early prohibition on murder – death – takes precedence over the equally present prohibition on incest – sexuality. This uses Pontalis on both death and fraternity 'as a kind of habitation' within which to think about these crucial subjects for siblings on a horizontal axis and as an important step towards an account of fraternity.

**Part 3: Fratriarchy** takes on the argument of the general thesis of the book but now from a political viewpoint. Rather than trying to fill out an absence – the lateral axis – it confronts what it has found to be there: Gender and gender distinction, the oppression of women under fratriarchy, death and life as the conditions of survival and – a task for the future – finding sisterhood.

First in order to clear the path to horizontal 'gender' we need to see the very different proposition of vertical 'sexual difference'. The thesis of 'sexual difference' applies to the woman rather than the man – women are different from men – as Freud stresses. A recent contribution by Rachel Chaplin to the thesis of 'bisexuality' rescues 'sexual difference' from this bias – but does it, or can it do so without the help of the concept of Gender? To consider the question we must add puberty to toddlers as will be done in Chapter 9.

With puberty we start adolescence with its prospects of adulthood which will give us the unconscious retrospective meaning of our childhood trauma and socialization. The all-important prohibitions on sibling murder and incest (as well as those on the incest and murder of parents) are engaged with anew and the resulting prescriptions of marriage and warring demand an elaboration of the concept of 'gender' and of the 'oppression' of women. These were both major theoretical offerings of feminism in the late 1960s and early 1970s. *Oppression, wherever it is collective – be it of slavery, the colonized, of Black Lives Matter, of transgenders, of gays (women and men), of ethnic minorities, of women – is based on a covert and latent violence which is essential to the status quo until it is challenged, when it rushes out of hiding and is recognized for the forbidden murderousness on which it is based.*

Here I argue that puberty and its outcome – for better or worse – is a repetition of the toddlers' sibling trauma and its effect: of when a new baby was expected or born and the prohibition to the completely lost and enraged toddler was that there could be no murder nor incest – the 'mother's law'. In the toddler's scenario there is also love, charm and joy. All this is repeated at puberty when the laws and their socializations on the horizontal axis centre on a 'gender' distinction. A brief and partial psyche of the adolescent needs to be added to that of the child. Freud, with his eye always on the Oedipus complex, considered that 'sexual difference' between women and men took its final form at puberty. This makes available the differential parenting – the mother and father of adulthood – based on their 'sexual difference'.

Vertical Oedipal-castration 'Sexual Difference' as what utterly distinguishes the sexes is one thing – 'Gender' as what describes their relationship on the horizontal axis is quite another. A gender distinction takes place at puberty which, as with the toddler, will be prior and different – marriage is supposed to come before parenting. For this gender distinction all the changes in the manifestations of the body-ego at puberty and in adolescence are additions to a repetition of the sibling trauma and the subsequent Law of the Mother. Above all, with the demise of the former self the latent question that arises again is: 'where is my place?' and 'who am I?'

As we will see, it is Narrative, the story which helps the transition. Social media takes up the place of the story – but narrative has always asked for social participation – of oneself as oneself, like and unlike everyone else.

# Part I

# The Toddler's World

The toddler loses its being and place as baby of the family. This had defined who itself and the world had thought it to be. Someone else now is, or could be, the baby that the toddler thought it was – and everyone thoughtlessly agrees to this usurpation. An account of the sibling trauma and the law of the mother follows. The toddler wants the baby to be more of itself and simultaneously to get rid of it for good. The mother prohibits her older child's desires for what would become incest and murder. Around three years of age, no longer a baby or even a toddler, the infant becomes a small child and more-or-less forgets the problems of its past. 'Infantile amnesia' – forgetting our pre-child years – commonly associated with later Oedipal desires, commences at this earlier point.

The original sibling trauma is an 'actual' trauma. This was a concept widely re-visited with the vast killing in World War I which seemed not to have any childhood precedent. Although there are plenty of traumas in babyhood it is argued that the sibling trauma is different: it is its actuality which is 'foundational' with no historical precedent. After this, on the absolute prohibition of the mother, the sibling trauma itself becomes the precedent to be repeated in the traumatic vagaries of future life.

The mother, or her representative, has all along been introducing reality to her offspring. Differently, her prohibitions against incest and murder constitute an absolute 'law' – the Law of the Mother. The child develops psychic defences such as 'splitting' which will be socialized – friend or enemy – and/or become pathological – schizoid tendencies or schizophrenia – psychotic pathologies which are widely acknowledged to be the flipside or on a continuum with social normality.

The toddler's world is one where following the new sibling's birth, or ever-expected presence, the task is to develop an understanding of self and other – an uneven process through identifications, mirroring, feeling empty and alternatively full of itself, mixing fantasy and actuality. Part 1 concludes with a description of the toddler's crucial transition from the pre-social to social group within the framework of the always social world into which we are born – the horizontal axis.

DOI: 10.4324/9781003347125-2

# Chapter 1

# From the 'Sibling Trauma' to the 'Law of the Mother'

The individual and the social are one and the same person or people – yet in nearly all analyses our entire focus is the vertical axis of the individual in the family – child to parent, parent to child. This individual who is always also a social person in lateral relations is acting as such on a horizontal axis. What should we make of the individual in the social world? Only the child has to make the transition from its pre-social immersion in the society into which it is conceived and born to becoming itself a social being. As such, in its turn, it shares and constructs that social world.

In the family a new or expected sibling has stolen the toddler's precarious identity as the family's one-and-only baby. The universal expectation of a new baby is the *sibling trauma* and its effects on the toddler provoke the *Law of the Mother*. The toddler loves the new baby to excess and simultaneously wants to get rid of it forever. With her more urgent emphasis on the latter danger, the mother prohibits both behaviours. The open explicitness of the toddler's need and wish at once to assimilate and to exterminate the imposter makes it quite clear that we are dealing with the omnipresence of what would be incest and murder and their prohibition – the mother's law.

The so-called 'Law of the Father' operates on the vertical axis, *between* generations; preventing incestuous sexuality with the mother is its primary target. The Law of the Mother, on the other hand, operates only on the horizontal axis, between siblings *within* a generation. It too forbids incest but between her children – sister–brother, sister–sister and brother–brother; in this case, however, it is the prohibition on murder that carries the greatest weight. Death, not sex, is first and foremost the focus and therefore needs to take precedence when we try to build a picture of the horizontal axis from the sibling trauma and the mother's law.

Of this experience, Freud wrote:

> What the child grudges the unwanted intruder and rival is not only the suckling but all the other signs of maternal care. It feels that it has been dethroned, despoiled, prejudiced in its rights, it casts a jealous hatred upon the new baby and develops a grievance against the faultless

DOI: 10.4324/9781003347125-3

mother which often finds expression in a disagreeable change in its behaviour ... we rarely form a correct idea of the strength of these jealous
impulses, of *the tenacity with which they persist and of the magnitude of
their influence on later development.*

(my italics)[1]

The argument is regularly made that the toddler does not know the meaning
of its desires and would-be acts. This is precisely the point – nor, all too frequently, does the subsequent rapist or murderer, nor the seductive charmer
who makes no distinction between truth and fantasy, assimilating all to his
lying and faking in the desperation of getting what he wants by whatever
means. The child itself produces a melange of real and imagined events with
an energetic liveliness of infectious joy, useful aggression and lovingness.
However, this toddler who persists in the psyche of all of us for the rest of
our lives has a lot of the worst and the best to answer for in our social world.
What counts is the prohibition which makes us social.

In sum, with a first sibling the excited and terrified toddler is asking
'where' it is placed and 'who' it has become. The two-year-old is expecting a 'replica'. Instead, someone else is, or could be, now the family's only
'baby'. The response to the 'sibling trauma' necessitates the prohibitions
on incest and murder of the baby through a 'Law of the Mother'. Together
this *double* blow makes this particular trauma – like the later 'shibboleth'
of psycho-analysis, the Oedipus-castration complex and the Law of the
Father – foundational. The foundational nature of the construct entails being repeated when any future trauma occurs.[2]

The event of the new sibling influences the future and this general experience of all of us is universally traumatic. The toddler is 'dethroned, de-
spoiled, prejudiced in its rights' to so extreme a degree that it is rarely that
we 'form a correct idea of the strength of these jealous impulses, of the tenacity with which they persist and of *the magnitude of their influence on later
development*' (my italics; see above).[3]

---

1  S. Freud, 'Femininity', *New Introductory Lectures on Psychoanalysis* (1933), *SE XXII*,
   p. 123.
2  For the actual absence of siblings in the western world, we can draw on the observation,
   made trenchantly by psychoanalyst Melanie Klein, that the child without a natural real
   sister or brother has more siblings in conscious and unconscious fantasy than the child
   with a sibling. Within psychoanalytic practice, the significance of compensation for what
   is absent immediately registers, but outside this particular knowledge, the missing sibling
   can also easily be grasped. 'Only' children have imaginary friends, so-called 'lonely-onlys'
   may be preoccupied with the sister or brother who is not there. What is actually there does
   not need to be consciously imagined or unconsciously fantasized; what is absent, does.
3  'Tenacity' is an important word for Freud – it is what he claims for himself as an intellectual 'conquistador' – someone who never gives up on charting pastures new. The toddler

The new and all-pertinent *generic* and 'foundational' trauma which hits the toddler makes use of and picks up the random and prolific traumatic experiences of the helpless baby, separate and, at the same time, inseparable from its mother. At the very moment when the infant is gaining a first sense of a coherent self, these previous experiences – won't it be fed, will it be dropped – are gathered and reconfigured in the dramatic, indeed cataclysmic experience of being replaced, annihilated by the new baby. With the arrival of the new sibling, the toddler has its babyhood-status shattered from outside (the new baby) and feels internally chaotic. Overwhelmed, it responds with a tantrum. We have the screaming, kicking toddler who won't eat, sleep, walk or talk, and whose body so often expresses the trauma but who also then attempts, compulsively and repetitiously, to gain control of the unbound energy with which the shattered body-ego bursts. The toddler originates the notion of a 'body ego': our 'me' or incipient 'I' starts in our bodily emotions.

## The 'Terrible Twos'

The 'terrible twos' is an understandable misnomer for what is an undoubted trauma at this age. Something terrible happens *to* the toddler and it cannot cope. The interest here is not simply the trauma *qua* trauma but the significance of the enormous work of the transition which the toddler must make from being the one-and-only baby of the family to 'fitting in' and becoming, with a group of friends and enemies, *an active member of a social community*. Both of the toddler's forbidden wishes are latent all our lives – informing our normative as well as our pathological behaviour. The wish to eliminate the baby forewarns of the total indifference of future murder and of assimilating two into one, of the stranglehold of abusive coupling in which the fratriarchal oppression of women occurs (Chapter 10).

The two prohibitions set up our psycho-social world. What does the toddler-past mean for the good and the bad of our social future? Does the effectiveness of the mother's and toddler's joint transformation of the trauma into a 'rite of passage' enable everyone to miss the significance of the toddler's experience for the future society and to label its trauma simply as a 'difficulty'? Do we trivialize the problems or emphasize only the undoubted humour and charm of the sometimes raging toddler? Do we want to forget its serious experiences because its future in our adulthood, when we behave like toddlers, holds us in thrall? This is the toddler's plight; it is the dilemma of the hysteric present in all of us. The toddler's trauma was once called 'infantile hysteria'; it is as though it foresees its future in individual

---

conquistador may bestow its tenacity on our future ability to make use of trauma in general for human social life.

and social outbreaks of hysteria and this ever-present future establishes that there is an important toddler-past which we need to address in our thinking.

Like an unwelcome immigrant, this new baby occupies the unique place from which the toddler had acquired its only certain identity. Imagine if someone claims to be you in your entirety! It is a sensation beyond the uncanny. The toddler's mother will not tolerate her toddler-child's response, apparently she welcomes the replacement. As well as the normal narcissism and grandiosity inherent to this developmental period,[4] frustration, guilt and the need for punishment have also been noted in the toddler's temper tantrums. However, without invalidating these possible responses, the tantrum would seem to indicate something that goes beyond these observations: the toddler who felt annihilated is protesting its condition as a being-in-fragments, a 'death' of its 'body ego', of 'itself'; it is 'itself', its 'me' no longer.

'Not being' is salient but any aspect of this syndrome of the trauma and the prohibited response can be experienced throughout life. In a television interview about the devastation wrought in regions of England which were without resources or assistance for the Covid-19 pandemic, a young mother unable to get a job (which hitherto had never been a problem) or to feed her children (which had also never been a problem) very quietly summed up her current state of existence: 'I feel I am no-one'. Somehow it was clear that she did not mean she was no-one important or no-one that counted, but that she felt *internally* that she was not *anyone.* Another young woman, bereft by Covid of her entire family, used the same words. The survivor lives but, at first, as 'no-one'. We need to imagine this for the toddler as well as also to realize that excessive loss, depredation and, above all, violence and oppression can produce a repetition of the toddler's death of itself.[5]

## The Body Ego and Trauma

The artist Louise Bourgeois, who on marrying moved from France to the USA, would spend hours making real French meals for her American family. Her sons and husband would come home from school and work and regularly go straight to graze from the fridge; Louise felt she was not there – all her long life she had tantrums:

> For dinner which is prepared there is soup
> meat soup with peppers and string beans – It is in the
> pot ready to be served. The bowls are on the stove –
> Jean Louis rings the bell, looks at the soup
> and says – I am going to open a black bean soup
> can – Robt says – that is fine there is also Pepper

---

4   See *International Journal of Psychoanalysis* (hereafter *IJPA*) June 2020 for different recent accounts of this developmental period.

5   A first-time mother can also re-experience the enormous life-change as another moment of her own toddler heritage: 'Who am I?'; 'am I anyone?'. Unkinged, King Lear asks who he is – 'Lear's shadow' answers the Fool.

ridge – I am completely forgotten, dropped out of
sight – I have the strength to throw away the
meat soup and also the beans – I feel you said it
rejected all right – ignored as at Chartres
    as at the ATA – as at the Club –
to feel rejected is certainly a way to be placed
in the wrong, unable, unable to please or even to
be tolerated[6]

Bourgeois later became the artist who has to feel the traumatic absence of self for something new to emerge; her tantrums were a feminist expression of what can be usual in male artists. A trauma which shatters the body-ego is *simultaneously* physical and mental. An adult survivor prematurely bereaved of a life-partner described it thus: 'the full-frontal *internal* attacks … had overrun me, blown me out of sight, and drowned me in the hole torn into my life'.[7]

With the body-ego in mind, we can use a physical trauma as an analogy or image for a psychological trauma. An overwhelming blow breaks through the psychic skin, the 'defences'; it turns the inner organization to an 'unbound' chaos. At the same time, the violence of the external blow is also experienced as something from the inside going in the opposite direction and coming out as in bruising and bleeding.[8] This 'something' is the desire and prohibition of the earlier foundational trauma. With a physical wound, hit from outside, a broken bone pushes up to the surface and through it. The psychic 'bone' is the long-ago desires and their prohibition struggling to push out of unconsciousness into consciousness. The threat to the integrity of the emerging 'me' or incipient 'I' is absolute; the fragmenting of the body-ego is shattering; one can feel 'in pieces' psychically and physically.

What there is of the 'I' desperately tries to bind the chaotic, unbound energy (analogous to bandaging the unstoppable blood-flow in a physical trauma). This unbound psychic energy released within the organism has produced a condition of involuntary, automatic anxiety. In this, the 'I'/ego, in a state of hyper-alertness ('ego anxiety') repeatedly tries to get hold of the chaos so that it can use its activity as a warning signal to fend off further attacks. 'Ego anxiety' is an excessive vigilance – a state of being on the lookout, binding and re-binding the internal wound and trying to take control of the inner chaos over and over again. In this repeated effort there is an essential element of what is known variously as the 'compulsion to

---

6  Louise Bourgeois, loose sheet of writing, 5 January 1967 (LB-0095); Courtesy the Louise Bourgeois Archive and © The Easton Foundation/VAGA at ARS, NY.

7  T. Mathews, *Chronicles* (forthcoming). This book is now available as *There and Not Here: Chronicles of Art and Loss*, London: Ma Bibliothèque, 2022.

8  See J. Mitchell, 'Sibling Trauma: A Theoretical Consideration', in P. Coles (ed.), *Sibling Relationships*, London: Karnac Books, 2006, pp. 155–174; Damaris Athene oil paints trauma from photographed physical bruises. https://www.damarisathene.co.uk/.

repeat', 'repetition compulsion' or 'compulsive automatism'. It is commonly known that people constantly put themselves back into an unmanageable traumatic situation. 'Catastrophes come in threes' is perhaps a weak (and over-hopeful) recognition of this phenomenon. The compulsion to repeat is more complex than this because it is an entirely unconscious defining feature of a traumatic reaction; it is not a characteristic of any lesser assault.

When the physical trauma is translated to the category of psychological trauma it is helpful to classify it as both a simple 'actual' and also a complex 'psychogenic' occurrence. In such a schema the sibling trauma in itself is 'actual' but combined with the prohibitions of the elicited wish for incest and murder and the threatened punishment of desertion for not obeying the mother's law, the totality is 'psychogenic'. The shift from actual to psychogenic retains both features.

### Actual and Psychogenic Trauma

The toddler's experience should not be compared with the unendurable and perpetual terrors and horrors of the world; rather it is a violence which is essential and structural to the conscious and unconscious psychological dimensions of the construction of the social world. On the whole the toddler survives and is the stronger and wiser for it. The prohibition from the mother's law is as crucial as the death experience of the sibling trauma in making this experience 'foundational'. The transition is the move from the 'actual' sibling trauma into a psychogenic trauma with forbidden desires. Co-operating with the mother's law turns the move from infancy to childhood into a rite of passage.

A 'psychogenic' trauma is one in which a new traumatic experience at any point in life elicits a repetition of the foundational trauma undergone in childhood – following my analogy for psychological trauma, this is the 'bone' that pushes through the skin: the prohibited and repressed desires for incest and murder which are always pressing up, urging acceptance. World War I had seen a re-vitalization of the notion of an 'actual' neurosis.[9] An actual neurosis relates to an 'actual trauma' in the present rather than the repetition of a trauma that took place in the past. Initially the term was used to describe present-day sexual trauma in which there was no relevant

---

9   Note also *'psychose actuelle'*. Charles Myers, who was the first to note this in World War I, dropped his interest in Freud's work because of Freud's insistence on a childhood aetiology. This may well have contributed to Freud's re-considering the question. Peter Jackson has found and reconstructed previously unknown footage of the war violence and devastation of Normandy – almost unwatchable, it seems 'beyond representation'. See my lecture to the Lima Psychoanalytical Association 25.11.21 Freud's concept of a death drive is his making conscious the unconscious denial that we are a very violent species.

preceding history of childhood trauma. In the later use, rather than sexuality, it was the war's violence which was so extreme that no previous trauma from childhood was discoverable in the unpredictable emotional–mental reactions of surviving combatants – at that point, no foundational murderous Oedipus-castration complex that had gone wrong.[10] Nor would we find a causative sibling trauma. The horrendous actuality of the war trumped the earlier actualities as well as psychogenic manifestations of both foundational traumas.

It is frequently observed that a satisfactory survival of childhood trauma is a good platform on which to rest later survival. In Winnicott's terms the mother has left her baby for a manageable Y, not an unmanageable Z period of time. Logically this would make sense; but has anyone studied whether this is true of social survival as for instance in wartime? We might see the engendering of a resilience – a 'tenacity' that can be re-used as with an artist like Louise Bourgeois who as a small child had been taken round the field hospitals of World War I and like Freud was very proud of her 'tenacity'.

The actual trauma may translate to a later version rather than become fully psychogenic. A recent talk about an adult patient at the London Portman Clinic who had a teenage history of knife crime was entitled 'Peter Rabbit was a thief'. The title indicated the commonality of lateral delinquent violence which we need to reach by way of the child who persists in our older selves. It is the toddler who, on the sibling-horizontal axis, demonstrates the crucial fact that sexuality is not added to violence or violence to sexuality as in the Oedipus complex; in the sibling trauma and its effects they are identical twins, the love–hate born effectively in the same moment. After the beyond-nightmare of World War I, the renowned psychoanalyst Wilfred Bion, a war hero himself, recurrently 'dreamt' he saw a child who had clean vanished from his sight with her feral eyes, and belly pregnant from rape.

The sibling trauma is a perfect candidate for an actual trauma in and of itself – there can be no previous 'childhood' history to the expectation of a new baby when one is the baby oneself – it comes out of the blue. The death-like experience of the trauma for the toddler is 'primarily repressed'. The primal repression has entailed an 'anti-cathexis' or 'negatived' attachment, a violent *opposition* to the existence of the trauma which is hurled away into outer darkness, hopefully never to be remembered. We recall loving and/or wanting to get rid of the new baby but no-one remembers feeling annihilated by its existence – instead it is repeated in later life either in an up-dated version or by total denial. In these ways it is an unknown aspect of the fabric of our lives.

---

10 It is widely recorded how war survivors experience their 'mates' actual deaths as their own deaths. The death drive features throughout this book but particularly in Chapter 7.

However, primary repression, the 'obliteration' of the first actual trauma, provides an historical precedent to the trauma of the mother's law. Room is made for the psychogenic trauma's new lateral defences such as splitting, denial, projection, foreclosure, dissociation and projective identification, all of which can be both psychotic and/or socialized rather differently as everyday behaviour and anywhere in between. 'Splitting', for instance, as in an adolescent's 'splitting' its desires at the prospect of having to leave home, desiring above all to go and desperate to stay; to love one's friends and hate one's enemies may appear as a quite normal social demand, or it may develop, commonly in late adolescence, into schizophrenia.

We think of thinking as an individual activity, but is not social thinking also normative? Apparently for some Afghani tribal women thinking as a group-self is quite usual; the Chinese can also think of themselves as pairing selves.[11] I remember collecting a gang of young teenage girls from a Chuck Berry concert – they may each have been saying different things but there was no way of telling because the incredible speed with which they gabbled their excitement made it literally 'one-voice' – is not this collective thinking? The terrible twos characterize toddlers as a group but when the tantrums are over the child is seen once more as an individual. The traumatic experience is forgotten, and forgotten along with it is the fact that it was a generic, social experience of all toddlers.

## Is a Trauma Really Just a 'Difficulty'?

Only a trauma and not a difficulty produces unconscious processes and is therefore of interest to the unconscious component of the psycho-social world. This is not of course a reason for claiming it as a trauma – that belongs to both the death experience of the sibling trauma and to the threat of 'deathly' desertion by the prohibiting mother: together with the wish to, and prohibition of, murder, these deaths are interdependent and traumatic.

Once obedience to the Law of the Mother, with her threatened desertion, has transformed the sibling trauma into a rite of passage, it will retrospectively be remembered as just a temporary 'difficulty'. The tantrums are over, the murderous hostility largely displaced– the infant is a child, all can be forgotten – in practice as in the theory: 'Hostile feelings towards brothers and sisters must be far more frequent in childhood than the unseeing eye of the unseeing observer can perceive'.[12] This may help explain why the experience of the terrible twos is frequently denied as a trauma. But a difficulty

11  A. Macfarlane, *Understanding the Chinese. A Personal A-Z*, Cambridge: Cam Rivers Publishing, 2020.
12  S. Freud, *The Interpretation of Dreams* (1900), *SE.4*, p. 252.

can be individually thought about, which is not the case with the instant shock which characterizes trauma and the toddler's violent reactions.[13]

When in *Beyond the Pleasure Principle* (1920) Freud famously observed the reaction of his small grandson to its separation from its mother, it was not the importance of separation that Freud elicited from the observation. Indeed he only used the game because from Ernst's toddlerdom he found a possible explanation of two clinical experiences which had hitherto been puzzling, the one of concern here being: why would anyone want to repeat something which was horribly traumatic ('compulsive repetition')? A sibling 'trauma' can help with this fundamental clinical observation – a 'difficulty' cannot.

Vamik Volkan (a specialist on trauma) and Gabrielle Ast were the first to write fully of siblings and unconscious processes, where they noted: 'the mother's pregnancy and the sibling's birth may act as a traumatic stimulant if internal or external conditions disturb the child's reaction to these "average, expectable events"'.[14] In other words, the new sibling was not a trauma in and of itself. Certainly, the notion of trauma is over-used and over-discussed – but that does not mean that trauma has ceased to exist. But what we have with the toddler's tantrum seems to be a carefully thought-out resistance to the idea; it would appear that within the framework of the production of unconscious processes something else is also at stake. I suggest that what is at stake is the near monopoly by much of the therapeutic community to account for the toddler's future with the over-worked notion of Separation Anxiety.

'Separation' is undoubtedly important as a contextualized experience, but as a concept it too easily denotes a pre-determined future.[15] The temptation to predict the future is a seduction to which it is mandatory to resist. Psychoanalysis can only work backward from the present to a past which contains its future. Latent within the current symptom or pathological problem in adolescence or adulthood is its onset in childhood. This onset has been transferred and produced in replica in the later clinical encounter.

13  Claudia Lament makes an important case for 'difficulty'. See C. Lament, 'Introduction' and 'Three Contextual Frameworks for Siblingships: Nonlinear Thinking, Disposition, and Phallocentrism', in the excellent 'Siblings: New Perspectives', *The Psychoanalytic Study of the Child*, vol. 67, pp. 3–13, and 84–99, 2013.
14  Thus, two psychoanalysts, V.D. Volkan and G. Ast, *Siblings in the Unconscious and Psychopathology*, Madison: International Universities Press, 1997. Volkan and Ast seem to be hedging their bets here. The suggestion that it is particular experiences which make the sibling's birth either traumatic or just a difficulty for the older child may be because unwittingly they realize that not to do so would necessitate a basic fundamental re-think of some of the premises of psychoanalysis.
15  It is a definition which, however complex, presupposes an answer where it should be an observation.

Its future can be handled in a new manner by the patient – or things can stay the same as in a 'negative therapeutic reaction'. Much of infantile sexuality only has meaning later than its advent. The future cannot be predicted – it is an 'afterwardness' – a past that, deferred, can be activated in a time ahead of its happening.

Freud describes how he would watch his grandson play a repetitious game after his mother left the house. He noted something that differed from maternal attachment and therefore from maternal separation. The child did not just miss its mother and cry, nor did it just 'master' her absence. Instead, he enacted both her going away and her returning in a self-sufficient game of throwing and retrieving his toy, a cotton-reel on a string. The little boy could not stop his repetitive play for something unconscious was driving him.[16] The game has been richly and variously understood but the particular clinical issues to which Freud addresses it can also be considered through the centrality of death on the horizontal axis.

It is notable that Freud's grandson repeats two comparable but different compulsive acts within the one game, giving it two parts. The significance of the difference between the games seems to be unremarked. A thrown-away and retrieved cotton-reel on a string represents the disappearance and recovery of the mother. Ernst, however, also plays at finding and losing *himself* by staring in a stand-alone looking-glass and then withdrawing from it over and over again. For the first game, Freud and his grandson were more interested in the cotton-reel which Ernst was throwing away (fort/gone) than they were in his retrieving it (da/there) – together with the mirror game, was this a try-out of the experience of the distinction between death and absence? They were surrounded by world war and with its end, the overlapping flu pandemic which was to kill more people than the 'war to end all wars'. Death was the air one breathed and the near future included the death of Ernst's and his brother Heinele's mother, Freud's deeply loved daughter Sophie.

The implication is that death, obliterated in the primarily repressed sibling trauma, may be grasped through another: his mother and/or her- or himself as 'other' because either of them could go away and might or might not come back. Only through the presence of others can death have meaning. The meaning of one's own 'dying' comes unevenly when one is another

---

16 Winnicott describes this early trauma retrospectively: it lies behind the not uncommon adult fear of an imminent breakdown in the future. In this 'inexplicable' fear of a *future* breakdown, the patient cannot realize that the breakdown has already occurred during a period before it could have meaning. Winnicott's concept of 'a separation trauma' is absent from every index or Concordia of his work. As mentioned, each and every one of his case-histories explicitly notices the traumatic nature of the new baby but Winnicott himself never makes this omnipresent sibling a part of his theory.

to oneself as Ernst was in the mirror. I watched on the television news a similarly pre-verbal toddler stumbling, whimpering in the total destruction of its home in bombed-out Aleppo, Syria – when it suddenly came across its broken drinking cup the toddler collapsed into heart-rending sobs; its mug was a stage on its route to self-representation. The other side of the knowledge of one's dying is some sort of survival – as a fragmented cup.

The first game of Ernst, in which the mother's absence seems prominent, thus refers to a vertical axis; however, the second refers to the horizontal. Babies love looking at themselves in mirrors well before the whole gestalt which they are given by the mother-figure naming them in Lacan's famous notion of a 'mirror-stage'. When an animal is looking at its reflection, it mostly sees itself as another animal and proceeds to search for it in vain behind the mirror. Instead, Freud's human grandson is typically fascinated by himself appearing and vanishing from the tall looking-glass. This 'mirroring' of the other-as-the-self is a relationship intrinsic to the lateral axis: the 'sameness' of siblings will be its retrospective endorsement and hence its future pre-condition. What is known as 'transitivism', when small children physically echo each other, is its enactment. Ernst is repeatedly reassuring himself that he too can disappear, not exist, 'be dead'; but he also can come back again. Although his father and uncles had fought in the war, it is likely that a possible new pregnancy was in the minds and conversation of his parents at this time, and that their toddler was therefore already anxious about his own unique existence as the family baby. What must it sound like to hear your parents talking about a future baby when that can only mean more of you? Or not another you, but another than you?

Characteristically, Freud had encapsulated his new and difficult idea of the 'repetition compulsion' in a graspable prosaic everyday incident – his own grandchild at play. It was likewise within a framework of maternal separation that was not his prime interest that Freud had set out his key observation of a death drive, a driven unconscious force which importantly can address the lateral relation. Pertinently, Freud first proposes a death drive in the war-permeated *Beyond the Pleasure Principle* which, as we will see, is crucial for the sibling trauma and its consequences.

Whether or not a new actual baby arrives, the possibility or impossibility of another child will be in the minds of one or both parents as well as in the expectations of the surrounding culture. Both the arrival and the non-arrival of another baby in the toddler's stead drive the mind of the two-year-old to work for explanations: where did this baby come from? How did it come? Or: don't my parents like babies? Have I been or done something wrong to explain why it failed to arrive? Whichever way, through its own endeavours and the mother's help in turning her strictures into a rite of passage, the toddler who becomes a small child takes its huge curiosity about life into the social world it must try to forge. This is so different from the fate of forbidden relationships with parents.

The all-prevalent, and of course crucial, vertical axis of ancestors, parents and children – the family in its various forms – utterly dominates our thinking. But this is, like the horizontal, a subset of the social, not its one-and-only *fons et origo*. However, when Freud first proposed that everyone sexually desired their mother, as Oedipus had, he meant *everyone*.[17] Indeed, what would be the point of the theory if one person had to repress and make unconscious this particular desire and another did not. The demand to repress the desires for what goes under the notion of incest and murder is general. In other words, although conditions may make some sector of the population, or a different population, more prone to a particular psychopathology, every girl and boy, woman and man world-over must share the basic unconscious way of thinking.

Obviously, there are enormous and growing numbers of individuals who have no biological siblings.[18] Thus, when thinking about siblings and the horizontal axis, the question of universality in the practical sense of the term must be addressed. In many cultures, other kith and kin such as cousins are considered to be sisters and brothers. In various times and places such as late sixteenth, early seventeenth centuries in England, it had been common to give a child from a large to a small family. Sometimes this was a formal requirement, sometimes it was the interesting effect of how a blood sibling (usually a brother) becoming a social brother went into reverse so that a social brother joined the family when, say, a blood brother died. Under the Russian Czar, Jews would transfer second sons to become first sons in other families to avoid the age-long servitude of the oldest in the Czar's punitive army. Social siblings do not have the same degree of the genetic pool as biological sisters and brothers, but it is likely some social equivalent such as a religion or oppression stands in as a substitute for genetics. As we will see, despite assumptions to the contrary, the universality does not have to be tied in a one-to-one relationship with biological data. Although biology plays a part – is indeed a very important reference point – the unconscious of psychoanalysis is not determined by biology, which is related but also altogether another discipline or 'knowledge'.

Various physical issues, although not determinative, have a role to play in the psychic experience of dethronement which always occurs around toddler-time. Breast-feeding has some contraceptive effect, and traditionally

---

17  Much ink has been spilled on the absence or the diversity of cultural expressions of the Oedipus complex. Arguments for its absence usually miss the nature of unconscious processes, and, *vice versa*, psychoanalysts are sometimes too rigid and miss the diversity of actual practices. We needn't. Diversity in no way affects the general claim.

18  That is, according to a definition of the sibling as a child of the same parents or sometimes just of the same mother or the same father. Historically and cross-culturally, definitions of siblings vary – but, though important, that is not the issue. Currently no- and one-child families have overtaken two child families in Singapore, the USA, UK and Europe.

weaning took place when milk became less abundant at around the baby's eighteenth month. A new baby might be desired or not, but whether to allow or prevent a new pregnancy would at that point be in the mind of one or both parents. Psychically, whether consciously or unconsciously, even in a family where the child has been adopted, or where, for social, medical or age reasons, a further pregnancy is not viable, the possibility or not of another baby needs to be reckoned with. It is generally accepted that there is an unconscious transmission of emotional affects and thoughts between people who are intimate, and in particular of mother-and-baby; this means that the infant is likely to sense that something is going on in the mind and body at least of the mother and maybe of the father.

If the 'replacement' baby arrives when the older child is just a year old, the infant is likely to be confused and chaotic and not yet able to take in this arrival, thus the trauma will be activated later when it has acquired some language and is beginning to walk. The 'terrible twos' happen around the age of twenty to thirty months and not much before, even though there may be an existent baby. If the sibling arrives much later, after the toddler has undergone the drama of a fantasized sister or brother, then, as with the Oedipal complex, as it is a persisting element later in life, the toddler trauma will be re-awakened and the reaction can be just as intense, even if it is dealt with in a later age-appropriate (or inappropriate) way. However strongly positive subsequent sibling relations might be, the psychical experience of the sibling trauma is 'terrible' for two-year olds and for everyone's two-year-old psyche which, because it is a *foundational* trauma (equivalent to the vertical Oedipus complex), remains within us all our lives. This does not mean that the older child will be traumatized all over again but rather that a foundational trauma never entirely vanishes, and it is this element that is awakened as a persisting factor when a new trauma arrives.[19]

The replacing baby will have all the baggage of the loved and hated younger child, but its own trauma will only come when it itself is a toddler threatened by a new or possible baby. As important too is that the sibling trauma and its effects, like the Oedipus complex with its effects, is repeated in the dramatically different trauma of reproductive potential at puberty. Again, what happens at puberty is generic. If siblings are a general factor, whether present or absent, then the consequences of this will also be universal psychological processes – and this again goes to the heart of the importance of siblings in our unconscious thinking.

---

19 It is the prevalence of difficulties in, say, adolescence that may, in part, explain why so many people regard the toddler as also just having 'difficulties'. See C. Lament, op. cit., and Volkan and Ast, op. cit. The later difficulties repeat the psychogenic sibling experience which follows the mother's law.

## Death and Murder

The murderous feelings and wishes for violent action that the child experiences in response to its sense of its own annihilation with the arrival of the intruder are quite real and there can be no mitigating circumstances. The toddler might indeed kill the baby. As a psychologist quoted in Stephen Pinker's *The Better Angels of our Nature* points out:

> Babies do not kill each other, because we do not give them access to knives and guns. The question … we've been trying to answer for the past thirty years is how do children learn to aggress … [that's] the wrong question. The right question is how do they learn not to aggress.[20]

The possibility of access to knives and guns arrives when toddlers are teenagers who, again fearful of their own annihilation, in certain times and places can resort to killing each other. Above all (and primarily), the toddler learns not to aggress through the mother's absolute prohibition. We have asked the wrong question because we have so widely foreclosed on the possibility of a Law of the Mother.

Everyone except the toddler whose being is at stake knows that the new baby is now the *only* baby. Above and beyond the jealousy noted by Freud and the rivalry noted by everyone, there is an indiscriminate need to eliminate the being who is exactly whom the toddler knows itself to be. Everyone nominates this other person 'baby' – unless it is got rid of, the toddler itself will be eliminated. Eliminating would be murder; but baby and toddler-self are also the same, so being killed and killing are mirror reactions. This can be seen later in adolescent gang warfare, where killing in order not to be killed and a distinction between being killed and murdering has once again not been perceived.

With the Oedipus complex, the father's prohibition on incest with the mother came to take precedence over his prohibition of the murder of himself (Laius in the Greek story); this emphasis on incest necessitated that the research focus was infantile sexuality. Differently, on the horizontal axis compulsive repetition is an effect of trauma in general so that the experience of 'death' is at the core of the 'sibling trauma' in particular. But also the subsequent prohibition of violence is strong – the new baby can all too easily be killed. The toddler experiences annihilation, desires to murder and the prohibition against its raging impulse refers above all to death. On the horizontal axis, death rather than sexuality takes precedence.[21]

---

20  Richard Tremblay in S. Pinker, *Better Angels of Our Nature: A History of Violence and Humanity*, New York: Viking Books, 2011, p. 483.

21  The responses of the toddler to these manifestations of death fall under the aegis of the notion of a death drive, which includes death and is analogous and opposite to a life-drive (subsuming sexuality) with which it also amalgamates.

For Freud, the never resolved challenge was the interlocking of the hypothesis of a death drive within the metapsychology or theoretical super-structure and his utter but misplaced conviction that, as we are alive, the experience of death was unknown and therefore could solely be signified and represented by castration. Instead, with the sibling trauma and the mother's law, the death experience is confirmed by the horizontal new sibling-baby taking over its being – annihilating its hitherto existence – and then with the separating mother threatening desertion; these change the field of enquiry.

The mother's threat of abandonment, like the father's later threat of castration, constitutes a further traumatic fear under which, in this case, both sexes continue to live. When the actual sibling trauma becomes psychogenic it provides an infantile history of the actual sibling trauma behind the demand on the toddler to become a social child. The toddler-becoming-a-small-child will therefore experience the mother's threat of desertion as retaining this actuality. So death in the sibling experience, even when psychogenic, also always has the immediacy, the present-ness of the 'actual'.

It may be that the importance of the sibling trauma has been overlooked in part because even those psychoanalytic authors who acknowledge the trauma of the arrival of a sibling see only the 'actual' present-day madness of the toddler. They fail to see the possibility of a 'psychogenic trauma' which uses the actual trauma as the historical basis for this more complex trauma which is inaugurated by the prohibitions from the mother.[22] Because the mother's prohibition on murdering the sibling is more urgent than her simultaneous forbiddance of incest, the focus on death implicates the 'death drive' – the *driven* return to the inorganic – is at stake (Chapter 7).

## Same Trauma, Same Law, Different Gender?

Of course, a gender bias one way or the other always features: girls or boys may be preferred, with the mother's own Oedipal psychic history directing her preference strongly towards the boy. Against this, her narcissistic heritage in her relation with the siblings may orient her to favouring a girl like herself. Most importantly, although mothers are of course individually infinitely various, the mother – or whoever stands in her place – as such is completely even-handed in her Law with her girl and her boy. Intrinsically, the trauma of the sibling's birth, the toddler's incestuous and murderous reactions, the prohibitions and punishment of desertion are the same for both.

---

22 When I discussed 'Siblings' with René Kaës and Louis Kanciper for a panel of an IPA congress and again in a conference in Montreal – no-one heard me when I proposed a Law of the Mother. Committed to there being only a Law of the Father, my Lacanian friend and colleague at UCL, Lionel Bailly, is still running a seminar he convened three years ago to prove me wrong! It is as though for those who do engage with siblings the death drive, a horizontal axis and the 'Law of the Mother' are knotted together and produce a bundle that is either inconceivable or unpalatable.

The toddler's 'actual' *experience* of death in the sibling trauma applies equally without any discrimination to both sexes; through our toddler selves we all have an experience of death in our lateral psychic histories. Death and the death drive are notions of great importance and the phenomenology of dying, being dead and the meaning of death which comes under the law of the mother needs to be further investigated (Chapter 7). Of great significance is the fact that the later vertical Oedipal girl who is considered 'already castrated' is bypassed in psychoanalytic thinking. This omission will be of concern in Part 3.

It is under the law of the mother that the girl learns she is a sister and the boy that he is a brother. In terms of their future these become structurally different places. The sister has to want to be married and the brother to be prepared for warfare. On the vertical axis there would seem to be a psychological 'sexual difference' between the biological sexes in relation to the experience of death as well as with its main thesis, in regard to sexuality as we will see in Chapter 8 – what is the situation on the horizontal axis?

The future Oedipal sexual division holds the egalitarian mother and equal children in thrall. Does this hold true for a gender division? Boys and girls equally have the same degree of intense, incestuous love towards the new baby, and both love it as though it were literally one and the same as itself. This incest sets a programme for the two-as-one of future coupling. Both sexes are also equally set on eliminating the new baby – this murder is a model for killing in future warfare. However, to use an outmoded but still pertinent term, under patriarchal 'modes of reproduction' sisters 'inherit' a future of being married and brothers of being fighters. Even where women are officially called up to fight equally with men as in today's Israel, a characteristic gender division of tasks prevails and few women fight. None of this happens till puberty when the bodies of the 'body egos' differentiate not just sexually and reproductively but also in terms of body size, with the girl's relative smallness being taken to signify the 'weaker' baby of old and the boy the 'stronger' larger toddler of those by then far away gender-egalitarian days. The different future casts its shadow backwards.

As small children, boys in the family want to marry their mothers but after the prohibited desire is repressed, few men go on to marry older women – the prohibition has been effective. That generational trajectory is reserved for women, whose very different Oedipus complex has enjoined that they pursue the father's love for them, and thus in some sense, their fathers. The male Oedipal desire for sex with the mother and murder of the father is so deeply repressed or demolished that the story of the original Greek Oedipus utterly *not knowing* who are his biological parents is a perfect descriptor. The universal Oedipal situation produces the unconscious defence mechanism of 'secondary repression', keeping the core prohibited desire for incest with the mother completely unconscious in an underground psychic habitat to which the techniques of psychoanalysis are so far addressed.

## Siblings in Psychoanalysis

Group, child and family psychoanalysis as opposed to individual adult therapy have continuously demonstrated or paid tribute to the importance of siblings. However, they have done so within the theoretical framework of the vertical axis. This has resulted in a failure to appreciate the maternal contribution of the horizontal axis to the social world and, importantly, the role of the mother in the installation of the 'reality principle' that makes this social world possible.[23] A horizontal pre-social, proto-social and *social* axis does not replace the vertical *family* axis, but rather it is *interactive* with the contemporary pre-Oedipal and subsequent Oedipal situation.

The toddler may envy the baby who is engrossed in mind and body with its mother's breast, but it also gets a boost the other way. The suckling baby is not envious of the older sibling and will interrupt its feed to watch, entranced by the other's playfulness. Together the baby and older child are contributing to the dynamic of the self and the group. In this paradigm, the social becomes not just a later extension of vertical child–parent relations, but also a product of distinct and independent lateral psychic processes that move directly from sibling to social peer. Push the same baby in a pram in the street and any dancing passing-by school child will provide the same two-way inter-relating joy and curiosity. Against this varied interactive background of the construction of the horizontal social world, the issue at stake then becomes how the sibling trauma and the mother's prohibitions which relate to the sibling experience can be understood as analogous to those that operate Oedipally on the vertical axis.

The vertical and the horizontal will make use of diverse unconscious defences. The different axes are always there but become prominent at different stages of infant–child development and this affects the use of unconscious defences. What is unconscious always persists; repression, repudiation, dissociation, projection, splitting and other defences merely try to prevent the universal illicit desires for incest and murder becoming conscious. Classically, what is called 'secondary' repression instituted by the Oedipus-castration complex creates the so-called 'repressed unconscious'.

---

23  The 'horizontal' has been the object of negative criticism in psychoanalysis; see, for instance, Christopher Bollas' discussion of 'horizontalism' in 'Psychoanalysis in the Age of Bewilderment: The Return of the Repressed', *IJPA*, vol. 96, no. 3, pp. 535–51, 2015. Bollas describes horizontalism as the increasing replaceability, equivalence and lack of differentiation of current social and cultural principles and practices. The purpose of the intervention is to place it in direct opposition to the hierarchical, more complex and structured, creative, vertical organizing processes which Bollas so favours. My own position in these debates is that arguments against 'horizontalism' mistake the pathologies that may (and indeed inevitably must) exist on this axis for a horizontal axis which is posited as *in itself* inherently pathological. This is an important disagreement. It is not, however, the argument that I am interested in exploring here.

(This designation of 'secondary' will be considered later with the elaboration of the proposal of 'primary repression' for the sibling trauma.) Secondary repression is replete with the desires for parental incest and murder which have been driven underground at a stage when the child has enough of a sense of reality to understand how to deal with the efforts of the unconscious desires to re-activate themselves and become conscious. This sufficient sense of reality marks a normal to neurotic moment. It is precisely what is missing from the earlier 'narcissistic-psychotic' and also perfectly normal toddler stage of development – life is somewhat different where the toddlers who have to become social take their stand.

If, as proposed, toddlers become social at this normal narcissistic-psychotic stage, then it is exactly this stage with its psychic characteristics and its uncertain grasp of reality which they take with them to form anew the social world around them. To account for the crazy 'unrealistic' behaviour of the crowd, the madness of the mob does not need only the factor of masses of people but also the determinant that beneath the collectivity is the age and stage of the toddler who started anew the social process that was always there. In entering and re-forming the social for itself, the toddler of the horizontal axis is socially engaging in a new group with its lateral peers who are psychically contributing their own 'social unconscious' psyche to the formation of society itself. That society is ours.

# Chapter 2

# Taking It like a Toddler

Humans are born too early. Our prematurity makes us dependent on adequate carers so that there is a tussle between our helpless passivity and our innate activity – our 'drive'. Species that are born more developed seem to be able, in widely varying degrees, to rely on instinctual behaviour. For us, rules and regulations replace instincts. Parents are usually the first carers and so we have their 'laws'. On the horizontal axis this can be called a 'law' if we allow the term to indicate the fact that an essential rule is the prohibition which comes from the mother along with the threat that she will no longer love or care for her toddler if it does not obey. The presence or possible presence of a new baby forces the toddler to become a small child together with its age group of other older siblings.

## The Law of the Mother and the Law of the Father

Because both the mother's and father's laws must be effective in childhood, if the actual parent is unavailable or the local social structure is such, the laws will be 'uttered' from whomsoever is in the position of a parent in the wider world. In both laws, the two prohibitions – against incest and murder – are absolute; both are universal, and both have threatened punishments which are death-threatening and thus if effected would be devastating for the dependent child. For both, the psychogenic trauma of the law's punishments rests on a previous actual trauma. Unconscious defences which are foundational for the human psyche are established.

The pre-Oedipal male child has not taken any suggestion of possibly being castrated too seriously. The possibility and the terrible shock are supposed to come when he discovers that his mother does not have a penis. From there it is only a quick step to the terror and horror of all women being by definition 'castrated'. His father's threat of castration becomes all too plausible – it has happened to over half the world. Such a dread haunts the patriarchy. In fact, it does this so thoroughly that the next step is to ensure that women as castrated have to bear the nightmare for everyone. The sister,

DOI: 10.4324/9781003347125-4

however, does not appear to feature in this,[1] as only the mother is of interest. Nevertheless, as women in general are seen to be castrated like the mother, what is called 'sexual difference' is established – one sex cannot be the other sex. It is this that transgender challenges from the inherent subjective bisexuality of the horizontal, social axis.

Not only the Oedipal but also the sibling trauma with its prohibitions are repeated at puberty with its enormous changes to the body and the body-ego. Indeed, this can seem forecasted by the insistent independence of the two years old who considers itself fourteen years old and rising! It is at puberty that social gender distinctions join the Oedipal construction of 'sexual difference' between female and male and ensure the oppression of women (Chapters 8 and 9). For the toddler, it is acquiring the knowledge of different genders from its likeness or difference from its younger sibling.

The two actual traumas – the absent penis of the Oedipus and loss of babyhood for the two-year-old – involve the establishment of unconscious defences and are foundational for the human psyche – both individual and social. Obedience to both prohibitions can – and will – go wrong, producing the psychic range from the normative to the pathological. In addition to these important similarities between the two laws, there are, however, commensurately important differences. The actual trauma unleashed on the social toddler is quite different from the Oedipal trauma: someone else is now really the only baby and its own babyhood no longer exists or is wanted.

The Law of the Mother, operating entirely between her children on the horizontal axis, takes the form of an *absolute prohibition* – a Law – which puts a complete check on the toddler's murderous and incestuous desires. As well as desires, these would be enactments in the here and now of toddlerdom. A mother can be seriously terrified when her older child tries to push the baby off a seventh-floor balcony or shove the pram under a passing car.[2] Lesser desires are also forbidden but these are not laws. The omnipresent 'no' that characterizes her interaction with her toddler also can be intensified by various physical threats and punishments. The only or last child will not escape these desires about which it will fantasize or which it will displace onto other children receiving commensurately displaced threats and/or punishments.[3]

Compensating for our lack of instinctual responses and substituting for this, these verbal laws have to become part of who we are as though they

---

1   But see Chapter 10.
2   These are two among very many instances told to me– once mothers are asked to remember, the memories come tumbling out. See also Jean Miller: *Relations.* Penguin Books, 2003.
3   In many so-called 'simple' cultures the law tabooing sibling intimacy is explicit and conscious as well as unconscious (Chapter 10). And where it is not, it will lie behind the rules of the future bride and groom not seeing each other.

themselves were instincts. They thus have to become unconscious and yet known without any verbalization. (Psychoanalytic practice re-verbalizes them.) They have to be consciously enforced when we first become social in our childhood, where they are verbally uttered by the person who stands in the place of a responsible parent. Obedience to the prohibitions can – and will – go wrong, producing the psychic range from the normative to the pathological which because of the age difference will be normal-neurotic with the foundational Oedipal situation under the Law of the Father and normal-narcissistic-psychotic with the earlier foundational Law of Mother. By the time the child is Oedipal, language is well established. But the transition from pre-verbal to verbal happens at toddler time; the movement from pre-social infant to social child occurs with the recognition of a metaphoric world – a gain that can also be lost.[4]

In later life, at one end of the process the psychotic and neurotic will merge into each other, but at the far end of serious pathologies there are profound differences: a full-blown psychosis substitutes a private sensory world – a delusion instead of reality – whereas a neurosis knows the difference between reality and a dream. We all navigate both sibling and Oedipal traumas and between the mother's and the father's laws. However, along with important similarities, there are of course important differences between the two laws.[5] Neither law displaces the other: each is different and autonomous, and each operates on a different axis.

The Oedipal law is effected by the patriarchal father (Chapters 9 and 10). The mother's law is our concern here. When the sibling trauma hits, the toddler in actuality is no longer a baby. It would be inappropriate for the mother to accept the projected dispersal of the toddler's traumatized being as she had done when it was her old baby but now must do so with her new one. The mother can explicitly and consciously reassure her child but also has to explain that however bad it feels about its new sibling the reality is that this baby is here and has come to stay – it is now the *only* baby in the family. This can fail and the tantrums that signify the traumatic fragmentation will persist in some new form in the social world of lateral friends

---

4  This is not speechlessness but may be a feature of autism which, if so would endorse the need for the likeness and un-alikeness of siblings to underlie the capacity for metaphor.

5  This is a further reason why the horizontal axis must be defined separately from the vertical. If nothing else someone has to stop the toddler killing or even damaging the baby. And indeed to stop incest if the title of a current talk for nscience.uk by Christiane Sanderson is anything to go by: 'The Hidden Nature of Sibling Sexual Abuse. When Sexually Harmful Behaviour Masquerades as Consensual Sexual Experimentation', https://www.nscience.uk/product/the-hidden-nature-of-sibling-sexual-abuse-when-sexually-harmful-behaviour-masquerades-as-consensual-sexual-experimentation-video-course/; as indeed it does.

and enemies.[6] Many a grown-up cannot handle the world if they are not the centre of attention. With the story-telling of the mother and her ancestors behind him, Don Quixote is to this day the most brilliant portrait of the toddler of either gender grown up in a world (a mother) that has failed to accept and transform its traumatized despair – Cervantes (like Shakespeare) generously does this for the reader (and watcher) through art.[7]

The mother cannot prevent the toddler's first actual trauma of the 'replacement' baby – whether it happens in reality or fantasy, it is a universal expectation and experience. She can help with both, but not cancel it as trauma. The process of primal repression is *sui generis* with its all-powerful anti-cathexis in which it tries to eradicate the trauma from any consciousness; it is a force in itself. Indeed, it is this eradicating act of primal repression which may be why we underestimate the tantrum and, along with Freud, forget that as toddlers, and therefore ever after, we experience 'death'.[8]

A toddler would not be able to kill the mother, who may indeed be inclined to laugh at its threats and rages against herself. It might, however, and indeed sometimes actually does, seriously damage or even kill its baby brother or sister.[9] Parents, including the mother who is always intent on imposing her law, usually whitewash the violence as an 'accident'. A colleague whose toddler had sat heavily on the new baby's leg and broken it, insisted that the older child loved the new baby 'to bits' (he did!).

However fraught or hoping for the best, the mother has been trying insistently all along to impose a knowledge of reality on her offspring since or indeed before birth. 'Reality' demands consciousness. The mother as lawgiver thus has to make two competing necessities complementary. The prohibited desires must become unconscious and 'reality' can only be grasped through consciousness of it. The toddler too has these competing tasks. Attaining this consciousness depends on the relegation of the desires and their prohibition to unconsciousness: incest and murder are the ultimate

6   As an immediate response to trauma, the baby instinctively saves itself by *projecting* its shattered, fragmented self into its mother. Bion calls these its 'beta elements'. In understanding her baby by a necessary identification with its traumatized distress which however is not her own, the mother psychically coheres the pieces for her terrified child offering it 'alpha elements'. Alternatively, the mother fails to do this in which case the baby has returned to it the projected fractured self which is yet more terrifying as there is nowhere safe to put it.

7   See J. Steiner, 'Learning from Don Quixote', *IJPA*, vol. 101, no. 1, pp. 1–12, 2019.

8   Freud's own brother Julius who replaced him died at six months old when Sigismund was nearly two – he later knew that the experience had profound effects. It was his sibling trauma which he knew about through an identification with the 'sibling trauma' of Goethe. See this chapter and Chapter 5.

9   Robbie Duschinsky suggested that I look for examples in the popular press – he was right!

anti-social forces which must be banished from conscious knowledge – they thrive unconsciously. The observable mark that they have 'quite properly' become unconscious are the psychic defences. Of these, only 'repression' is regarded as sufficiently strong to warrant that a person is sufficiently social. This repression – 'secondary' repression – is the signature of the later castration complex. That the sibling trauma is subject to 'primary' repression is argued further at various points (e.g., Chapter 4). Other defences are 'shallower'. However, it seems that complete amnesia has only overtaken the primarily repressed actual sibling trauma. For the rest, if we think hard about what is subsequently forbidden to us as siblings, somewhere we have an inkling, at times a pre-conscious knowledge of these prohibited desires – the defences that hold these outside consciousness are weaker than either primary or secondary repression.

This weakness of the lateral defences is not all bad news: it enables the forbidden desires for sibling incest and murder to develop a socially acceptable other side – the everyday 'splitting' of likes and dislikes versus schizophrenia.[10] These numerous unconscious defences are weaker when they are nearer to their social expressions and untouchable when they simply must not on any account be known. With the toddler's stage of existence, the near-consciousness and the absolutely untouchable are both present. This is the proximity of normality and psychosis referred to earlier. It is one way of seeing why Freud always argued that although psychoanalysis well understood psychosis, it could not treat either it or the psychotic patient – for Freud, but not subsequently, psychosis had to be brought up to a neurotic level of understanding reality. As a still latent belief exemplified in the entire dominance of the Law of the Father this contributes an additional motive for obliterating the Law of the Mother from any acknowledgement.

Whenever the material gives evidence of a Law of the Mother, it is either ignored or converted to a lesser status. Julia Kristeva describes the mother in a vertical position as an 'authority'; this undoubted authority is distinct from a Law. Vertically it has been argued that instead of a Law the mother makes a covenant with her children.[11] This too in no way addresses the issue. It is *murder between siblings* that the mother utterly forbids – neither her authority nor a covenant would be anywhere near sufficient. A further issue which will be considered wherever it becomes pertinent is that a 'superego' needs an internalized law. Only with a Law of the Mother can sisters and

---

10 As a major theme that will be developed particularly in Part 3, murderousness and incestuousness feature in domestic sexual partnering and murderous legal warfare.

11 Lionel Bailly substitutes a 'covenant' for a law'. I am happy for the mother to have a vertical authority and make a vertical covenant. However, a 'covenant' whereby a toddler agreed to not feel the need or make the attempt to murder the baby is a pleasant but implausible wish.

brothers and the mother herself provide the core need for a superego. A superego is a presence in the self of someone authoritative who originally was an external person but who becomes one's own internal guide. This is analogous to but is not the same as that provided later for the Oedipal boy by the castrating father.

The mother's Law operates only *on the horizontal axis.* As mentioned earlier, the social implications of siblings have been well recognized by analysts practising group psychoanalysis.[12] However, this has occurred without a theory of the horizontal axis. To miss the latter is to miss the former: without a theory of the horizontal axis, we will inevitably miss the mother's Law and vice-versa. We may more easily miss it because as an established paradigm and social practice, the mother is always subjugated to the Law of the Father. The source of the mother's authority may be vertical like the father's, as a parent to children, but her Law is horizontal, between the siblings. The mother's 'Law' must be insisted upon because what is being prohibited is murder and incest between siblings that, for society to exist, cannot be allowed.

A major problem is that the mother who so obviously utters this Law is simultaneously idealized and *excluded* from society by her own 'female' Oedipus complex (Chapters 8 and 9). Her paradoxical position inside and outside society can only be understood with an analysis of a horizontal axis. There has never been, and cannot ever be, a society without some taboos or prohibitions relating to sexuality and killing. The mother's prohibition, which is as much to sisters as to brothers, automatically allows the small girl along with the boy into society. Women could not exist if we were only excluded. Is the Law of the Mother unconsciously resisted because the oppression of women is a patriarchal necessity? This will be explored in Part 3, but meanwhile we may simply note that both professionally and popularly the mother is always held responsible and blamed when her prohibitions fail: children do wound and even murder younger siblings. If she can fail in such serious issues, then surely she is at the very least a failed law-giver! As Olympe de Gouges proclaimed in her 1791 'Declaration of the Rights of Woman': 'woman has the right to mount the scaffold, so she should have the right equally to mount the rostrum'.

The law prohibiting her toddler from murdering its sibling produces a culmination or critical apex to the mother's endless efforts to instil reality as one of life's abiding principles. The competing necessities are resolved. Prior to her Law, the mother had been introducing 'reality' with interminable 'noes' to her child. With the prohibitions of her law, reality becomes as well

---

12 See, for example, Earl Hopper in London and Smadar Ashuach and her colleagues in Tel Aviv. Explicitly making full use of my work, their book is forthcoming with Routledge in 2022.

the 'reality principle', which regulates how goals can be attained according to the conditions of the outside world, while the sexual drive continues to express the avoidance of unpleasure as a 'pleasure principle'. Thus, babies and infants in both the social world and the family come under the aegis of the mother with her constant assertion of 'reality'. It is mostly claimed that reality establishes itself through the baby's testing of it. Everyone misses the overwhelming fact that it is also the mother who is always insisting on it. For instance, Melanie Klein contended that accepting 'deprivation' is an important factor in the child's success or failure in grasping reality; she forgot to mention that it is the mother who makes use of deprivation – as she does of rewards. Her role is most easily perceived in its negative manifestations: she is forever saying 'don't do that' to her infant. In its babyhood, times for feeding, sleeping – and everything – underlie these forbiddances – which are not her Law.

The mother of the family demonstrates her love, care and authority between herself and her baby on the vertical axis, while the mother of the social intervenes with different allowances and deprivations between her children, thus simultaneously demonstrating that they are the same and different: 'you can stay up a bit later, have an extra sweet – but your little brother may not'. The forbiddances appeal to a conscious ego, but what will become prohibitions refer only to sexual and murderous desires that will need to become unconscious, part of the child's apparently natural 'instinctive' assumptions.

The primary vehicle – 'do not bite my breast' – moves to the horizontal family where a requirement – 'do not bite your sister or brother who is my new baby' – morphs into what will become a dramatic prohibition. The mother's vertical family authority, her rules and regulations and her lateral social prohibitions are all enjoined under her all-prevalent task of introducing reality. In psychoanalytic thinking, because inducing reality is the province of the mother, the importance of reality was, for a long time, missed. A distinct concept of 'reality' and a 'reality principle' was introduced into psychoanalysis as one side of the psychic conflict that is essential to its theory. This changed the course of its thinking but the mother's crucial role in it was, and is, omitted.

## The Sibling Trauma in Clinical Child Analysis

Is there something intrinsic to the vertical perspective that obliterates perceptions of the importance of the sibling? Freud's early perceptiveness in *The Interpretation of Dreams* turned to quite frequent but almost casual random observations. Thereafter there is an important contradiction: the clinical cases of child analysis repeatedly describe how in the context of siblings the toddler's involvement is with sex and violence, yet these are given no theoretical status. Can the prohibition on sibling incest and murderousness just be a further instance of the Oedipus complex as it is assumed to be? It would seem that through clinical attentiveness the toddler's reaction to the birth of its sibling – the sibling trauma – cannot be missed but the mother's law-giving role is obliterated, either because therapists assume it for themselves or because, as there is no place for it in the theory, it apparently cannot be found in the practice which describes it. To miss the mother's law is to miss the child's role and hence the significance of the toddler's experience.

Although by now joined by very many important others, Anna Freud, Donald Winnicott and Melanie Klein remain major initiators of child analysis. Winnicott has his own chapter (Part 2); Anna Freud and her adherents will be used for the advent of the transition of puberty (Part 3) and Klein will receive most attention here. Much of today's work is still carried out within the conceptual frameworks of these three major thinkers.[13] However diverse their intentions, they each have something which can be used differently as a contribution to building a picture of the toddler's *experience* of lateral relations on a horizontal axis. All three child analysts will have been cognizant of how in Freud's case of 'Little Hans' it was the birth of his sister 'Hannah' which produced the crisis that led to the formulation of a castration complex. The aim here is to pinpoint the problems in order to see whether the work can offer the social world something of use and importance.

Anna Freud was acutely aware of her own experience as the youngest of six siblings; her own work always involved a perceptive understanding of child–child interaction in a nursery school context. She started her working life as the equivalent of an elementary school teacher in Vienna and when she became a psychoanalyst, she was a pioneer of child psychoanalysis. Later, as a refugee in England, working with a small group of child survivors of the Shoah, she studied how, in the absence of parents, children protect and care for each other; lateral rivalry appears only when vertical caring adults become available. She described how '[t]he feelings of the six children toward each other show a warmth and spontaneity that are unheard of in ordinary relations between young contemporaries'.[14] Together with her colleague and companion, Dorothy Burlingham, she established the Hampstead War Nurseries; it was mainly from this work that Burlingham wrote up a richly observed and important study of twins – independent lateral relations.[15]

13  I am indebted to having studied Infant Observation with Rose Edgecumbe and reviewed the distinctive work of Anne Alvarez – *Live Company* and *The Thinking Heart*. In *The Thinking Heart*, Alvarez identifies three different levels of analytic work and communication with children: the explanatory level – the 'why – because'; the descriptive level – the 'whatness' of what the child feels; and the intensified vitalizing level – gaining access to feeling itself for children with chronic dissociation, despairing apathy or 'undrawn' autism.

14  A. Freud and S. Dann, 'An Experiment in Group Upbringing' (1951), *The Psychoanalytic Study of the Child*, vol. 6, no. 1, pp. 127–68, 2017.

15  D. Burlingham, *Twins: A Study of Three Pairs of Identical Twins*, London: Imago Publishing, 1953.

Leaving Donald Winnicott's work in the main to Chapter 5, one pertinent instance of his keen observation can be mentioned appropriately here: the New Zealand-French psychoanalyst Joyce McDougall described watching Winnicott with a mother who brought her completely out-of-control pre-verbal toddler to his clinic. Winnicott watched the onslaught of chaotic destructiveness and then asked the mother if she had discussed with her toddler her still completely imperceptible pregnancy. Appalled, the mother said that absolutely no-one in the world, in particular not the father, knew nor must know of it. Winnicott said her little boy was certainly aware of the baby. Having been extremely reluctantly persuaded to tell her toddler of the fact, the mother returned to the clinic two weeks later with a calm child.

Working as a paediatrician in a public hospital, Winnicott probably would not have seen this mother and toddler again (there is no further account of this quite ordinary situation which was grasped by Winnicott's extraordinary observational perceptiveness). Mother and child would only have returned if there had been a worryingly disturbed reaction to the actual arrival of the baby – or to its miscarriage or abortion if it did not arrive. Winnicott certainly knew that toddlers usually have strong responses to the arrival of siblings, which he considered they 'get over'; indeed he was explicit that this was far preferable to the situation of the only child who always had to deal with siblings in their fantasies. What he was not interested in was the effect or significance of the toddler's experience of its sibling's birth for future social relations – and this despite the fact that the pathologies he notes tend to be socio-pathologies such as stealing and self-harm which are in urgent need of being understood through the social horizontal axis.

Even with his child work, interestingly, Winnicott said that despite his extraordinary experience observing and working with babies and children, he ultimately learnt more of the psyche of childhood from his subsequent adult psychoanalytic patients. Both Winnicott and Klein, although very differently, started their life's work with children and then became revolutionary adult analysts. Almost every one of the child cases examined by Winnicott and by Klein involves a crisis on the birth – or failed birth[16] – of a younger sibling to a toddler. Whether or not one is an adherent of Klein's theories, their radical nature may be used as a contribution to the toddler's psychic world. Klein never loses sight of unconscious processes. Her main intention in her early presentation and first published paper is to argue

16 See Klein's case of Erna as described in Mitchell, *Siblings.* op. cit. I am giving a terse resume of Klein's theory as it is incidental to my argument which notes the squeezing out of the toddler of her practice from the production of her theory. 'Free Association' is the one contribution demanded of the patient – it is the requirement to say whatever comes to mind however trivial or embarrassing or for any other reason, without let or hindrance.

that children can be analysed just as well as adults if one changes not the theory but the technique. She makes a child's 'play' the equivalent of adult 'free associations' – uncensored talking – a direct way into unconscious processes.

For Klein, where adults *verbally* free associate, children *enact* in their play together with and in the presence of a transference 'mother' psychoanalyst. What one finds in children and adults is the same: the Oedipus complex. Where Freud's adults reveal the four- to five-year-old child in Oedipal straits, Klein's children display what she comes to determine as the Oedipal baby of six to eight months. For Klein the importance of the pre-Oedipus to Freud's Oedipus is matched by a commensurate pre-Oedipus for the baby – this is the normal 'schizoid-paranoid baby' of three months.

The first two child patients Klein spoke and wrote about will be privileged here as this may give us the material to regain a different outcome from the very young baby who became the centre-point of her work. As nobody can analyse a tiny baby, her theories about babies are necessarily constructions from the children (nearly all older than toddlers) whom she analysed: in this the analogy is that just as adults reveal the crucial child experience, so children will give us insight into babies.

In Klein's first work the toddler is all-important. Subsequently there are in fact many accounts of toddler pathologies in her presentations, but they have no distinctive status; their habitus becomes undefined as she focuses increasingly on the very young baby which the older child revealed to her in its regression to the babyhood that was still a part of its psyche. Rita, the youngest child whom she treated from the age of two-and-three-quarters together with the many babies and toddlers she knew personally, certainly offered her material about the ever-existent baby these toddlers wanted still to be – the baby discovered in the toddler was to be both Klein's focus and an important part of her originality. Toddlers were a gift for this enquiry because they themselves try to hold onto or recapture their lost babyhood.

Importantly many older children also enact a regression which I would argue – as Klein does not – is a regression not to the baby on whom Klein increasingly insists but to themselves as toddlers and from there to that toddler's terrible anxieties about retaining its lost babyhood. This is the traumatic compulsive repetition. As well as babyhood, because of their extremities, the pathologies of these often very ill child patients express the psychological state of the toddler and small child within the family. Winnicott's and Klein's theories are quite different, but the material of their case histories is not – although about babies they are redolent each with the sibling trauma for which their theories have no place. Trude and Rita – Klein's two earliest patients – interestingly exemplify how the transition from the toddler either as itself or as a regression from an older child behaving as the baby its toddler-self wanted to be.

## When the Illness Starts – Trude and Rita

### Trude

...at the age of not quite two [Trude] began to suffer from pavor nocturnus. At that time, too, she used constantly to run into her parents' bedroom in the night without being able to say what it was she wanted. When her sister was born she was two years old.[17]

At the age of eighteen months ... [Rita] began to suffer from *pavor nocturnus* and a dread of animals. She developed an excessive fixation to her mother and a very pronounced father-identification ... Up till the age of nearly two years Rita had slept in her parent's room, and the effects of the primal scene showed plainly in her analysis. *The occasion of the outbreak of her neurosis, however, was the birth of her little brother.*[18]

(my italics)

Trude could not say what she almost certainly knew was the focal point of her distress: the expected baby. Melanie Klein also seems to have known what the problem was for the anxious toddler but can only verbally enact it by a juxtaposition which is a bizarre parallel with that of her stymied patient: neither of them can speak about something so simple. For Klein, Rita's problem is that she probably witnessed and certainly imagined her parents' copulation which led to the pregnancy. The fantasy of the 'primal scene' which the incipient baby provokes becomes the important experience. Yet Klein also asserts that the central cause of these utterly typical 'pathological' night fears (*pavor nocturnus*) and subsequent neurosis was the birth of the first new sibling when the child was a toddler. The accounts of Rita and Trude follow the same lines but the portrait of Trude is fuller and so will be the focus here.

Klein presented Trude at a conference in Salzburg in 1924 and published a version of her talk as a contribution to the *International Journal of Psychoanalysis* three years later when she had just settled in London. This first 1924 paper is crucial for my purposes – which are different from Klein's. In it she says:

The analysis of one child of two years and nine months, [Rita] another of three and a quarter [Trude], and several children of about four years old, has led me to conclude that in them, the Oedipus complex exercised a powerful influence as early as *their second year.*

(my italics)[19]

17 M. Klein, 'The Psychological Principles of Infant Analysis', *IJPA*, vol. 8, 1927, pp. 28–9, ft. 1.
18 Ibid., p. 27.
19 Ibid., p. 26.

Two years old is, of course, the ascendancy of the toddler, and Klein's discovery that it is suffering from the privations encountered in an early Oedipus complex will give us an 'inside' look at the psyche of the tantrum on the horizontal axis.

In fact, although Klein was working within the framework of the vertical family, what she is describing is exactly the sibling trauma and its effects on the two-year-old toddler. She is not sure whether her child patient was already neurotic when the first stage of the early Oedipus complex struck or whether it became neurotic because it was unable to cope with the Oedipal deprivations forced upon it. These 'deprivations' included punishments for its normal 'naughtiness' and, interestingly, in the case of the ill child there is the violence of its hatred of the mother and the problem of the seductions which it wants with and from both parents – together these drive it crazy. And Klein includes the new baby: Trude dreams of being in a familiar restaurant and the waitress not giving her any raspberry syrup because it had run out. Klein comments that this was her experience of serious deprivation at weaning and her envy of the baby – a toddler phenomenon.

According to this initial paper, Trude had the one clinical session when she was three-and-a-quarter years old and commenced regular analysis when she was three years and nine months. Trude's parents will have told Klein when they think all her difficulties started and their report will be confirmed by Klein's understanding of Trude's enactments in the analytical sessions. The night fears Trude reproduced with Klein as a maternal transference figure were therefore her near two-year-old anxieties about what was going on inside her mother and between her parents. When four-and-a-quarter, Trude, on the cusp of becoming a Freudian Oedipal child, had re-enacted the night-time fears (the *pavor nocturnus*) that she suffered in her toddlerdom when she was not yet two and her sister was imminently expected.

Klein further comments that Trude's four-to-five-year-old raspberry syrup dream revealed the small child's pain at the withdrawal of her mother's breast and her envy of her younger sister. She analyses the dream as a punishment-dream based on death-wishes derived from Trude's oral frustration directed at her sister and mother, together with the sense of guilt which resulted from these wishes. Klein reads Trude's four- to five-year-old story back into her two-year-old self and then from this regression first to the toddler and next to the baby the toddler wanted to be. In the 1927 paper two other patients – Ruth and Erna – suffer respectively from the mother's chronic paucity of milk and from a violent reaction to toilet training. In the later chapter, identically to Trude and Rita, Ruth breaks down on the birth of her first sister and Erna, an only child of six years, is obsessed by the non-appearance of siblings.[20]

The Freudian Oedipal complex comes about when the child has a sufficient grasp of reality, which is somewhere around the age of four-and-a-half to five – Trude's actual age. Klein's argument at this stage is that the Oedipus complex starts some two and a half years earlier – in other words with the two-year-old toddler. Everything including pronounced 'sexual difference' between the female and male sexes is there *in statu nascendi*: this was the 'anxiety-situation' which is also a girl's version of a castration complex. That was the case which the parents reported of when Trude was a toddler before the analysis started. Klein is finding the Oedipus complex everywhere.

However, looked at from the perspective of the toddler, what we would seem to have is not an analytical construction of a toddler's babyhood but the typical regression of a disturbed older Oedipal child. The Oedipal child is being a toddler and that toddler wants still to be the baby. In Klein's theory the child who wanted and in her disturbed state still *wants* to be the baby has now behaving as the actual baby it urgently wants to be. In other words, the toddler is still very much around but becoming excluded from the emerging theory.

In 1932, Klein included Trude in a re-write of her 1924 and 1927 papers for a book chapter on the technique of child analysis. The crucial second year has become the second half of the first year. In turn this will transform into Klein's well-known concept of a 'depressive position' at approximately six to eight months when the baby feels guilt because of its previous three-month-old paranoid-schizoid attacks on the mother whom it has split into a good and a bad mother that it fears will retaliate. My concern is only the place of the toddler in this important change of scenario from four to five years at first to two years and then to six months. In the 1927 paper the Oedipus complex starts around toddler age and reaches its climax with Freud's exclusive claim for it somewhere about the fourth year of life when it 'reaches its zenith'. So initially Klein's ideas start with the toddler and the 'sibling trauma' but in the later theory, the toddler and its sibling, although frequently described in the symptomatology, are themselves omitted from a six-month baby wanting to make 'reparations' for its attacks on the mother whom it has 'split' into 'good' and 'bad' at three months.

The two-year old who actually has a sibling, although still present in Klein's material, is ejected from its place – from any particular place.

20 See Mitchell, *Siblings.* op. cit.

Indeed, the toddler whom this was about is now entirely out of place. In the expanded version of her initial Salzburg talk when she had settled in England, Klein elaborated a thesis which was to remain a foundation of her radical theories of the psychic history of the baby. The two-year-old has turned into the baby whom it yearned to be. Being replaced seems to be the toddler's fate! But we have learnt something about the toddler, such as its violence towards the mother and its terror of her retaliation which gives a new perspective on her threat of desertion.

### Rita

The 1932 book chapter starts with Rita, who featured second after Trude in the earlier papers. Rita, Klein's youngest ever patient, was aged two and three quarters when analytical work started. In a footnote this time round, Klein comments, as above: 'When she was two years old her brother was born, *and this event led to the outbreak of her neurosis in its full force*' (my italics).[21] Again, despite such an observation, it was the witnessing of the 'primal scene' of copulating parents that was to be at the forefront of Klein's theories. 'Primal scenes' (whether watched or imagined) are undoubtedly crucial, but Trude and Rita's despair and envy of the new sibling, the event that produced the breakdown, was now entirely subsumed under this.[22] What happens in the presentation is that two-year-old Rita is as Oedipal as is four-and-a-half-year-old Trude.

The toddler to whom Oedipal Trude regresses, and whom Rita still is, must always be the toddler of the primarily repressed sibling trauma. As this was a 'death' experience there is inevitably a danger when it is repeated in the suicide-prone-ness of adolescence. But two further propositions are implicit in Klein's shift of interest. First, this child between babyhood and latency (six months to five or six years old) is Oedipal and the Freudian Oedipus is too late to involve a traumatic sibling birth, but Klein's 'early' Oedipus leans on a still earlier position when the baby moves from its 'paranoid-schizoid position' at around three months to its 'depressive' position at six months.

The birth of a sibling when the older child is six months (or three months) is impossible – unless the father is counted as the sole parent – and therefore ruled out of any picture on offer. It may (like Winnicott's wild child described in Chapter 1) feel the presence of a pregnancy. Trude and Rita

---

21  M. Klein, 'The Psychological Foundations of Child Analysis', in *The Psychoanalysis of Children*, Vol. II, London: Hogarth Press, 1932, pp. 3–4, ft. 2, and p. 11, ft. 2. Later Klein drops her suggestion of a girl's castration complex and with its omission the castration complex quietly slips out of Kleinian theory.

22  The model for the importance of the primal scene was Freud's account of the Wolfman – a younger child.

played not only their terrified night-time toddler selves but also the baby that they wanted still to be – an identity they needed to retain as threatened toddlers – their baby selves. Trude, an Oedipal child, can regress to her toddler-self who in turn can regress to babyhood. Who is this baby the toddler is playing? Is this some 'memory' of her own babyhood well before any other baby has appeared on the scene? Or does it resemble the babyhood of the sibling that had stolen her place, who is receiving the mother's attention while the toddler is receiving her prohibitions? Klein's toddlers want to be three and six months old. Klein usefully coined the term 'memories in feelings' – it would have to be these feeling memories of their own baby selves that Trude and Rita enact. But they cannot be free of the 'sibling trauma' that Klein herself nearly always recounts as the cause of the breakdown.

What Klein is finding in her babies is splitting, rage and depression. She emphasizes feelings of guilt that result from the murderousness towards the mother whose punishments it hates. To this can be added the sibling whom she continues to mention. But we can also retrieve the experiences for the ousted toddler whom the baby has replaced in this revolutionary theory of a schizoid-paranoid phase at three months and a depressive phase after six months. The tantruming toddler may well split the mother into the good mother that continues to help it and the bad mother that no longer does so because she is giving all the milk to the new baby. It may well identify with the father whose belly and being does not produce a baby. It knows enough about punishments to fear the mother will retaliate.

Realizing its fate as no longer the baby is now set and sealed, the toddler will doubtless become depressed. When they had a new baby girl sibling, the toddler boy twin whom I observed become worryingly withdrawn and self-isolating; the angry girl twin, who attacked the baby, favoured any helper rather than her mother. But these characteristics are also more than this – the splitting, paranoid and depressed manifestations are also features of a social world. And, as with Klein's portrait of the tiny baby, they all have their good sides in that there are ways in which the becoming social toddler begins to realize that there is good and bad in everyone and that there are more people in the world who are like and unlike itself.

Is it the material of the clinical observations or the different logic of the developing theory of an early Oedipus complex in babyhood that determines the exclusion of the sibling trauma which Klein knew so well? Glimpses of her future assignment of envy and the death drive to our innate heritage are visible. To be explored further this question would need to take in Klein's commitment to the direct unmediated psychological effects of a biological death drive and the direct psychological effects of a biological difference between the sexes. If, instead of the child in the adult, it is the baby who is to be found in the child, then it can be found through direct clinical observation (Winnicott) or through the baby in the psyche and actions of the child

(Klein). In this case it will need to be not the new baby but the baby in the child and this child must include the toddler who is on the cusp of the social. What matters here is that the many vital portraits of toddler and small child pathologies in her clinical work have become untethered from any status and therefore have been lost not only to the toddler's world but to the unconscious psycho-social existence in which we all partake.

# Chapter 3

# From Toddling to Walking; from Speaking to Talking

Babies are born into two distinct psycho-social structures that are importantly distinguishable but tightly linked, interactive and above all muddled up together within us: that of the *family* and that of the *social*, the wider society. From her work with small children whom she saw as reproducing the family in their play with the toys which she provided, Melanie Klein hypothesized that the six-month baby already had a very primitive superego. It will have been the many children and one toddler patient in what we know of her clinical practice who revealed this to Klein. Whether or not a superego is a possibility for the baby, by toddler-and-child time an internalization of the mother's strictures as a family pre-Oedipal and social early superego is certainly possible.

For a superego-proper there will need to have been a law to internalize – and although much has been forbidden, there is no universal prohibition for the baby. It is the lateral law between the mother's two children which is emphatically and essentially all-present. The transition from toddler to child, from sibling trauma to rite of passage to the peer group, can be seen as the internalization of the mother's law (accompanied by all her strictures) as the commencement of a social superego. This will be a marked feature of the individual in the group – but the need to find others to share one's societal beliefs is also intrinsic to the social situation. No man – nor woman – is an island....

The law is necessitated by a universal 'sibling trauma' which affects the toddler independently of whatever its mother might or might not do. In addition to its prime role in annihilating the toddler's being, the left-over effects of the trauma join the psychogenic trauma of the mother's threats which aid the implementation of her prohibition of murder and incest. All this entails a useful challenge to the subject's sense of uniqueness and omnipotence. Following the effective primal repression of the sibling trauma, the mother and child contribute together to the acceptance of the reality of the new baby who has really come to stay. Some very varied *modus vivendi* must be acquired for better or worse in the family, while the small child undertakes the transposition of lateral siblinghood into equally lateral social

DOI: 10.4324/9781003347125-5

friendships and enmities. Although it is something usually insisted on by parents or by the customary habits or by rules and regulations of the circumambient culture, there is no prohibition or law from the mother to the toddler if it fails to enter the social. This task is for the toddler who now must make its own absolutely crucial contribution to becoming a small child in its increasingly equal interaction with alike and unalike others.

## A Psychoanalytical Perspective

It is not that sibling events and relations are absent from psychoanalytic child studies, quite the contrary – it is that because they are undeveloped in the theory, where they are present, as such they go nowhere. Twins, for instance, suggest the possibility that from the beginning lateral interaction may take place independently of the necessary mother; as we will see, this was a passing 'flash-in-the-pan', never pursued thought that momentarily worried Winnicott (see Chapter 5). I am not a child analyst so I will make use of the work of those who are and add my own training in 'Infant Observation'.

I have done weekly hour-long observations of one set of girl–boy twins and their new sister from their pre-birth to three years old and then monthly for a further eighteen months. This was in no way a psychoanalysis of any of the children – quite the contrary – but rather a very particular method of non-participant observation which can be used here for the focus of this chapter, which is not on the psychoanalysis of the toddler but on where and how the toddler as a highly active pre-social and subsequently social child *proceeds* from its 'sibling trauma'. And what are the implications for the social world in which it partakes? Can we, however, also wrest a contribution from other psychoanalytic work that nevertheless ignores the question?

## The Mother's Narrative and the Toddler's Metaphor

Under the auspices of the mother's law, the toddler makes the psychological move towards a recognition that there are others like and unlike itself in the world. This is a co-construction and the child's side must be considered. Learning that it is not the baby, and that the baby is not it, involves the complex idea that both are different children of the same mother. The degree to which the distinction can be grasped introduces time and space into linguistic practice as Maurice Merleau-Ponty recognized:

> The jealousy that is manifested at a younger brother's birth can be interpreted as a refusal to accept the change in situation. The arrival of the new-born supplants the previous role. This stage disappears due to the constitution of a kind of past-present-future schema … The child

learns to think of reciprocal relations: he distinguishes between the concept of role and that of individual. He learns to relativise the actions of the youngest and oldest.[1]

For Merleau-Ponty the 'stage disappears', as though the new actual situation by itself produces the mental result. Rather, I would argue that it is the hard work of the child and the mother; in particular, the priority given to the mother's offer of narrative and the toddler's insistent search for metaphor together produce this all-important past–present–future shift.

Narrative and metaphor induce a new logistic competence and psychic grasp. It is the story which has 'the constitution of a kind of past-present-future schema' and the storyteller who mimes the social world by splitting herself into several characters with reciprocal relations to each other, and the listener who independently follows suit. It is said that the ability to symbolize comes with what Lacan called the Symbolic – language and all the rules and hypotheses that organize human thought and human society. However, prior to this, the mother offers stories and on its own her toddler has been proceeding to a very young child's profound interest in a metaphoric world which it is undoubtedly keen to understand.

Metaphor, which marks the transition from an infant who may have started to speak to a child who discourses, changes the world. The toddler's constantly reprimanded enactments leave its desire still highly active as though its body's 'doing' is in the immediate present and its mind's 'wanting' persists into the future. Its body can be controlled but its mind is freer; what may be a particular human disjuncture or flexibility between acting and thinking within the body-ego is initiated.

As the toddler is automatically socialized with the advent of the new baby, its murderous and incestuous desires are not only utterly prohibited, but they are also socialized as 'allowances'. What is allowed the child in its play and its work will match what is forbidden until puberty which is when the sibling trauma and the Law of the Mother have to be renewed along with the Oedipus-castration complex and the Law of the Father. At puberty, the 'allowances' on the horizontal axis which match the prohibitions will be future marriage instead of incest for girls and the brotherhood of legal warfare instead of murder, for boys.

How does the individual child first leave the vertical family (in which of course it also remains embedded) and take on its social being on a horizontal axis? Without doubt very variously, yet every human being is, or needs to be a 'terrible' toddler, whether or not an actual sibling arrives either at the

---

1   M. Merleau-Ponty, *Child Psychology and Pedagogy: The Sorbonne Lectures, 1949–52*, trans. T. Welsh, Evanston, IL: North-Western University Press, 2010, p. 244. Robbie Duschinsky gave me this quotation for which I am most grateful.

due date or never or at some time later. After coping with the first new baby (actual or expected) the toddler becomes a social child with its age-mates, lateral peers and friends and enemies. We have to take the toddler's terrors and tantrums, its charm, its walking and the nature of its talking very seriously. The toddler is going through a seismic shift in which what starts as an 'actual' sibling trauma becomes a complex rite of passage. The pre-social toddler, participant in the social world since pre-conception changes as it realizes its world can be imaged in metaphor. The child's access to the metaphoric depends (among other things) on the sibling experience of the simultaneity of alike and unalike.

## Siblings: Selves and Other

A metaphor is about what is alike and unlike; the post-toddler is grappling linguistically with its psycho-social dilemma. The sibling is the 'other' who is also the same as oneself in sharing a same parent, and with whom one must become a participant within a *series* of potential near endless siblings instead of a dyad or triad.

The argument that sibling relationships play not just an autonomous role, but also a fundamental organizing one, focusses on the developmentally necessary struggle to find a place vis-à-vis the new sibling. But 'finding a place' and all the emotions which that entails is at war with another prime factor – the toddler's continuing dependency. Its situation and its experience of its situation would seem to be a mass of contradictions. It has to be both a dependent individual in the vertical family and an independent socialite on the horizontal axis.

Underpinning the vertical axis is the claimed condition of the prematurity of human birth and, although the biological boundary is different for siblings as we saw in Chapter 1, it is undoubtedly the case that our premature birth also has a bearing on the sibling situation. At the time of the arrival of a new baby, the toddler is still highly dependent on the mother whose care is now divided between itself and the totally dependent newly born infant. Both its separation from the mother (the 'separation trauma') and the mother's subsequent threat of abandonment if the toddler harms the baby highlight the effect of this prematurity and its consequent dependency. But this vertical individual dependency is set in the social context of the new sibling and the mother's lateral law and the child's social metier; the combination underpins the contradictions in the toddler's predicament – dependency versus independence. We must not let the first continue to ignore the second. What is going on for instance in the toddler's sudden food-fads?

The psychoanalyst, Marion Milner, when training to become additionally a child analyst, had a three-and-a-half-year-old patient who was in very serious danger of starving herself to death. In the case history as usual, the mother's pregnancy was mentioned only in passing and instead what

Winnicott would have called a 'false self' was understood to have developed in the space of an 'emptiness' in the little girl's psyche. There are major issues to be raised about this emptiness, but here the not-eating is all-important. The pre-toddler and just-toddler puts everything it can in its mouth, suggesting that eating is a model for the growth of the mind as well as the body. The prevalence, or rather the Western normality of the toddlers' food-fads and the extremity of Milner's patient's starvation prompts further questions. Only the mother is usually considered with regard to the later pathological anorexia. But the social factor of a sibling also impinges on the family relations. The new baby receives the desirable food. Siblings may play a too often neglected part in the aetiology of anorexia as it has been shown that they do in self-harming. Again, its advent along with its suicidal characteristics are marked in the repetition of the sibling trauma in and beyond puberty. Or is it the sibling murderousness that the anorexic girl in her lethal femininity has turned inwards on herself?

On the horizontal axis the biological situation referred to more crucially than human prematurity is that siblings share more genetic material than any other relationship. What is considered the right closeness or distance within this contiguity always matters. Even when there is no knowledge of genetics, cultural requirements referring to the too close similarity will affect the behaviour of toddlers. As with the clans and tribes of *Totem and Taboo* and the matriarchal, matrilineal Trobrianders in the work of Malinowski, the only taboo is on sister–brother contact and sisters must hide in the bushes if a brother comes into sight. Everywhere a social factor can impinge on, or get backing from, the reference to what is in fact a genetic similarity. The strength of the brother's desire for excessive closeness and the compulsory demand for the sister's avoidance are paramount. Yet more generally the salient fact is that one cannot literally stand in the same place as another person – this is what the adult social imposter frighteningly tries to achieve. Impersonation and stalking have become prevalent in social media and wherever there is a post-truth world. This originates with the new sibling who is standing exactly where the toddler uniquely had its being.

A trauma marks a break between baby and toddler but there is also a developmental continuity. This is the focus of individual work – but what of the continuity of the social baby? The pre-social baby sleeps and apparently dreams – looking at and feeling things? When it opens its eyes, it looks around with increasing interest; it tests its limbs in the air, movements in space and seems to agree that there should be glory to God for all dappled things: sun through leaves, a shadow on the wall. It goes easily to other people until 'stranger anxiety' sets in at around ten months. But it also screams in pain and rage and fear/terror. The baby would seem to be psychologically related to the external world and to its own body as well as to its internal feelings. And this world is full of other people. The rapidity with which a baby's mood changes from joy to despair and vice-versa makes it seem that it can enjoy and fear the lateral relations in which it is immersed. A small group of un-related babies can socialize with each other.[2] Often the child's first word or phoneme is addressed to a sibling as well as or instead of a mother. But this babyhood is brought to a dramatic close when another baby arrives in its space as it did for Klein's Trude and Rita and, potentially, for all toddlers.

Omnipotence – the feeling of grandiose all-conquering power so endearingly displayed in the puffed-out chest of the newly standing baby – reaches a height in the toddler who is grasping that there is something/someone that it does not want to exist. It is easy to see that in the infant's life, as in the child-in-the-adult whom we meet in the later clinical encounter, the child of this age normally foregrounds itself, loves itself, promotes its narcissism to cope with the presence of the new baby who has shattered its omnipotence. Or, perhaps rather it is that omnipotence comes into being with full force at this point as a reaction against the toddler's own sudden experience of utter impotence, of 'nothingness', when it is de-throned by the new baby.[3]

When the mother sends the toddler off into the social world, the toddler both reciprocally repudiates the mother and begins to walk away, but it also clings to her more than before, wanting to be carried, to wear nappies, to gurgle instead of talk – acting more than ever like the baby. Paradoxically, it is the simultaneity of both psychic states – wanting to leave and wanting to stay – that will lead to and make possible the later Oedipal crisis. The toddler's insistent, indeed now urgent, love for its mother will provoke the process of becoming phallic and Oedipal-incestuous with the mother (at first as much for girls as for boys) on the vertical axis. At the same time, it will be the toddler's curiosity and exploratory nature that will lead to the beginning of the discovery of the role of the father, of whom Oedipally the child will want to be rid.[4]

The horizontal axis and its lateral practices have always been there for the child in, and as, the world into which it is born; physical baby–baby interaction such as mutual foot-playing even with baby-strangers has been noted from four months onwards. However, for the child itself the peer group comes into its own once the Law of the Mother is in place. Life in the group can be absorbing: the three-year-old can be 'in love' with its friend of either gender, ganging up against lesser beings, often the younger sibling of one of the pair. Where it replaces its vertical mother, apparently thinking it could

2   Jane Selby and Ben Bradley. As well as my own and friends' and colleagues' observations, references to written observations of early sociability are to my long-standing extensive acquaintance with the work of Selby and Bradley.
3   Winnicott recommended that patients be allowed their omnipotence till they feel safe. See Chapter 7.
4   'Go to the fwont' in the words of Freud's grandson.

give birth 'from itself' as Little Hans told his questioning father, now it also happily plays laterally at acting a family and enjoys pretend-parenting a baby with its friend. Other children may be designated mother or father but in fact are like each other as couples and partners – as indeed are the actual parents too. When his sister was born, one three-year-old insisted unrelentingly that they would share a bed just as their parents did.

The death-effect of the first actual trauma of the new sibling, who has taken both the place and the potential ego-being of the toddler, forms a deeply unconscious bedrock of the social unconscious. This has been touched on previously but in looking not just at the toddler but also at its world, the wider consequences need to be considered as a prelude to Chapter 7, where the importance of death will be considered through the contribution of J.-B. Pontalis. Wilfred Bion (whose work is used for the social in Chapter 6) was to call a death-like experience, a 'nameless dread' – a dread of being dead if dropped, unfed, un-held, cold and untended, utterly helpless in our prematurity. The later accumulation of this huge baby-precarity in the toddler's sibling trauma, which is 'primarily repressed', helps how we think about death. That suddenly every infant is no longer who or where it was triggers a primal repression of an experience of death. Through the sense of an annihilation of whom it is, the toddler fears its own death and through the act of primal repression tries instantly to abolish this fear.

Subsequently we can repeat having the experience while we also miss the meaning. We all carry inside ourselves the 'meaningless' but profound experience of death. In its turn, this suggests the complexity of the toddler's normal so-called narcissistic-psychotic position in the social world. Psychosis is loosely defined as not having a grasp of reality; insofar as this persists in later life, how much does this process become an avoidance of the reality of one's own death? A person kills excitedly but also so as not to be killed, rather than knowing the reality of the death of another person which entails discovering that killing, like being killed, is irreversible, final. In the childhood social group, acquiring the meaning of being killed and killing takes place in games which are as often about this as they are about becoming lateral mummies and daddies. After the Law of the Mother, through these games, death begins to acquire its meaning which it does only through understanding the death of others who are alike and unalike.

However, as well as eradicating the toddler's babyhood, a new baby indicates more baby, more of itself, until it means none of itself. Being two in one – the concept of later being in love – is effectively simultaneous with the sense that it has been killed by another person, whom it is claimed is exactly that which it is itself. The same problematic – that this person claims to be you – informs both loving and killing. The toddler who thinks the new baby is 'more of me' has a narcissistic boost which is instantly countermanded by 'now I am no-one'. The narcissistic 'me' and the trauma which annihilates are completely entangled and through the means of primal repression will be anti-cathected. This anti-cathexis is an energetic counterforce absolutely as strong as the violent trauma that broke through the psychic defences in the first place, and which it thus counterposes and arrests – landlocks. The trauma of feeling non-existent and the counterforce to this are in a fixed and permanent struggle, with the same strength being exerted on both sides. This is a game of locking hands (or bodies) but with neither ever winning the struggle, even though for a time it might look as though one side is ascendant. Primarily repressed, the 'I am no-one' will be a kind of 'hole' in oneself sometimes filled with a negative narcissism that can have the strength of suicidal compulsions – as with Marion Milner's three-year-old child or the teenager whose anorexia is suicidal. But there is another side to this.

Milner, a psychoanalyst with a long-standing strong and productive interest in art, felt she needed to find her independence from Klein to whom she had gone for supervision in a further child training.[5] She considered that the 'emptiness' manifested by the dangerously ill little girl she was treating was also the emptiness that an artist must reach and use. What we could call an anti- or non-narcissism is the important space of 'no-place' for new creativity. The sibling trauma will not be the only *actual* trauma that is anti-cathected but as a foundational trauma, this absence within the emptiness may be the effect of an un-recalled, primarily repressed 'missing' sibling. This could be the source of the need for fellow-artists that is well-recorded in fact or fantasy in the psychic economy of creativity. The preliminary emptiness of art, as well as science and knowledge, would then be the other side of the omnipotent grandiosity which the toddler must assume if it is to establish its presence in the context of its threatened annihilation. If allowed the space and time, the toddler is wondrously curious about life and things.

If this understanding of 'emptiness' is roughly correct, then the landlocked sibling trauma, with its imprisoned but explosive energy, is also ready and waiting for the Law of the Mother and the transition into the large demands of social life. Currently, there is considerable emphasis on how narcissism is not a single entity but a wider syndrome and how 'good' narcissism has to be a marked feature in survivors. The toddler surely shows us that a survivor (like a creator) is able to experience the non-narcissism of apparently dying and yet still live. Social life can come out of this individual death. Bion pinpoints the shuffling loss of individual self as the group is formed (Chapter 6). Is this why social life appears to come out of nothing and is assigned to being already there? And, therefore, analogously to God and religion – which it is not – yet seems to be created from something outside itself?

---

5   Marion Milner, initially as, pseudonymously, Joanna Field, had written *On Not Being Able to Paint*. She was one of my own two training supervisors.

## Lateral Mirroring

The social baby and its heir in the toddler offer rich ground for many instances of varied interaction. For instance, mirroring is an early form of lateral sociality. However, it is theorized mainly on the vertical – thus, as we saw in Chapter 1, Lacan coined the notion of a 'mirror-stage' when the infant that feels itself as a bundle of loose parts is given a whole gestalt by having its coherent mirror-image labelled Jenny or Johnny by a mother-figure. Told of this by a patient, while still maintaining only the vertical axis, Winnicott altered Lacan's thesis to suggest that it is the mother herself who acts as a mirror in which the baby can find its true or false self, according to how well it is the baby's self and not her own projections that the mother sees. But what of a healthy twin described so vividly by Dorothy Burlingham as not eating at all until a literal mirror-image of itself tricked it into believing its sick twin was eating too?[6] As mentioned above, twins have a primary lateral relationship to each other as well as the vertical maternal interaction. Can they provide a residual model for all lateral relations in this respect? On first thoughts, this seems unlikely.

The relationship of the toddler to the baby is predicated on their different ages and developmental stages, yet this is only initially and only from an objective perspective. Subjectively, at the moment of the trauma when the toddler feels the baby is the same baby as itself, this is a twin-like mirroring which we will find persists as a characteristic relationship. Even though the mirror observations of Lacan and Winnicott pertain to the vertical axis, Lacan drew for these on the subtleties that the child analyst Charlotte Bühler had previously designated as 'transitivism' – a lateral relationship.

Transitivism is a special kind of identification frequent with small children who reverse or mirror their own image: one child hits the child who faces it on the left cheek and simultaneously clutches its own right cheek and complains that the child it has just hit is the hitter. This age children do not distinguish between themselves so when a child falls another one will cry. Taking this up, Lacan instead argued that the ego was formed not from itself but from its interaction with the external world.[7]

What is crucial here for building a picture of the toddler's world on the horizontal axis is that this is uniquely a mirroring child–child experience. Once a younger baby itself, the toddler will both have experienced and witnessed lateral interaction – for instance, as mentioned, its lateral parents if they are partners. On the field of these lateral equivalences, from the side of experience when a baby cries when it sees another cry, we can imagine it

---

6   D. Burlingham, *Twins*, op. cit.
7   For Lacan this is a part of the infant's 'imaginary' mirroring formation and is where he places siblings with their rivalry, jealousy and envy.

feels that it *is* the other person. This could be called a process of 'projective identification', but that term, discussed below, carries a rather different freight. Instead, this is an instance of what I have called 'identality' – a state in which the toddler feels it really is one and the same as the other – or the same as a cat. 'A child who was unhappy over the loss of a kitten declared straight out that now he himself was the kitten, and accordingly crawled about on all fours, would not eat at table, etc.'.[8] 'Identality' shifts to its opposite when the young infant will look completely blank at the distress of another. The other baby is regarded as a rock might be perceived. In this phase, the infant moves through complete 'dissociation', in which two mental processes co-exist but do not connect or to a type of 'splitting' where the onlooker is in two places which it cannot relate to each other. This state of utter non-connection may be repeated in later life with a total absence of concern in killing, torturing and the dire cruelties of later life.

Projective identification, another common experience which is particularly well understood by Bion, is the projection into someone else (for Bion, the mother) of a self in fragments. The fragmented self is always a traumatized subject.[9] The projection is then identified with either by the receiver or by the sender. If the receiving mother understands the terror of her traumatized baby, she can psychically cohere the baby's self; however, if she does not accept the projection the baby will identify with its own projected fragmented self and will feel far, far worse. By the time a toddler wants its mother to cohere its traumatized self she has another baby with just such a need – now the mother can help her toddler but not by accepting the projection. The toddler will have to manage this itself – but is likely to seek help elsewhere as well, classically from the father whom the new baby has also de-throned. Again, the mother as intended recipient may not want the projections of a toddler who is supposed to be growing up. If the toddler has survived this experience as a baby, it will still fear its repetition in normal separations not only from the mother but also from peers and in couple relations. However, following on from the anti-cathexis of its trauma, its taking charge of its own recovery is a momentous step; it will start to remember instead of enacting its love and hate for its sibling.

With the Law of the Mother, the baby who has been indifferent to the other person's tears, the toddler who has persisted in demanding the mother for itself alone and behaved as though ego and other are the same is becoming

---

8  S. Freud, *Group Psychology and the Analysis of the Ego* (1921), *SE XVIII*, op. cit., p. 109. 'Identality' is a coinage from long ago when I was teaching English literature. The wonderful literary critic, Geoffrey Hartman, was very supportive when I introduced this term at the Whitney Humanity Centre, University of Yale in 1982.

9  Stunningly portrayed in E. Ferrante, *Frantumaglia*. trans. A. Goldstein, New York: Europa Editions, 2016.

the child who, from feeling her friend's distress as her own, can approach a concern for someone who is the same and not the same as itself. She grasps that the other person has feelings; this is the individual finding its way in the 'multi-person' concern described by Enid Balint in her work with Michael Balint:

> We are now considering a process which starts in the two-person mother-child relationship but needs, if it is to develop fully, a particular kind of multi-person relationship, the structure of which has not been described but which deserves serious study.[10]

The structure of this 'multi-person relationship' is a lateral *social* experience. The baby of Balint's observation can be added to the toddler; it adores the older child to the benefit of both: with energetic delight it can cohere its own body into an ego dance from the playful antics of the older child. In a social context – going into a room, meeting in the street – the baby's eyes are far more for the toddler (or older child) than they are for its parents. Taking in the other lateral child helps to produce part of the ego, of the 'I' itself for both or all participants.[11] While we must never underestimate the mother and her breast, there are also specifically lateral relationships which are always out there in the world to be internalized as contributions to the self.

This lateral mirroring does not invalidate the processes described by Lacan or by Winnicott on the vertical axis, but it does suggest that there is a further process taking place horizontally. It has long been understood that we 'internalize' the authoritative nature of our parents to form our own superego and, as we have seen, Melanie Klein has proposed that this is a process that takes place already at a few months old. But the fact that our 'I' is also constituted in part through lateral others sets up a different scenario. It is one that must encompass what goes wrong as well as right, for there are, of course, failures as well as successes on the horizontal axis.

'Decomposition', a term which has come to be used in relation to borderline and narcissistic disorders, is a quite frequent problem. In this case, the lateral friends and peers who have become composed 'inside' return to the 'outside' and are heard as critical voices. Now decomposed these peers were not enemies, but the child's friends and admired contemporaries who now seem to demand that the child, teenager or adult accounts for their failure to be as good as the others – a social phenomenon. If they had stayed composed internally, they would not have been parental-type critical 'superegos'

---

10 E. Balint, *Before I Was I: Psychoanalysis and the Imagination*, eds. J. Mitchell and Michael Parsons, London: Free Association Books, 1993, p. 69.
11 This is a different suggestion from Lacan's 'ego-ideal'. Different too from Klein's proposal of a superego.

which need to take in a 'Law', but rather 'ideal egos' – crucial determinants of emulation and aspiration. These instead are lateral models or heroes placed by the child above its own level for whose admiration the child has yearned in mirror fashion; now externalized and decomposed their voices have turned painfully critical. Thus, the structure of the shift from baby to toddler to child gets caught up in the web of lateral relations and their intersubjectivity.

## Intersubjectivity and the Narcissistic-Psychotic Toddler

Here at last – even if by accident – with 'intersubjectivity' we have a conceptual term designed for the individual in their social persona on the horizontal axis – a term that has for the most part been used willy-nilly for lateral relations and coined for mainly lateral group interaction. Psychoanalysis has long been interested in inter-relational phenomena. It has, for example, carefully attended to the baby and mother's mutual but different identification on the vertical axis, and to what Winnicott famously described as the 'transitional' stage of separation-in-relationship between mother and baby; the baby can be alone in her presence. And yet these instances would rarely be described as intersubjective.

Because there is no framework for it, 'intersubjectivity' is used either loosely or in incompatible ways. A prominent example is its deployment by 'Relational' theory, mainly in the USA, which considers it to mean the interaction of two existent subjectivities-in-process, each being shaped by and shaping the other. Emanuel Berman, an eminent Israeli psychoanalyst, gives a clear definition of this use when he describes how psychoanalysis is both a 'one-person' psychology (studying *intra*-psychic processes) and a two-person psychology (studying *inter*actions). The concept of intersubjectivity for Berman and Relational psychoanalysis attempts to integrate both aspects.[12]

However, for the horizontal axis there is no 'one' or 'two' person psychology to be added together; there are always *more than two*. Or, if apparently only two as in the prevalent 'pair' which we will see haunts our study, there is always a dialectical opening which constitutes a 'third' around them. Freud's theory has never been, as is often claimed, a 'one person' theory. Furthermore, especially after World War I, he was emphatic about the importance of the social dimension of the psyche, as for instance in the following oft-cited passage:

---

12  E. Berman, 'Psychoanalytic Supervision: The Intersubjective Development', *IJPA*, vol. 81, no. 2, p. 273, 2000.

The contrast between individual psychology and social or group psychology, which at a first glance may seem to be full of significance, loses a great deal of its sharpness when it is examined more closely. It is true that individual psychology is concerned with the individual man and explores the paths by which he seeks to find satisfaction for his instinctual impulses; but only rarely and under certain exceptional conditions is individual psychology in a position to disregard the relations of this individual to others. *In the individual's mental life someone else is invariably involved, as a model, as an object, as a helper, as an opponent; and so from the very first individual psychology, in this extended but entirely justifiable sense of the words, is at the same time social psychology as well.*[13]

(my italics)

Extremely important as this is, Freud's observation describes this interconnection in one direction only – the group embedded in each of us as individuals. However, each of us is also an individual inside the social group, as Bion's *Experiments in Groups* (see Chapter 6) illustrates. René Kaës, whose remarkable work with therapeutic groups in Lyons, France, has always, and increasingly so, highlighted siblings, emphasizes that the individual 'I' is one among others in the inner world as well as outside, socially:

The issue of intersubjectivity opens up a central question of psychoanalysis: it concerns the intersubjective conditions of the formation of the unconscious and of the subject of the unconscious. In these conditions, I call intersubjectivity the dynamic structure of the *psychic space between two or several subjects.* This space includes specific processes, formations and experience, the effects of which have a bearing on the accession of the subjects of the unconscious, on their becoming *I at the heart of the We.* This definition is very far removed from a perspective that reduces intersubjectivity to interactional phenomena.[14]

Kaës' definition explicitly contradicts Berman's perspective but neither psychoanalysts engage with the difference. Berman proposes a state of being which is already formed and constituted whereas Kaës highlights the unconscious which by definition is an open, un-constituted to-be-discovered way of thinking. What happens unconsciously in the intersubjective space, the space between two *or more* people, is not a fixture but will vary in different circumstances and at different psychic stages.

13  S. Freud, *Group Psychology and the Analysis of the Ego*, op. cit., p. 69.
14  R. Kaës, *Linking, Alliances, and Shared Space: Groups and the Psychoanalyst*, London: Routledge, 2007, p. 8.

Intersubjectivity can never be a static condition of our existence; it melds in with the age and stage of the participants – here the narcissistic-psychotic 'being' of the toddler in the toddler's world. Crucially, where Freud sees the 'we' in his individual patients, working with the social not family person, we need to trace the individual 'I' in the social 'we'. The toddler has lost its family 'I' so it needs to 'grow' a new 'I' which it can take to the group it is forming. This new 'I' is offered the empty space of its loss which is lying in wait, ready to be filled by the individual child as it forms and is formed in its rite of passage from its mother's law. We will see in the next chapter how its own determination to grasp the metaphoric world of unlike and like siblings is ready for its mother's narrativizing stories to offer it a future.

When the pre-social babyhood and infancy are relinquished, the still narcissistic-psychotic mechanisms of the toddler are socialized through the Law of the Mother becoming a rite of passage. This entry into the horizontal axis of sociality occurs at a time when the dominant psychic mechanisms fall along the *narcissistic-psychotic* spectrum rather than as *neurosis* with its greater recognition of reality. Thus, an implication of the fact that the toddler enters the social before it reaches the Oedipus complex is that the main psychic mechanisms that it first takes with it into the social are different. Taking its new 'I' into the 'We', what is labelled as narcissistic and psychotic become characteristics of all our social life.

## The Narcissistic-Psychotic 'I' in the 'We'

The narcissistic condition of the toddler is associated with sexual playing and physical auto-erotic self-love, as Klein (after a lengthy interpretation about parental intercourse) picks up from three- to four-year-old Peter's repeated insistence: 'When I told him that the chickens were his and Fritz's thingummies bumping into one another and spitting – that is, masturbating – he agreed with me after a little resistance'.[15] At the beginning of the twentieth century, a new recognition of the prevalence of childhood masturbation gave plausibility to Freud's revolutionary concept of an omnipresent infantile sexuality. Toddlers love to touch and play with parts of people's bodies – our hair, our nose, our mouth.... Auto-erotism features in narcissism which in turn manifests as the group of 'others' within oneself – all the people whom one is, in one's dreams. Positive narcissism gives confidence and contributes to self-esteem; it usefully re-surfaces in later life and is essential for recovery from any illness. In the last analysis, there must be sufficient narcissism to ensure survival. Crucial in times of need, this love provides a

---

15 Klein, *The Psychoanalysis of Children*, op. cit., p. 18. Overall, Peter has seemed relieved rather than resistant to interpretations of his sexual fantasies about his parents. He probably could not articulate these but would know that masturbation was not allowed.

foundation for the self/ego and features centrally on the horizontal axis as loving *others as oneself*. This is different from the Oedipus complex where the issue is the love of others *per se*.

In addition to a positive narcissism resting on the life drive, with the character of Narcissus in mind, the toddler's psyche also illustrates the fact that there is a destructive or 'negative' narcissism linked to the death drive. Here, as a feature of narcissism, if auto-erotism becomes compulsive, fixated and extreme like an addiction, then, as in the myth of Narcissus, it can threaten a decline and the death of the self. With adulthood the otherwise satisfying masturbation can shift into a driven series of meaningless 'one night stands' or abusive relationships. In negative narcissism, the 'other' features as another aspect of suicide, as the killing of the 'other' in oneself – 'O, what a rogue and peasant slave am I!'[16] says Prince Hamlet, king of intellectual would-be suicides.

Narcissism and psychotic phenomena are closely interrelated in late infancy and early childhood. A great deal of Winnicott's work is based on his thesis that in young children both narcissistic and psychotic responses are inevitable and normal defences against the impingement of reality and that a degree of this must be accepted in clinical work. This 'reality' on which the mother must interminably insist is always a step too far for the baby-self who emerges in the adult of the clinical context. Where for Winnicott the mother needs to get it reasonably right – she must be 'good enough' – in Klein's cases of Trude and Rita, the knowledge of reality is dependent on the child's ability to accept the 'deprivations' of life – most particularly those of the all-embracing very early Oedipus complex. With the sibling trauma it is different: the toddler experiences the mother's love for the new baby as the loss of love for itself. The negative narcissistic defences of the toddler attack the other baby in the toddler's self-defence and the positive ones act in the interest of the necessary love of the individual toddler for its own emerging social self – the 'I' in the 'We'.

Hurt by the total loss of the mother's erstwhile baby-love, threatened with the very real possibility of her life-threatening withdrawal, the toddler by means of a tantrum protest will make use of these narcissistic-psychotic defences. Its first social self will be a collective narcissism with all the excitement – the excitement of kids on the block and the later football crowd – that that entails. The psychotic too will be socialized so that the psychic 'splitting' will turn into social splitting – the 'divided' self, sugar and spice, very, very good and equally horrid. It will also quite normatively split its social group into friend and foe, thus moving from the pre-social

---

16  W. Shakespeare, *Hamlet*, II.ii.485.

to socializing the narcissistic-psychotic defences which are clearly distinct from neurotic defences.[17]

In popular understanding 'neurosis' is usually paired with 'psychosis' so that a neurotic orientation to 'reality' trumps the failures of 'mad' psychosis. Both concern defences together with the conflicts engendered by these defences, and both raise the question of how and what they are defending against. For neurosis the origins lie in five-year-old Oedipal childhood where, in addition to a better grasp of 'reality', something has gone wrong in the libidinal tie to a sexual object so the present-day sexual relations will be traced back to disturbances in childhood relations with the mother and/or father. In psychosis, on the other hand, there is a disturbed relationship to the outside world, the 'reality' of which the mother never ceases to insist on, and which the child's ego attempts to reconstruct, for instance, by socially acceptable shared illusions or private delusions that create a second 'untrue' reality. Unconscious and conscious are blurred. Thus again, what is crucial on the horizontal axis is different.[18]

The psychotic defences of the toddler gradually develop so that they merge into those that are dominant in the creation of the social person from its socially embedded pre-social self. 'Reversal into the opposite' can be the quick switch of loving and hating which otherwise happen at exactly the same time – what Pontalis (Chapter 7) specifies as beyond the banality of much vaunted 'ambivalence'. Socially, reversal into the opposite can be having disturbed mixed feelings about someone. 'Dissociation' can be a psychic cut-off, whereas socially it may be a necessary indifference to something one is powerless to influence. Foreclosure, denial and disavowal are all ways of psychically or socially refusing a reality which seems untenable. Projection is to be psychically lost in the other person and socially a way of understanding them. All these have negative social applications as well. For example, racism disavows or denies the reality of another person's existence. Sexism forecloses on the possibility that in positive ways a man could be like a woman. Fascism projects hatred of the other into a paranoid fear that it is the 'other' who is doing all the hating. These all have a source in the toddler's transition from infancy to childhood.

---

17  In one sense it can be claimed that psychoanalysis is about understanding neuroses. Thus, Laplanche and Pontalis write:

> The task of trying to define neurosis, as revealed by clinical experience, in terms of the comprehension of the concept of neurosis, tends to become indistinguishable from the psychoanalytic theory itself, in that this theory was basically constituted as a theory of the neurotic conflict and its modes.
>
> *The Language of Psycho-Analysis*, op. cit., p. 269

18  It would be interesting to see if there could be an exchange here with the propositions for consciousness offered by Mark Solms in, for instance, his latest book, *The Hidden Spring*. London: Profile Books, 2021.

There are important implications for the narcissistic and psychotic expressions of the baby, infant and very small child on the horizontal axis of sociality. In the vertical attachment of mother-and-baby, we allow the baby (and to an extent, temporarily, the mother with her essential 'maternal preoccupation') its madness. But this is not so with the toddler: here the new baby has claimed an exclusive right to all that is crazy. The toddler is not ready for this transferral; the charm of its illogicality may now become an irritant to the mother and as such assist the implementation of her Law. The infant does not just grow up – it also *has to grow up*. No longer allowed to express 'madness' in its tantrums, the child's earlier baby-infant mechanisms and defences are transposed onto the horizontal axis as social adaptations. All our lives we have neurotic, perverse and psychotic potentials. Our normal personalities can regress to – or express – these states any time of the day or night.

## Lateral Relations in the Clinical Setting

Because the difference and autonomy of the horizontal is not credited, most accounts consider social life as taking place on the vertical normal-neurotic plane. This means that when something goes wrong it is explained as a *regression* from the normal-neurotic to the psychotic-mad which should have been left behind on the vertical axis. In fact, the axes co-exist, and going wrong is as much a characteristic of society as going right; that right and wrong are two sides of the same coin is evident on the horizontal axis.

Our reluctance to acknowledge the importance of the horizontal may lead us to miss important dimensions of the transference in the consulting room. With the omission of the sister or brother in the transference the particular and crucial toddler-infantile experience of becoming one among alike others is left out of the picture. Because the analyst in the transference is considered a parental figure, the psychosis too must be understood on the vertical. If the analyst were to see that he is the sister in the transference, then it might be realized that it is the social group or couple relationship rather than the parental dynamic which is causing this particular difficulty and it is this that could be helped. Male violence against females is largely a lateral affair. Psychotic and narcissistic aspects of lateral relationships – including work relationships, marriage, violence with enemies, quarrels with friends – get ignored or folded into the certainly also valid vertical paradigm. Not only the potential origins but also the current problems and future psycho-social maladies of lateral interchange remain untouched.

The infant's wish to kill and its illicit sexuality return from the un- or preconscious 'elsewhere' to which they have been relegated through the lateral defences, as can be witnessed in the ease with which the legitimated violence of later life spills over into abusive excess. In rape and domestic violence, in the torture and other abuses that accompany warfare, it is these toddler desires which break through into adult life. They can be directed to the self or to the other – both demand that (as well as vertically) we think laterally. When the effects of the trauma of war persist through the lifetime of the sufferer, we are likely to be looking not only at the horrors the victim experiences, but also at the bursting through from unconsciousness of the murders its toddler-self wanted and, in traumatic circumstances, still desires to perpetrate. The law against sibling murder and incest is made real by the trauma of annihilation in the sibling trauma which preceded the prohibition.

The 'primary repression' aims to make only an 'anti-knowledge' of the 'sibling trauma', as previously described. The prohibited effects of the trauma on the one hand will be socialized and made into the truisms of everyday behaviour (splitting into friends and enemies) and on the other hand because its effects are also the desires for incest and murder, they must be defended against and made sufficiently 'unknown'. This will not be the same either as the primary repression of the sibling trauma nor the secondary repression of the later male Oedipus-castration complex, but instead appropriately lateral defences that do not go down into the unknown depths, which Klein discovered but Winnicott thinks are not yet there. The primary repression of the initial sibling trauma will be impermeable and iron-hard, but the prohibition on sibling incest and murder will make use of both shallower and weaker defences than on the vertical.[19] These lateral thoughts and feelings will shoot off sideways into elsewhere. At the younger toddler age, these lateral psychic defences against the prohibition of sibling murder and incest very much merge with the wider unconscious which we all bring with us into the world – this, rather than any weakness of the law, particularly against murder, means they can be socialized. Socialized they will be preconscious, available to be known about and, if required, ultimately conscious. In part this accounts for the persistence of the dynamic unconscious being missed on the horizontal axis.

Children enter sociality at a time when they are toddling and chatting away to each other. To think of siblings and their 'nursery' as coming after the parents is obviously logical from an adult perspective – parents exist before their children. But psychically the child in us precedes the parents. Furthermore, the child's perspective is different: children are obviously members of the family, but they also endeavour to repudiate it, as they will do so again yet more demonstrably when as teenagers they repeat these features of their toddlerdom. We need not to forget the toddler-sibling origin of this partial rejection of the family so striking in adolescence, but we must remember too the ever-available excitement for good and ill of being in a 'same person' group with 'other' people.

---

19 Are these the defences of her child patients which Klein assigned to the three-to-six-month baby on the vertical axis?

# Chapter 4

# From the 'Sibling Trauma' to the Horizontal Axis of Social Relations

The birth of a sibling – or its imagined existence – brings the social foursome into the family; but at the same time the toddler exits to become a small child with other soon-to-be happy refugees. Still in the family it is also repudiating, the same toddler on the vertical axis, will do its utmost to get its mother's love back again until the Law of the Father prohibits this at Oedipus time. Meanwhile with other children she or he will form a new and creative social group within the social world of which they have always been a part. Most importantly, with the Law of the Mother, the sibling trauma is transformed into a rite of passage so that each three-year-old together with its peers can proceed to make its own individual contribution to the horizontal axis. This concluding chapter of Part 1 scoops up the mainly descriptive preceding accounts and explorations and places them in the larger, radical thesis of the whole argument. I shall not signal each repetition as they will be used anew in this different context.

To summarize the first stepping-stone: the Law of the Father operates on the vertical axis, *between* generations; incestuous sexuality is its primary target. It applies to the threesome of the family. The Law of the Mother, on the other hand, operates only on the horizontal axis, *between* siblings within a generation. Its range applies to all the biological siblings and their social heirs. It forbids incest between her children, but in this case, it is the prohibition on murder that carries the greatest weight: death not sex is the first and foremost focus of the Law of the Mother and therefore needs to take precedence when we try to build a picture of the social world on the horizontal axis.

The interaction of the toddler with its first actual or expected sister or brother is the 'sibling trauma' which, together with the prohibited reactions to it, establishes a specific 'foundational' social trauma very different from, but in this foundational status, analogous to the Oedipus complex for the individual child in the family. The toddler will willy-nilly have had to accept the mother's prohibition of sibling incest and murder; its failures will make it in different degrees 'a-social'. If it fails to become sufficiently social, at its core will be the 'death' experience of the sibling trauma which will have been

DOI: 10.4324/9781003347125-6

converted to the prescribed punishment of desertion – no more care and protection for its still highly vulnerable dependence – the danger of actual death for an abandoned two-to-three-year-old. As noted previously, Freud is clear about the identity of the individual and the social: 'In the individual's mental life someone else is invariably involved, as a model, as an object, as a helper, as an opponent; and so from the very first individual psychology, in this extended but entirely justifiable sense of the words, is at the same time social psychology as well'.[1] Rene Kaës calls what Freud is describing the 'We in the I'. If instead we follow in the footsteps of the toddler, it is its individuality which it is taking to and managing in its social group – not the 'We in the I' but the 'I in the We'. This is equally paramount with its social 'We in the I' self. In a way that seems paradoxical but is not – it is this 'I in the We' which psychoanalysis omits in its theory but practices in its clinical work. Whatever its orientation, the practice of individual analysis takes the struggles of the individual ego for granted and forgets its necessity in constructing the social world in which it partakes.

The toddler's foundational experience is repeated at puberty when a huge surge in psychosexuality accompanies the major physiological changes occurring at the onset of the capacity for procreation. The repetition and transformation of the Oedipus complex for the individual within the family is well charted but the significance for the social aspect of the coming of adolescence is no less major on the unreported horizontal axis. There is a crucial repetition of both the sibling trauma and the implications of the 'Law of the Mother'. This time around a gender division of future marriage (girls) and fighting (boys) is added to the part they play in the construction of the social world. How does this change operate unconsciously as well as consciously? As with the toddler, born into a larger society no less than into a smaller family, the 'world' with its structural gender expectations is there for the adolescent to make its contribution.[2]

Once again, it matters here that the originating sibling trauma is a trauma simply because only a trauma (and not a 'difficulty') sets in train crucial unconscious processes. Hitherto psychoanalysis has largely followed sociological thinking such as that based originally on Gustav Le Bon or Elias Canetti in suggesting that something in the numbers, the massification, intrinsic to the social world changes its unconscious modalities. Thinking about an interdependent but also autonomous horizontal axis necessitates, to the contrary, considering a 'social unconscious' which comes about at the very site of the construction of the social. The social unconscious is now variously defined particularly by group analysts but

1  S. Freud, *Group Psychology and the Analysis of the Ego*, op. cit., p. 69.
2  This will range from the unorganized crowd or small group to organizations such as school and work and their accompanying institutions.

introducing the notion of a horizontal axis offers a special case. Where other definitions consider what an already formed society contributes to our psyche, instead a horizontal axis of lateral social relations asks almost the opposite: what is the interaction between the individual and its always present collective social context which *produces and reproduces* the social in the first place?

In *Totem and Taboo* (1912), Freud had accorded just such a structural constructive position to *brothers*. This quasi-anthropological speculation or 'mythology', a favourite of Freud's, but a much disputed (and today under-used) book, contended that at a certain point all the sons of an hypothesized original or *Ur* father realize that instead of being only sons they can act as the brothers whom they also are.[3] Together they can, and do, murder their father because he has insisted on keeping all the women for himself. They claim the daughters of the father as sisters who, with the father dead, are sexually available to themselves. The brothers then realize that, like their father before them, each one of them will want all the women for himself. As a consequence, laws regarding whom a brother may or may not marry are instituted. Freud argued that a *contract* ensuring this between the brothers is what initiates the social world – prior to this contract all belongs to 'pre-history'. But we need to ask: and what of the sister?

It is the woman as sister not as mother who marries. In *Totem and Taboo* society is formed by the brothers on the basis of a prohibition on sibling incest; a prohibition on murder of rivalrous others is implicit and secondary. The picture changes when we look from the side of the sister. How and whence does a gender distinction arise on the horizontal axis and under the Law of the Mother, a law which emphatically does not – as a law – differentiate in any way between her girl and her boy? These sisters and sisterhood will conclude this study (Chapter 10), while suggesting there is much future work to be done.

Although one can feel its presence behind the revolutionary *Moses and Monotheism* created near his life's end, the placing of brothers as founders of the social in *Totem and Taboo* was not developed further. So that, despite the propositions about the fraternal social contract, these lateral relations have ever since been treated as relations within the vertical family axis. Brothers and sisters are simply woven as follow-ons from fathers and mothers in the Oedipal situation – the killing of the unrecognized father Laius and the un-witting incest with Jocasta, his mother (the ignorance indicates that Oedipus is unconscious of his acts). This enactment with the mother-wife is forbidden from the position of the father in the 'castration complex'. The drive to commit parental incest and murder will continue to exist unconsciously but it

3    Gillian Gillison: *She Speaks Her Anger: Myths and Conversations of Gimi Women. A Psy-chological Ethnography in the Eastern Highlands of Papua New Guinea.* London: Palgrave Macmillan 2021.

should not become conscious. The girl like the boy represses her so-called 'male' incestuous desire for her mother before her specifically female Oedipus complex urges her instead to seek out her father's desire (Chapter 8). Incestuous love and murderous hate among siblings have been understood, then, as an extension of the desires and prohibitions at play between children and their mother and father.[4]

With the birth of children, the Oedipus complex becomes a 'family complex', and only then in turn, a 'social complex'. Though this may well be so on a vertical axis, at the very same time the social horizontal axis of lateral relations implicit in Freud's thesis of a fraternal contract in *Totem and Taboo* instead gains aid as a crucial separate trajectory for siblings. Yet, so clearly, the role of the sibling trauma and Law of the Mother for the social world is very different from the threat of castration which ends the 'male' Oedipus complex for both sexes roughly two to three years later. But, as already argued, it is also in some ways equivalent, or at least analogous, to it. Both are all-important structures for the psychosocial world, but not in the same way.

As clinical practice and as the theory that arises from and makes use of this, psychoanalysis is bounded not only on the physical side by biological conditions but also on the social side by sociological determinants. Although this is also true of the Oedipus complex, I am arguing for an autonomous horizontal axis of lateral relations, the social peer-group dimension of those relations must loom particularly large. But its significant biological condition also differs from that of the vertical axis. The extreme prematurity of the human baby, so significant a biological factor within the family – which the paediatrician and psychoanalyst Donald Winnicott makes his province (Chapter 5) – differs in importance on the horizontal axis. Unless the age gap between them is as great as that of a child from its parents, siblings potentially have the longest live relationship.

However, although this lifetime relationship is important, what we need to select for their biological constraint is the fact that they have what anthropologists describe as a 'minimal difference' between them. This concept is a relational way of describing how, if they are full siblings, they receive and share genetic material from each parent – this gives them a double quantity which makes them more genetically alike to each other than to either parent. This genetic near 'sameness' provides the biological reference point of the psychological need to do the opposite – in other words, to establish their

---

4   The implications of the vertical Oedipus-castration complexes are wider than the fundamental prohibition and desire becoming unconscious; today it is *de rigueur* to argue that with their advent prohibiting maternal incest and paternal murder, 'third-ness' is realized: every child has two parents whether or not they actually know them and this places then in a triangular situation. With this, the *huis clos* of the pre-social dualistic baby-and-mother comes to an end. However, although very differently, there is already a third position with the dynamic presence of two siblings and a mother.

difference. From within the sibling dynamic, sameness and difference rather than the notorious rivalry haunts our picture of the sibling world.

## Unconscious Defences

Certainly before, but more particularly from birth, the mother has been introducing her offspring to reality. By the time of the Oedipus complex and the Law of the Father, the child has a sufficient grasp of the unpleasure of not acknowledging reality to realize that repressing its illicit desires in a satisfactory manner is a good idea. Before this, such a recognition had only gradually come to the toddler after the Law of the Mother had become effective. In the case of the desire for parental incest and murder during the Oedipal phase, the defence mechanism in operation is that of repression, and this means that the symptoms which are the expression of whatever is trying to escape repression will be described as taking place on a normal to *neurotic* spectrum, which simply indicates that a sufficient grasp of reality has been achieved.

Because the desire for sibling incest and murder and the defences that follow their prohibition have usually been understood to function as part of the Oedipal constellation, it is assumed that they should function in the same way. But of course, they do not – the toddler is younger than the Oedipal child and 'reality' to start with is chiefly a persistent and mostly annoying flash-in-the-pan from its mother's insistence on it. The toddler partially tries (without success) to keep its 'naughtiness' secret. In kind-enough circumstances, this will be part of its charm. It carries its toddler features with it to act as a major aspect of our social life. The reaction to the mother's law is both to use psychological defences other than repression and simultaneously to socialize these as common sociable behaviours.

Thus, as mentioned previously, other psychological defences shape the lateral relations of friends and foe that come to constitute the social world on its horizontal axis. Because siblings enter and contribute to the social earlier than the Oedipal child, they therefore use a wider range of psychic defences than repression. These lateral psychic processes contribute to their own provenance of being likewise 'everywhere' in the theoretical material. In the clinical material these defences are 'shallower' but no less present processes than the vertically deep secondary repression of the castration complex.[5] Because of the toddler's lost babyhood and its need for its own survival, they are psychically self-interested, narcissistic, and because of its still tenuous relationship to 'reality', they are it is technically 'psychotic'. This, the narcissistic-psychotic, for better as well as for worse, will be socialized as an aspect of our everyday life. We may no longer shout loud and clear for what we want but certainly we use behaviour which is the equivalent.

---

5   Contributing to Winnicott's counter to Klein that 'early is not deep'.

Because as older children and as adults we have been both toddlers and Oedipal children, we will have both a poor and a good grasp of reality available to us depending to a degree on our individual history. So too at different times, we will use both one and all the defences available to us.

The structures of these early stages are crucial. It is the infant or young child's transition into being social that constitutes the psychic nucleus from which our psychological being, in sickness and in health, as individuals and as social beings, develops. Pathology, infancy and childhood are the equally crucial scenarios for all enquiry into unconscious processes. But what are the implications of the rite of passage whereby the toddler–infant transitions to the small child? Psychoanalytic thinking goes in for descriptions rather than diagnostic categories. As a short-hand illustration, the world-renowned analyst Otto Kernberg, in his extensive work with 'borderline-personalities', suggested that within the general category of narcissism there are three positions – normal, malignant and pathological – and so will there be with the transitioning child. At the extreme pathological end are what psychiatrists know as psycho- or socio-pathic individuals who completely lack the ability to conceive of the feelings of another person. Causes may be many and various – but here we can add that the syndrome may be the result of a failure of the sibling trauma to be survived in a rite of passage from infancy to childhood.

Quite normally for the toddler, there was at first no concept that the new baby had its own existence; if it was not part of itself then all the toddler wanted was for this imposter baby to vanish from the face of the earth. The Law of the Mother with its threat of desertion changes all that or fails to do so adequately; the social world is bound to have criminals. Rather than widen the problem to multiple causes of criminality, narrowing it to the persistence of the sibling trauma in lieu of a rite of passage might offer a path to understanding. There may be many reasons that cause this failure but this failure may be the cause. Certain circumstances may foster an excessive response to an experience of death and also an extreme reaction of murderousness which, for some reason, the Law of the Mother has been unable to transform. Is the sociopath so mindlessly fearless and endlessly danger-courting because he is so terrified of the death that has happened to him?

Meanwhile psychoanalysts join the crowd of experts who by and large cannot help this extreme end of human behaviour. And we are left with noting that as the relationship of the narcissistic-psychotic to reality and the type of defences used to keep what is unwanted at bay differ at different stages, so too, to a degree, will this necessitate diverse modes of clinical investigation. It is said that extremities of anti-social behaviour such as socio- or psychopathy do not present as such in toddlers[6]; however, in the

---

6   The Mayo Clinic (USA) considers that anti-social behaviour appears after age 18. *The Washington University Review* notes that sociopathy and psychopathy have only been regarded as treatable in the last twelve years.

UK it has been noted that mental health concerns such as self-harming are affecting younger and younger age groups. This is most likely linked to the great increase in the divide between the seriously poor and worryingly rich, with swathes of England having three out of four children living in severe poverty – as has long been the case in the USA. The sibling trauma will leave its legacy and the crucial benefits of the mother's law will be urgently needed – the question will be what causes the transition from one to the other to fail?

## Clinical and Observational Methods

In very schematic terms, there are two broad roads through which we can try to understand unconscious thinking and the defence processes which are utilized to keep what is forbidden unknown. Psychoanalytic theory re-lies on the use of the pathological; this is not different from the normal, it is only an exaggerated and hence more visible version of it. There is also an understanding of the child to whom the adult patient regresses or where he has remained fixated. In the petri dish of the clinical encounter there will be either an infantile fixation or a regression to the child transitioning from the pre-social to the social – both at the time of the mother's law and of the father's law. In the consulting room with an adult one waits for the moment when, as the analyst Joyce McDougall put it – 'the child is coming'.

It would be surprising, however, if child analysis, vertically as practised, horizontally as proposed, did not use some different modes of clinical work. One difference would be Melanie Klein's introduction of the means of special play to the young child as the equivalent of adult 'free associa-tion' which is speaking without censorship. Through its play with the toys she provided, Klein could discover the baby in the child's regression. As we have seen, the toddler and small child was the present-day child through whom she found yesterday's baby still active. Very differently Winnicott saw playing as the 'royal road' to culture; he watched babies and children playing and himself played in diverse ways such as drawing exchangeable interpretable 'squiggles' with his patients (Chapter 5) and being playful in his personal life. For the horizontal axis, the toddler itself and then the child–child interaction until puberty, the lateral adolescent and then adult, is the patient within whom we need to find the hitherto neglected psycho-social toddler.

Particularly useful for the toddler-in-all-of-us is the prevalence of the un-discussed and un-named sibling trauma that permeates the clinical reports of such innovative analysts as Winnicott and Klein. After this is actual infant observation. Such observation is practiced by allied fields[7] and observational

---

7  Jane Selby and Ben Bradley. See also the work of Colwyn Trevarthan.

genius bears testimony to its ground-up perspective in any science. The cy-togeneticist Barbara McClintock went down her microscope to join in the social activity of her maize germ cells – then she sat on rough grass outside the lab and closed her eyes in order to see the cell world in which she had been participating over the years. She was considered somewhat mad by her fellow scientists until she received a Nobel prize.[8] Comparably, the practice of the psychoanalytic pioneer of 'infant observation', Esther Bick, was de-scribed by a student:

> As she delved into the world of the infant, it was as if she went underwa-ter, and swum around in a world of the infant's mind and then surfaced and related what she had found there. She would be piecing together some information that she'd noted. When she told us what she had seen, it then gradually emerged to become clear for us students.[9]

Bick, like McClintock, was exceptional; they both learnt from their subject – with this immersion so-called 'participant observation' (which is sometimes too intrusive with its own ideology) becomes non-participatory because it is seeing the whole rather than identifying with one or a series of individuals.[10]

Clinically or observationally, we can listen to toddlers. Just as they 'toddle' rather than walk so they may speak but as yet do not usually 'talk'. It would seem that they need the experience of one-becoming-two of the sibling trauma to reach an awareness of metaphoric knowledge. They are driven to work hard to understand the nature of metaphor which transforms language. Meanwhile they forewarn us of our later mental and physical stumbles; foreign metaphors are the last verbal acquisitions for immigrants.

## 'Constructions' in Analysis and Primary Repression

Sigmund Freud wrote:

> ... it is a 'construction' when one lays before the subject of the analysis a piece of his early history that he has forgotten, in some such way as this: '...up to your $n$th year you regarded yourself as the sole and unlimited

---

8   Of her own history with this very comparable observational ability and training, McClin-tock pertinently observed that one must await the right time for conceptual change. Have siblings found the right time as the social and horizontal triumph and their own numbers decline in the prosperous world?

9   A. Briggs, 'The Life and Work of Esther Bick', in A. Briggs (ed.), *Surviving Space: Papers on Infant Observation*, London: Karnac, 2002, pp. xix–xxx.

10   Letters from and discussion with my late husband, anthropologist Jack Goody.

possessor of your mother; then came another baby and brought you grave disillusionment...'[11]

Is Freud's late introduction (1937) into the theoretical literature of an implicit clinical practice of some standing – 'constructions in analysis'[12] – more than an interesting description? Is there something intrinsic to the nature of a 'construction' that made Freud – very near the end of his work and life – perhaps unconsciously or preconsciously select this sibling experience in the quotation above to illustrate his argument? A latent theme of this chapter is the biographical knowledge that underlies the impersonal statements. As Chapter 7 on J.-B. Pontalis will demonstrate, every psychoanalytical writer has their self-analysis permeating their objective thinking. The subjectivity is objective.

I suggest this 'construction' repeats the story which the mother tells her eager child; it is the story which will come to save the day for the traumatized but metaphor- and story-seeking toddler. A construction is a story, a generic one – something that happens to all of us. Aspects will be unconscious but can become available to the pre-conscious and consciousness. They can help – 'you are not dead or demolished; like almost everyone else you survived this take-over by your new sibling'. What, then, is the significance of Freud's choice of the sibling trauma to illustrate a psychoanalytic 'construction'?

Israeli psychoanalyst, Rachel Blass proposed that initially Freud equated 'truth' with 'reality' but that this shifted with his introduction of the concept of making 'constructions' through which 'truth' was then verified by the patient's 'conviction'. Is this correct? Convincing or hoping to convince a patient is always problematic and indeed is counter to the ethics of the analytic endeavour. It is highly pertinent that it is the experience of a new sibling which illustrates or elicits something that can invite not conviction but reflection and change. Freud's early equation of reality and truth persists with this late introduction. On the horizontal axis a 'construction' is indeed itself a union of reality and truth, as is a true and realistic story – however fantastic.

At the turn of the nineteenth and twentieth centuries, what had been the hysteric's re-construction of the trauma of paternal abuse turned out not to be the case – to be 'unreal' or 'untrue' as described earlier. This was a trigger for a turn away from the actuality of trauma into the all-importance of desire. 'Constructions', however, are essentially not the always popular 're-constructions' which lay claim to a supposed factual ('real') personal history: 'Johnny's mother ignored him...' etc. Such re-constructions of likely

---

11  S. Freud, 'Constructions in Analysis' (1937), *SE XXIII*, p. 261.
12  Ibid., pp. 255–70.

facts should be recognized so that the relationship to them, but not their actuality, can be changed.

An analytic 'construction' on the other hand is something altogether different from a re-construction – it relates not to an individual actual event or experience, but to an important, plausible and *general* 'historical' truth of which everyone has their different individual experience, in which other unconscious and conscious factors as well as what quite probably may actually have happened are all in play together. Each person will have their own very particular experience of this shared human happening. Where a re-construction particularizes – 'this happened to Johnny but not to Jane' – a construction, to the contrary unites the particularity; the same thing happens differently, but to everyone – the mother's story and the toddler's transition. There is no cure for what has happened, no changing it, but there is the openness to changing how it is experienced.

The generic fact is that the toddler has a baby sibling which the mother cares for. Johnny may remember his individual experience of how much he loved his new sister, what a happy event it was. But a construction refers to the particular experience of a generic occurrence of something that will have been traumatic or painful. This aspect will have been forgotten, subject to amnesia, and a story produced around it; the construction can counter the oblivion and any falsity. The generic event which is constructed is something unconscious and universal: by way of illustration Freud offers us the sibling trauma.

Pain and trauma have been forgotten because of infantile amnesia – we do not easily remember our illicit sexuality or murderous violence, our wish both to assimilate and to eradicate the new baby. The notion of 'infantile amnesia' generally refers to forgetting the pre-Oedipal phase; in fact, it is before three years rather than five – the pre-social – that has succumbed to this universal omission.[13] But more totally than this, the pain and confusion of the sibling trauma which annihilated our toddler identity have vanished, leaving only its effects such as a persistent jealousy which can also motivate the older child to strive for what may feel like a life-saving superiority.

Forgetting the 'death-like' experience of one's own vanishing brought about by the accepted presence of a complete substitute for oneself needs to be factored in as a specific feature of the recorded 'amnesia'. A few get near to the experience with intimations of mortality. A friend can clearly remember in her adult present, her feelings as she looked at the young woman who had been brought into care for her when her brother was born at home. She lay in her child's bed watching this woman standing in her pyjamas looking

---

13 Infantile amnesia is very widely recognized and very variously explained. The primary repression of the sibling trauma associated with the instantly prohibited sex and murder of the response is a good candidate for amnesia.

pensively, meditatively out of the window. Still today she can have the feeling of her two-year-old self: translating the felt-thought – 'that is what it is to be big and grown-up and I don't really understand it'.[14]

Mothers and others may tell the toddler that they are now 'grown-up' – a strange idea to have to grasp when one so clearly is not an adult, 'a grown-up', and not that much bigger than yesterday. Toddlers often look meditative. This may be why a toddler unrealistically tries to assert its independence. But in fact, the toddler is thrust into metaphor. The multitude of emotions that take the toddler forward into the mother's law or backward from its success to an undiscoverable hole suggest that something else underlying the feeling-thoughts is at stake. Klein wrote of 'memories-in-feeling' as defused throughout babyhood. However, if we link the phenomenon of feeling-thoughts to the pre- and post-sibling trauma we have a structural possibility. Are these feeling-thoughts our first memories and what has gone before the advent of an actual or a possible sibling that is not only the result of amnesia but also of a pre-history before metaphorized memory? When people describe our babyhood it has no self-referential resonance; when they recount incidents from our forgotten toddlerdom we find ourselves listening to a story.

The movement from infantile amnesia to cognizance of a metaphoric story-telling world is momentous, but the whole issue of memory is so complex that only a question or two can be raised here. For instance, the Oedipus-castration complex succumbs to what is sometimes called 'secondary repression' as a primary repression of some sort clearly precedes it. As we have seen, the suggestion here is that the earlier experience of the death of the 'self' is the primary experience which will be 'primarily' repressed – it is cast out to a place that is also beyond or other than memory. As we saw in Chapter 2, a traumatic force that breaks through the protective barriers of our psyche can be 'anti-cathected'; this is a psychic energy that is glued to any idea or object – anything – that can *oppose* what has happened ever coming to consciousness. There is a powerful investment that is capable of rejecting something becoming conscious; every force possible is deployed to prevent the trauma taking up residence inside us. 'Primary repression' is used to explain various experiences that can only be pulled out of a black hole of total amnesia into a recognition that it was likely to have occurred.

14 What Laura Cumming in *On Chapel Sands* has beautifully written and constructed is in fact based on the completely false belief and therefore false construction that there was something mysterious about her mother forgetting the first three years of her life. Infantile amnesia has to happen and is completely, universally typical. Cumming was intruding into a way of life which she failed to understand was normal. Her mother's single memory of jam-tarts is the typical, one real memory or 'screen' memory we all have.

If, however, we relate this to 'no memory' in the pre-history before and the advent of memory which comes afterwards, then the artist referred to by Milner in Chapter 2 or the everyday, everybody creativity emphasized by Winnicott, pulls something of the no-memory pre-history with them. Subsequently, such a recognition of pre-history and history would come from a successful construction-in-analysis. At the time of the toddler's transition, the mother's 'narrative' and the toddler's incipient grasp of its new metaphorical status as being now 'grown-up' are able to make the absent primarily repressed sibling trauma into a plausible story.

Yet of the many traumas of babyhood and infancy, including, possibly, birth,[15] only the sibling trauma which is primarily repressed also produces illicit desires that have to be prohibited. The procedure of anti-cathexis applies to the sibling trauma itself but not to the prohibitions the mother utters. These must be defended against but not as totally as with primary repression; the defences against the wish for incest and murder will be split off, dissociated from, but are also available for the help which the mother (or her equivalent) offers as a further story, a 'construction', her narrative.

'Constructions', then, are immeasurably important for a reason that goes well beyond engendering a 'conviction' for the patient. A construction, in referring to 'historical' truth, suggests how the individual's distinct and particular idiosyncratic history fits into a generic or universal one. A construction is a new *representation* of the 'facts'; as a representation it stands alongside fiction, a fiction based on a universal fact and a likely particular individual history. Without giving it a title, Freud offered the sibling trauma as a classic case to illustrate his introduction of the concept into the theoretical praxis of psychoanalysis. A 'construction' is an analytic story used to re-think the earlier stories of sibling infancy and childhood. Through this, the trauma of the mother's potential desertion if her prohibitions are not adhered to can become the key factor in a rite of passage to a stage of social childhood. The unremembered sibling trauma passing through the mother's law joins the rite of passage through which the small child will contribute to the horizontal axis of social relations.

## The Toddler's Metaphor and the Mother's Narrative

Early on, Freud worried that his case histories read like stories and indeed psychoanalytic listening from one unconscious to another unconscious can only start when the story stops. What then is the relationship between the claim that the toddler is socialized through narrative and the coming into

15  See the theses of Otto Rank.

being of psychoanalysis only when the story no longer has a place? I suggest that it is the written case histories which are the 'I in the We', the theme and the story that Freud eschewed in his own work. For instance, the 'female homosexual' of whom in 1920 he wrote a story-like case-history is a teenager demanding her place in a promiscuous social world in the hope of escaping her mother's new pregnancy which was taking place in the strictures of the family.[16] The 'unsuitable' woman she adores, like Dora's Frau K before her, could be a sister rather than a mother substitute. Repeating her toddler experience as does every adolescent, her parent's actual repetition of a new sibling was an 'insult' too far for this teenager who could herself have been expecting the baby– she heads out of the family and into dangerous pastures new: a florid social world. Freud says she is normal and should be left to work out her own subjective bisexual nature.

An 'hysteric' – or the hysteric in all of us – will twitch his facial muscles to indicate what a 'slap in the face' felt like. He is returning metaphoric language to the body where he had initially understood it as literal. He is, once again, a toddler before it grasped that we live in a metaphoric world. Freud wanted his patients to talk instead of twitch – so they told him the stories they thought he wanted to hear and sometimes insisted on telling the ones they themselves wanted to tell.[17] This was a toddler trying to tell a story to a mother who knows the general narrative. It does not matter to whom the narrative belongs as it is everyone's story of what they want. What we all want by definition is exactly that which we most cannot do or have – to be the baby it was and at the same time the infant who plans to practise the forbidden incest and forbidden murder.

The mother's law helps the toddler to move on linguistically. In a nutshell, the new sibling, on whose hopefully permanent presence the mother insists, is the same and different from the toddler – the essential condition of metaphor. And reciprocally metaphor enables the serial positioning of siblings and their social heirs. The toddler, realizing something is going on in the conceptual world, tries out its literalness. Famously, one of Bion's patients recounted finding her small daughter on the large bed with her profiled head on the tummy of the baby that the mother had placed there for safety. Questioned about her posture, the little girl replied: she was keeping an eye on the baby. I recall my own then same-age daughter jumping with total concentration from side-to-side of a wooden-brick wall she had built – like her departing baby-sitter, she was 'fencing'. In my own childhood, my small brother would not eat the orange he loved and that my mother had peeled and prepared for him; she tried another and another; having joyfully

16 S. Freud, 'The Psychogenesis of a Case of Homosexuality in a Woman' (1920), *SE XX*, pp. 145–72.

17 See Frau Emmy in S. Freud: *Studies on Hysteria. SE II*.

gobbled my fill of the rejects, I was suddenly inspired and said: 'this one is a plum orange' – it was the 'blood' oranges he had not been able to stomach.

In time the metaphorical world and the ever-available narrative mitigate the anxiety latent in the compulsively repetitious demand the small child makes that the same story be told with minute accuracy over and over again. The wish to have what one wants can be left to dreams and the story gives us what is allowed. We can have a mother who is still one's own mother even if she belongs as a mother to someone else as well; there are siblings and playmates who are not quite the hero who is oneself even if in the disguise of a giraffe. The story re-configures that the world is full of other people. And later it tells us 'we won the war' and 'Reader, I married him'. As this book moves forward the mother's Narrative will be seen as different from the Symbolization that comes from the father. Narrative insists on a future.[18] The storyteller is embedded in the collective world; the mother and toddler have two different perspectives on the same experience, which is a condition and a quality that for Walter Benjamin characterized the social story in contradistinction to the 'lonely' novel which is from the viewpoint here, the refuge of the feeling so alone social teenager who needs her own story yet again.[19]

## Socializing the Psychic Defences; the Interacting Horizontal and Vertical Axes

Within the family the toddler's move is from the pre-Oedipal relationship to the mother to the Oedipal triad of child, mother and father, but the transition from pre-social infancy to social childhood is different. Horizontally their younger selves as sisters and brothers start to convert their infantile narcissistic-psychotic psychic existence into the type of psychological defences that we practise in order to get along in our everyday world. For instance, intra-psychic 'splitting' of the 'good' available breast that comes and the 'bad' refusing breast that fails to do so becomes inter-psycho-social divisions of good friends and bad foes. The psychic features of the normal toddler on the horizontal axis become characteristics of normal social life. In good time this socialization of the narcissistic-psychotic will join with the normal-neurotic perspectives of the post-Oedipal to produce the psychic

---

18  'Then my question was why, and in that tiny book I started to guess aloud on paper about what the connection is between the stopping of time and the impossibility of narration'; Denise Riley on *Time Lived, Without Its Flow*, London: Picador, 2019 (first published 2012). 'Lisa Baraitser in Conversation with Denise Riley', *Studies in the Maternal*, vol. 8, no. 1, 2016, p. 5.

19  This is described by Walter Benjamin in 'The Storyteller' and beautifully exemplified by Edith Wharton in *Souls Belated*.

melee of vertical and horizontal that makes up the social world. The family itself remains vertical – parents with sons and daughters who outgrow their narcissistic-psychotic and unrealistic psyches as, with the overcoming of the Oedipus complex, they move into the symbolic organizing world of the patriarchy. But the horizontal social practices will not be subsumed by the symbolizations of the vertical.

In both pre-Oedipal and pre-social cases, the narcissistic-psychotic defence mechanisms of the toddler are normal; so too are our post-Oedipal symbolizations and our post-sibling trauma socializations. Our theories need to make room for both. The vertical helps us or fails us in the process of growing up as individuals; on the horizontal, where the same narcissistic-psychotic defence mechanisms are instead socialized, they become rather the characteristics whereby we form communities or their obverse. Where the child on the vertical narcissistic-psychotic changes to become neurotic under the father's law, the same child on the horizontal does not change psychic modality – accompanied by its reality-inducing mother it instead *socializes* its narcissistic-psychotic way of being. The symbolizing patriarchal, vertical family must bear the responsibility for the world's dominant cultures and its dire oppressions – the we in the I. The initial toddler-age of this earlier socialization must take responsibility for the good and for the bad, for the fun, the creativity and the distressed violence of the social – the I in the we. And of course, each individual is born into both and bears both within them as they go; one may be born a black girl in a dictatorship or a white boy in the upper classes of a democracy.

The 'terrible twos' and the far less 'dreadful threes' continue to underpin the social world when it goes wrong – when it goes right it is thanks to the rite of passage producing a social grasp of reality. A crowd relives the excitement and fears of that earliest social formation of the toddler becoming a small child. At post-toddler time, the vertical has contributed the told-off worried or worrisome individual in the family and the horizontal offers instead the independent single child, whom the mother encourages to contribute its strength to its new social group. Our social single and our family individual selves overlap and co-exist but are not identical. When the two axes come together post-Oedipally, each have made this different contribution: 'he's so happy-go-lucky at nursery school; he is whiny and clinging at home' and any number of permutations.

If we see the vertical Oedipal and horizontal sociality as different structural lines, then what is called in anthropology the 'atom of kinship' is a split atom. The term 'atom of kinship' was coined by Claude Lévi-Strauss, who held that affinal (or marital type) relations framed the most basic and irreducible unit of kinship. Lévi-Strauss defined this unit or 'atom' as a husband and wife, their son and the wife's brother. Against this, theorists who privileged 'descent' defined a set of parents and children as the core of kinship relations. In our terms here, affinal relations are 'lateral' relations – the couplings that 'inherit' the relationship of siblings. While in Lévi-Strauss's 'atom', descent is subordinated to the affinal framework – the father and son to the son of the husband and wife – developing the horizontal along with the vertical hypothesizes a split atom; there are both affinal relations and descent of parents and children. For fleshing out a horizontal axis of social relations we need vertical descent and horizontal affinal relations to start from the same source, they split and then come together again! Psychically a culture has both an individual descent unconscious, as in the analysis of the *neurotic individual*, and an affinal social unconscious as in the analysis of *group narcissistic-psychosis* and of the individual in the group – the I in the we.[20]

To be psychologically 'foundational', the transition from one psycho-social state to another must take place *in childhood* through a confrontation with residual universal kinship laws which act against one's desires. On the horizontal, no-one can exist in the exact same place as another and must be totally assimilated or made to vanish totally – toddler-fashion. The father's castration threat for males on the vertical and the mother's threat of desertion on the horizontal both exemplify a foundational 'transition': a previous 'old' state must be demolished and a new one must commence. When successful, both the desires and the prohibitions are made unconscious. Later transitions repeat in their own manner the original, foundational procedures.

Although hopefully a child will acquire the Laws, even with a rite of passage a foundational trauma never entirely vanishes. The primarily repressed sibling trauma can only be reached in its effects which are subject to the law. No act of repression which is only designed to stop both the experience and the reactions to it becoming conscious is ever completely successful. It is a constant potential presence – hence the characteristic repetition. But in addition to this, particularly as a result of the socializing of the unconscious defences, there is always a slippage between the prohibitions and the 'allowances' or social expectations and injunctions which are the prohibitions' other side. For instance, the prohibition on sibling incest should lead to the socialization of marriage with a partner who is at some (but not too much) remove from the sibling with whom the incest was prohibited: your partner should be the actual or social brother or sister of your friend or friend's friend – a change but far from a complete break with the achievements of social childhood.

The so far 'acceptable' dimension of this need for the sexuality of incest is retained as the desire for coupling and bonding within the same or similar social group, which of course means that social classes, ethnic and racial groups still tend to inter-marry. The clearly negative side is the fact that around one third of women worldwide either realistically fear or actually

---

20 My thanks to Alan Macfarlane for alerting me to this possibility and to Sarah and Alan for their personal and intellectual hospitality.

experience serious violence from their male partner.[21] Could this be because he is too often the socio-psychological heir to the toddler's reaction to the new baby? Likewise, torture, a feature of the murder the traumatized toddler wants to commit, and which is accounted a differentiating mark of terrorism, is all too frequent in the legal warfare in which brothers are supposed honourably to engage.

## Gender, Male Hysteria and Siblings

A gender distinction is no part of the mother's law. How does it arise in the division of girls to marriage and boys to warring, which in turn ensures that the horizontal axis plays its part in the continuing world-historical oppression of women (Chapter 9)? Because unconscious thinking is universal, it is essential that it was recognized by psychoanalysis that men can be hysterical. On the edge of madness, King Lear felt the 'mother' rise in him. Yet the destiny of the awareness of male hysteria captures the dilemma.

Throughout its world-long life, hysteria – the wandering womb – has been assigned to women. Yet to specify a sex for an unconscious psychological condition is impossible. Any and every one can become hysterical. We can see the problem in its more local effect in the gendered disposition of hysteria as portrayed by psychoanalysis. In the first explanation it was thought that both men and women had been abused by their fathers – a traumatic origin to the illness. But though prevalent, abuse could not be universal, so the understanding began to take shape that the father's sexual love was what was desired. Trauma as the main factor was put aside, and from the insights of the clinic the observation of an Oedipus complex eventually emerged in its place. However, despite this, within its chequered history, whenever *male* hysteria has been acknowledged, it has continued to be associated with a traumatic occurrence – a fight in the street, an accident at work. But as trauma had been discredited as an explanation, the acknowledgement of male hysteria along with its trauma dropped out of sight.

Both sexes pursue what is described as the 'male' oedipal desire for incest with the mother and the murder of the rival father who possesses the mother. The girl's Oedipus complex then startingly differs, so that what she desires is the father's desire for her. This female Oedipus complex is exactly what Freud and Breuer's male and female hysterics had claimed in the 1890s. However, this changed, so that it was decided that the desire belonged to the girl, not the father. It is no accident that because of this every girl but no boy has what is called a 'positive' Oedipus complex which is that of a hysteric. In turn this explains why hysteria is covertly re-assigned to women and missed in men.

21  Report of the WHO 2019.

This is one source of the explanation of how, as soon as it is noticed, male hysteria constantly disappears from consideration: taking its trauma in tow male hysteria bifurcates both as practice and in how we understand it. It was considered to resemble female hysteria as a desire for the father and it thus became equated with homosexuality.[22] As with other oppressed social positions, homosexuality was labelled 'effeminate'. Two bullets from the status quo hit the mark of the gay man and the heterosexual woman at the same time.

As suggested, to counteract this stigma of the 'feminine' on behalf of the 'maleness' of male hysteria, more than a whiff of physical virile trauma remained attached to it long after the idea that trauma was a causative factor for hysteria had vanished. Introducing the hysterical and bisexual toddler on the horizontal axis counterposes this unacknowledged gender distinction of 'trauma' for macho men and 'desire' for hysterical women and effeminate men. In the sibling trauma, there is a trauma that occurs for both sexes at a time when, despite behavioural gender typing, both sexes are still dominantly psychological bisexual subjects.

We will never lose our bisexuality, but when we are toddlers the result of the sibling trauma is that we are meant to learn subjectively for the first time that we are either a girl like the new sister or a boy like the new brother – but not neither nor both. This lateral awareness is covered by the concept of 'Gender' introduced by second-wave feminism to distinguish social sex from its biological – female/male – manifestations. Gender rests on this psychic subjective bisexuality and the psycho-social distinction of sister and brother and their lateral heirs. It also makes the terms 'sister' and 'brother' crucial beyond their simple designation. While the exploration of omnipresent lateral relations initiated by sisters and brothers in their sameness and difference as siblings should be demanded more widely, it is mandatory on the horizontal axis. It is this wideness to which 'gender', as specified for the horizontal axis, can lay claim.

## Psychoanalytic Thinking and the Horizontal Axis

Psychoanalysis – as clinical treatment and consequent theory – in its concern with 'unconscious' or 'primary process' thinking (vs. conscious or 'secondary thinking' processes) asks how these are connected with the important hypothesis of the 'drives' (the specifically human version of

---

22  It would double the length and defeat the purpose of this book to go into details about the vertical Oedipal axis, so I only do so in so far as it is salient for the horizontal axis (Chapter 8). It is spelled out from the perspective of its use for an understanding of patriarchy in my *Psychoanalysis and Feminism: Freud, Reich, Laing and Women*, London: Allen Lane, 1974, 2000.

'instincts' from which they differ). Freud called the drives 'our mythology'. Drives 'are mythical entities magnificent in their indefiniteness'.[23] They are 'mythical' because they can only be a postulate of something obviously needed by the observable activity of the organism. A 'drive' is a force 'lying on the frontier between the mental and the physical' that is crucial to human life. It is the wild west wind of the soul – an energetic pressure which makes the mind work to eliminate instinctual tension by trying to get what it needs or wants by whatever means it can. Wanting what we cannot have might seem a condition of life! The hard-working mind finds that it cannot always have what it wants. But the drive persists and works to find another route.

Desires and their vicissitudes are many; what is universally prohibited and therefore repressed or defended against in some effective way is what counts for human society. Psychoanalysis addresses the repression of the prohibited desires as well as the resistance we display in our determination not to have any further knowledge of them – to forget they exist. With repression, the representations, the images and the ideas of both the desire and the prohibition become unconscious. The mother's prohibition of the desire for lateral incest with, and murder of, the new baby prevents the toddler from being the baby it has been. Realistically, in developmental terms, it is also impossible to stay as a baby at this point, but the psychological defence that indicates something has become unconscious is produced not by the developmental stage – crucial though this is – but by the prohibition of the desire. It is exactly at this developmental point that the prohibition must be activated – hence the all-importance of the Law of the Mother. The toddler must give up its unrealistic, impossible demand to be the only baby and pursue the drive within which it operates to find the satisfactions of being 'grown-up'.

Sexuality is there from the beginning: we 'sexually' suck the breast or bottle which is present and hallucinate or sensually fantasize or dream what is absent. But modifying sexuality as 'sensuality', as many instances may suggest, although it is a factor, will not do overall. Being sexual is an omnipresent human condition which, due to our extreme dependence on a human caretaker, leads quite normatively to an excess of the emotions of love and hate so that they become incestuous and murderous and must be prohibited. In addition, with siblings there is a further and different consideration: the toddler wants the mother so desperately because the mother seems no longer to want the toddler as her one-and-only baby. As she sends it away to play with its peers, it wants more and more of her love. It thus sets out on the vertical road which leads to Oedipal-incestuous desire, while at the same time it tries to take on the mother's prohibition of its lateral desires towards

23 S. Freud, 'Anxiety and Instinctual Life', *New Introductory Lectures* (1933), *SE XXII*, p. 95.

the new baby whom it must leave behind till it can turn it into a sibling friend (or enemy) – or sexual partner.

The 'death drive' and the wish to murder similarly underlie the milder expressions of everyday violence. Both sexuality and murder are expressed and satisfied in dreams and in the psychopathologies which we all display in common, perverse, narcissistic, psychotic or neurotic behaviour. They appear in their frightening forms as prohibited desires in the clinical encounter. Oedipally the child wishes to murder the father who possesses the mother. It is the same drive and desire but in a different context for the sibling. With the sibling, the object of these same sexual and murderous desires differs – so too does the structure. Differently from the mother and father who are separate, the sister or brother whom the toddler incestuously desires is also the very same person whom it wants to eradicate, to murder. Love and hate, sex and death are intertwined. There is no gentle 'ambivalence' here; instead, what we have is 'reversal into the opposite' (Chapter 7).

While all human societies utterly prohibit those sexual and violent drives and desires that go under the collective names of 'incest' and 'murder', the structural context affects the personal. The South Sea island matrilineal Trobrianders, mentioned earlier, occasioned a spat in the 1920s between the eminent anthropologist Bronislav Malinowski, who had studied them, and the well-known psychoanalyst Ernest Jones, who insisted that the universal Oedipus complex must be discoverable there. There would have been no quarrel if they had discussed what they knew: that as a *matriarchy* one needed to consider that the psyche of the dominant social structure passed through *siblings*. Siblings, not parents, were entirely the main objects of the prohibitions.

## Bisexuality and Social Allowances

The toddler who has felt incestuous and murderous to the new baby is a bisexual subject. It wants sexually to 'assimilate' and murderously to 'eliminate' the baby sister or brother irrespective of its gender and irrespective of its own too. This bisexuality needs to be emphasized because it is crucial always to bear in mind that this moment when toddler siblings acquire the sister–brother meaning of their gender is when their subjective bisexuality is the same for girls and boys and they are completely indifferent to the gender of the object of their desire. In both popular and psychoanalytic discourse bisexuality tends to be considered as a matter of someone wanting a partner of either sex – what is called 'object choice'. However, it is the bisexual *subjecthood* of the toddler that is universal – the sex and gender of its object choice is an individual and various matter. From the viewpoint of unconscious processes it is our permanent and persistent psychic bisexuality that underlies transgender, which has always been present as a position in human societies.

As far as the mother's law goes, it is a bisexual, gender indifferent small child that forms its social group. However, it is not only the unconscious forbidden desires and their prohibition which we take with us as we go, but also the pre-conscious and conscious 'allowances', effectively requirements, that are the 'other side' of prohibitions. On the vertical, these requirements are for becoming parents and exercising parental ruling – the girl must give up her 'male' desire for incest with the mother and in becoming the object of her father's desire, she should want to have a baby instead of a penis; the boy living under the threat of castration can eventually follow on from his father as a paternal rule-giver. On the horizontal, the allowances and requirements are for lateral marriage or its equivalent instead of incest and, instead of murder, killing one's erstwhile brother who has become the enemy in legal warfare.

Current reproductive technologies are widely regarded as potentially changing the vertical situation: biological women are no longer the only means whereby motherhood can be realized. Whether or not this is a new situation or a further realization of what has always been a social possibility for the vertical family, it is nevertheless the case that on the horizontal there has never been the tight tie-up with a biological determinant. Sisters and brothers are biologically distinct, but this has its effect where sisters are equated with mothers (Chapter 10). Depending on local legality, marriage and warfare have always been available to same or other sex proponents. At their core is the prohibited incest and murder and their allowed/prescribed other side. And of course, the separation of the prohibition and of the allowance is not as neat as this – legal warfare is also defined by what is not terrorism and marriage by what is not sex-trafficking, yet each constantly spills into the other. With this thought, we can open the discussion to use well-known psychoanalytic theorists to isolate the key features of the horizontal axis – how the narcissistic-unrealistic stance of the toddler effects all we do, its definitional sociality and the predominance of death.

# Part 2

# Three Theories

There are three distinctive features of the proposed horizontal axis as it is expressed in a fraternal system. These are: that clinical descriptions of a sibling trauma lie in the narcissistic-psychotic stage of social relations; that the social is distinct from the familial and that the prohibition on murder between siblings is stronger than that on incest and therefore death takes precedence over sexuality in the unconscious.

Part 2 discusses these three central constituents of the social horizontal axis through the work of Donald Winnicott, Wilfred Bion and J.-B. Pontalis. Winnicott's vivid and pertinent case-histories displaying the sibling trauma and his depiction of the narcissistic stage of development form the setting which we need to use for the crisis of the toddler confronting the new baby. Bion's *Experiences in Groups* is used to demonstrate that the social is entirely different from the family; J.-B. Pontalis' 'On death-work' is examined to show how death and the difficult concept of a 'death drive' must be foregrounded over and above sexuality. And in 'Brother of the Above', a booklet written some thirty years later, Pontalis describes 'frerocity' among pairs of brothers in literature, psychoanalytic instances and his own personal history – a hugely resisted but compulsory self-analysis. Is fraternity a hope or a disaster?

DOI: 10.4324/9781003347125-7

# Chapter 5

# Donald Winnicott

## Narcissistic-Psychotic Development. Do Siblings Count?

In the many years that I have been arguing for the importance of siblings and a sibling trauma, Winnicott's work has been a stand-by – a rock of stability in the choppy waters of the unexplored. I understood his infrequent but adamant certainty that there is always a 'separation trauma' for the two-year-old as the vertical effect of what was also at the same time a horizontal trauma for the toddler confronting the baby that stole its place. A reason for my grateful confidence in this equation was the fact that virtually every one of Winnicott's clinical cases and references claimed that the new sibling caused the onset of the toddler's breakdown and illness – often physical as well as emotional–psychological. Along with my own practice and that of colleagues and supervisees, Winnicott's clinical instances permeated my thinking – yet his intellectual superstructure seemed always to ignore this material basis in his clinical work which itself was paramount for his work in general. The observations which he made of his clinical acumen remained at a practical descriptive level:

> This boy has been coming to my department at hospital since three years old. He was well until his sister was born when he was 18 months old, whereupon he became violently jealous, especially when his mother was feeding the baby. He would rush up to his mother and pull down her jumper and try and get the breast for himself, or he would stand by furious when his mother was changing the baby's napkins or preparing her cot. His jealousy of the new baby slowly turned to love of her and great pleasure in playing with her.[1]

At a theoretical level, for Winnicott what is primarily universal is the specific fact that as human beings we are uniquely born prematurely into an

---

1   D.W. Winnicott, 'Children and Their Mothers' (1940), in L. Caldwell and H. Taylor Robinson (eds.), *The Collected Works of D.W. Winnicott, Volume 2, 1939–1945*, Oxford: Oxford University Press, 2017, p. 84.

DOI: 10.4324/9781003347125-8

environment and to a mother on whom – completely helpless – we utterly depend. As an orientation this 'universalist' condition of prematurity and dependence[2] can be deployed for babies but not, however, for the transition to sociality which the toddler must make. Nevertheless, I think we can insert pre-social siblings into his important contribution of the developmental narcissistic-psychotic stage which he depicts for his mother's baby. Dealing with the toddler's desires for murder and incest and their prohibition produces dynamically as opposed to descriptively unconscious processes where they have been missing along with a distinct horizontal axis which Winnicott had absorbed into his analysis of the analyst as mother.

Winnicott's emphasis on a specific maternal 'trauma of separation at two years'[3] highlights a different aspect of the same trauma as the 'sibling trauma' which he certainly knew about clinically, but which had no place in his psychoanalytic postulate. In trying to understand why this explanatory place is completely missing for these all-present siblings, I have come to think that in this instance there is a disconnect between Winnicott's practice and his theory – but that both are useful. I will indicate briefly the prevalence of a sibling trauma in his clinical material in order to introduce the nature of this disconnect, which arises out of his specific premiss for the foundation of psychoanalysis, and then will focus on two cases where the theoretical understructure needs to allow for siblings in a way which it cannot do.

These two cases are first a man with a 'split-off' traumatic internal 'foreign object' who is a psychically a penis-envying little girl, and second a teenage girl who is compulsively repeating her toddler sibling trauma which Winnicott had also treated. Thus, he totally excludes from any larger 'overview', theoretical or otherwise, what he has no shyness in constantly recording in his clinical work – not only the presence but also the effects of a sibling trauma which will be repeated in a person's later history. This is the case even when – as in the loss of identity – these are the very effects which characterize its impact.

## Some Siblings in Winnicott's Clinical Cases

The little girl who called herself 'the Piggle'[4] is an exemplary instance not only of the sibling trauma but also of how this will continue in impor-

---

2   One could usefully put this beside Otto Rank's proposal of 'birth' as the psychic determinant – paradoxically using Rank enabled Alfred Adler to put siblings in the driving seat where prematurity enabled Winnicott to put the mother.

3   D.W. Winnicott, *Playing and Reality*, Harmondsworth: Penguin, 1974 (first published 1972), p. 80.

4   D.W. Winnicott, *The Piggle. An Account of the Psychoanalytic Treatment of a Little Girl*, London: Hogarth Press, 1978. Also in Mitchell, *Siblings*, op. cit.

tance beyond its resolution with the Law of the Mother. The Piggle had a sister when she was twenty-one months old and Winnicott describes the annihilation of the 'who, where and what' the toddler felt itself to be before this subsequent baby took her place. He reports:

> The mother said there had been a great change toward ill-health ... [the Piggle] was not herself. In fact, she refused to be herself and said so: "I'm the mummy", "I'm the baby". She was not to be addressed as herself.

He continues: 'she was very conscious of her relationships and *especially of her identity*' (my italics).[5] An 'identity-crisis' notoriously surfaces in key situations or periods such as teenage years (see 'Sarah' below) or in the gender distinct history of women which we will come to in Part 3 (Chapters 8–10).

Siblings are so prevalent in Winnicott's practice, his lectures and his random publications that perversely their key role comes to seem to be a reason for ignoring them in his overview. A woman patient as a child had lived in an isolated fantasy world which Winnicott saw as extended into her habitual and serious adult dissociation. This had originated when, being much the youngest of many siblings, she always had to play assigned roles which she did not understand and so had spent her time as a child in her own 'make-believe' world. He describes this, yet his explanation is that only a badly handled maternal prohibition on thumb-sucking was the source of her adult problems – and so indeed it may have been. But the obvious is left hanging. Siblings which keep coming up in the material can only be a parenthetical factor in the 'separation trauma' on which he insists thus: 'the string-boy' as Winnicott refers to one worrying patient 'had recently tied a string round his sister's neck (the sister whose birth provided the first separation of this boy from his mother)'.[6] String, which could have throttled a baby, is only important because it signifies re-establishing contact or denying separation from the mother.[7] At age seven it still features in the boy's abuse of this same sister. Or again, as so often, his illustration of an argument is taken from the siblings omitted in his theory:

> In this case [that of baby Hannah] it happened that having a hot poker put against her neck corresponded with nothing already in the infant's mind. As a result little ill-effect can so far be noted. Nevertheless, when the child reaches a more advanced level of emotional development,

---

5  Ibid., p. 13.
6  Winnicott, *Playing and Reality*, p. 17.
7  The boy became addicted to drugs in adolescence and Winnicott hopes anyone dealing with his case will consider the history of maternal separation; I suggest that string-games always demand attention.

anxiety will quite possibly be referred back to the incident, which may then come to represent to her the cruel assault that it was.[8]

It was Hannah's two-year-old brother who at the height of his 'sibling trauma' attacked her with a poker. Ignoring the omnipresent siblings and privileging separation from the mother is a part and parcel of Winnicott's basic theoretical stance; it must bear the weight of the disconnect as far as siblings are concerned; a disconnect which is a necessity for Winnicott's successes and fame.

To repeat briefly and residually, the foundational proposal of classical psychoanalysis is that there are psycho-social effects of the defences against universal prohibitions: for both the vertical Oedipal and the horizontal siblings these prohibitions on desires go under the umbrella terms of murder and incest. The defences make the desires and their prohibitions dynamically unconscious – and the conflict between them produces symptoms that the therapeutic procedure tries to understand and help to resolve.[9] Childhood is the key period for the imposition of these prohibitions on these desires because it is when we have to become social human beings. Although implicitly engaged with Freud's work, Winnicott has no truck with this – instead, he took up the object-relational nature of our human species which is inevitably produced by our biological uniqueness. Helplessness, as a consequence of this, effectively forced his hands – there was no place for siblings or their trauma – except in his practice.

## Winnicott's Universalism

We are born so prematurely that our survival relies on older people to care for us; we are entirely dependent on these carers. Ignoring desires and prohibitions, it is on the terrain of this prematurity and dependency that Winnicott set up his tent, working as a necessary and brilliant replacement carer with the baby and infant, both in actuality in his paediatric hospital work as well as in his subsequent psychoanalytic practice for the infantile states of mind which persist in all of us all our lives. By the same token, our distinctive prematurity makes us equally dependent on, and vulnerable to social conditions which he calls the 'environment' – the world that is there – personified in the 'environment mother'.

Winnicott had always wanted to undertake what he called 'a classification of the environment', and although his training analyst, James Strachey, discouraged him, he made various attempts at it. 'Environment' has a locality

---

8  D.W. Winnicott, *Through Paediatrics to Psychoanalysis*, op. cit., p. 9.
9  'Late' Freud wondered if symptoms were produced when the 'life drive' predominated and 'guilt' when it was the 'death drive' that was ascendant.

and factuality which the 'social' as a general term does not have. What is achieved with 'environment' is a grounding in the everyday immediacy of the wide-open feature of prematurity which characterizes us as a species. The repercussions arise from the 'givens' of our bio-social condition, not from the constructions we make of this factor. The use of such an underlying principle embraces a very different *universal* from that of the prohibitions and defences – it is Winnicott's faith in the relational consequence of what he considers to be the unique biological pre-condition of prematurity and dependence that suggests this different 'universalism'. 'Universalism' in general became a bugbear of 'postmodern' theory, but this is not my critique.

Winnicott's 'universalism' has several pertinent ramifications which will appear during this chapter. It is both the producer of, and produced by, Winnicott's stance as a developmentalist. For now, we have to recognize that siblings cannot be fitted into such a perspective – *their dependence on each other does not and never will emanate from the universal prematurity of human birth*. In turn, Winnicott's orientation affects the meaning of trauma and regression and much else besides – 'trauma is that which breaks up an idealization of an object by the individual's hate reactions to that object's failure to perform its function'.[10] And: 'For me, the word regression simply means the reverse of progress... reversing the flow of time'.[11] When he does discuss siblings for themselves, then, it can only be in homely, on-the-side observations, such as his suggestion that they get over their problems and are always a good thing because it is better to sort out love and hate with actual relations than with fantasies. There is, then, a disconnect between Winnicott's acumen about siblings in his direct observations in the clinic and his framework of universal prematurity which can have no place whatsoever for them in their specificity.

## Narcissistic-Psychotic Normality

Nevertheless, very usefully Winnicott's always existent 'separation trauma' for the toddler from what is called 'the environment mother' crucially admits or re-admits[12] serious effects at two years old to a central place in psychoanalytic theory. Although Winnicott does not explore his own contention, yet nevertheless the absence of siblings from the overview still leaves this perspective as the context in which their clinical presence

---

10  Ibid., p. 145.
11  Quoted in L. Quagelli, 'Reading Winnicott: Return to the Concept of Regression to Dependence', *IJPA*, vol. 101, no. 3, June 2020, pp. 456–78. Followers of Winnicott rediscover buried concepts such as temporality –'afterwardness' (*nachträglichkeit*').
12  'Re-admits' because it is there in Freud's letters to Fliess and repeated in *Moses and Monotheism*.

is firmly set. Winnicott offers an inestimable portrait of the normalcy of a narcissistic-psychotic stage in which early defence mechanisms such as dissociation come to the fore to protect against what for him constitutes trauma – archetypically when the loved mother on separating from her toddler becomes overnight the hated mother.[13] In thus focussing on the baby and mother through his direct observations and through his psychoanalytic stance, Winnicott's work contributes a powerful portrait of the narcissistic-psychotic world of the baby, infant, toddler and small child in contradistinction to the neurotic perspective of the Oedipal and post-Oedipal child and adult. As we will see with Bion on groups and Pontalis on death, what Winnicott tells us about narcissistic-psychotic *normality* helps with siblings even though he placed them totally outside his theoretical frame.

Groups, death and narcissistic-psychosis are crucial features of the toddler's world on the horizontal axis. This chapter then is not a general account of Winnicott's contribution to the psychoanalytic field, but instead a narrower presentation both of where a sibling dynamic pinpoints something missing in his theses and of how his clinical work and the narcissistic-psychotic and traumatic conditions which his work presents can be harnessed for the horizontal axis. Furthermore, the narcissistic-psychotic phase can be considered in a social framework where the trauma which emanates from the 'environment' appears to produce social-psychological maladies as much or more than psychological symptoms, thus confirming the proposal that, when successful, the resolution of the mother's law is socialized – so too when it fails.

This superstructural relegation of the clinically all-present siblings can be best discussed by cases where they seem to matter, where they are not incidental but are potentially contributors to the unconscious social dynamic of the situation under scrutiny. For this I shall use the two pertinently different cases of the male patient who had a 'split-off' little girl as a traumatic 'foreign object' within his male 'self' and the teenager whose paranoid psychotic breakdown repeats her toddler 'sibling trauma' when her sister was born.

## The Clinic and the Theory: A General Background

Winnicott's way of presenting his work is highly particular and the presentation matches the argument. He could not be further from where we will end with Pontalis on metapsychology nor more strident in his opposition to the notion of a death drive which he described as equivalent to the notion of

---

13  Winnicott is giving an alternative explanation to the material of toddlers and small children from whom Melanie Klein secured her thesis of a schizoid-paranoid phase followed by a depressive resolution. Klein is concerned with the subjectivity of the baby, for Winnicott this is dependent on its relation to its object – the mother.

'original sin'. Of his own methods as a renowned psychoanalyst, he himself wrote shortly before his death:

> This work ... arises out of my clinical experience and is in the direct line of development that is peculiarly mine. I cannot assume, of course, that the way in which my ideas have developed has been followed by others, but I should like to point out that there has been a sequence, and the order that there may be in the sequence belongs to the evolution of my work.
>
> What I have to say ... is extremely simple. Although it comes out of my psychoanalytical experience I would not say that it could have come out of my psychoanalytical experience of two decades ago, because I would not then have had the technique to make possible the transference movements that I wish to describe...[14]

Winnicott's notorious 'simplicity' rests on his universalist premiss of the psychic importance of prematurity and dependency – this is not untrue or unimportant, but undoubtedly it is simple. On the other hand, his clinical work with its 'transference movements' can develop and become enriched in a way not available to his theoretical presuppositions. With this in mind, to show the progress which he suggests in the quotation above, I shall mainly use his final psychoanalytic book, *Playing and Reality*, published posthumously in 1971, with its theoretical claims, and also refer to his writings before, during and after World War II, which demonstrate his extraordinary observational skills as a paediatrician and his clinical work as a psychoanalyst. As he says, his work arises out of his clinical experience, and its interaction with explanatory modes will be the trajectory here – from clinical practice to explanation and theoretical claims.

## Psychosis

Where for Melanie Klein the three-month-old baby is dominated by an internal emotional experience of a paranoid-schizoid 'position', for Winnicott any 'position' is an external social fact. This perspective owes much to the forty years until 1962 when he worked at Paddington Green Children's Hospital which became part of the post-war National Health Service. Here and in his World War II work with evacuees Winnicott encountered the antisocial and psychotic child more frequently than the neurotic. For Winnicott, as for others,[15] psychosis in the adult is a completely *normal* baby writ large.

---

14 Winnicott, *Playing and Reality*, p. 86. Hereafter, references to *Playing and Reality* will be given in the text.
15 Though contrarily for Klein whose three-month baby was schizoid paranoid as a generic psychosis. The same observation with opposite way around consequences.

In the 1950s and 1960s schizophrenia and everyday schizoid states were the psychoses that were popularly greatly feared and professionally frequently ascribed.[16] Winnicott set himself against this trend:

> It is important for us that we find clinically *no sharp line* between health and the schizoid state or even between health and full-blown schizophrenia … In fact, if we look at our descriptions of schizoid persons, we find we are using words that we use to describe little children and babies, and there we actually expect to find the phenomena that characterize our schizoid and schizophrenic patients.
>
> (pp. 66–7)

For Winnicott, an adult who experiences psychosis or madness is someone for whom the temporarily and quite normatively 'mad' mother-and-babyhood somehow went wrong – the baby's mother must have been too absent, too depressed, not good enough, have had insufficient reverie – or *too* mad. In a hospital setting, Winnicott aimed to give the family itself (above all the mother and to a degree the father and any siblings or grandparents) the tools with which they could become the necessary therapeutic environment for the 'ill' child – an extremely important project.

As a young analyst Winnicott had very deliberately undertaken to treat 'a dozen or so' cases of full-blown adult psychosis. In his late life, renowned for his innovative work, many patients came to his practice because their hitherto successful defences of dissociation and splitting were breaking down. Between the two periods, his practice as a child analyst made him very aware of how the two-year-old child patient with its 'trauma of separation' from the mother reveals its babyhood – all the variations of maternal identifications and separations that make up the mother-and-baby's life. He could use his knowledge of actual babies and children in observations and in clinical work to chart the progressions and regressions which reveal the psychological child within an adult patient. All too often an analyst and patient can conduct an apparently successful therapy of the neurotic problems while avoiding not only the psychological baby but also the underlying psychosis.

## The Environment and Play

The aspect of the thesis which matters here is that in psychosis as distinct from the psychoneuroses, it is the environment which forces the recipient of its impact to muster various psychological defences before the secondary

---

16  R.D. Laing sent *The Divided Self* (1958) to Winnicott saying he owed everything to him.

repression of the Oedipal crisis comes to dominate the situation.[17] Winn-icott considered that it was the environment that had failed these children but that, while the environment could be improved for the future, its past failure could only be treated in the illness of the child. These early defences are attempts to resist the traumata which disrupt the illusion of omnipotence which is the baby's essential self-protection. The baby and its successor – the patient in treatment – should have felt omnipotent: it is its world and its world is it.

In the context of the 'environment' it is social behaviours and delinquen-cies such as stealing that characterize the psychotic psychopathologies which burst out when these early defences fail. They break through the de-fences that characterize the 'too good' child – a dilemma of Sarah in the second case to be considered here. In these breakthroughs we witness a bid for health, a statement that the environment has been at fault, not 'good-enough' in specific respects.

Dependency entails something on which to depend – even in her desire for conception, as well as post-natally, the mother is the baby's first envi-ronment. Notoriously, Winnicott claimed that there is no such thing as a baby without a mother; the baby cannot exist outside the environment on which it depends – the 'environment mother'. At a neonatal stage there is a primary identification with the mother/the breast – the breast should be an element of the baby's 'being'. A period of non-differentiation and mutual identification is necessary if the baby is sufficiently to trust the environment on which it so utterly relies. The possibility for creative living in which one feels one is oneself instead of being compliant with others' demands rests on the 'environment mother' seeing her baby for what it is in its particularity.

Different dependencies will be necessary at different times. Winnicott claims for instance that a baby of a certain age can tolerate 'x' amount of the absence of its mother; the amount 'y', which is intolerable, can still be repaired by the mother on her return, while 'z' cannot, and the baby will become mad with an un-mendable anxiety. From the baby's 'z' perspective the all-essential mother is dead – 'this is what "dead" means'. At this stage mother and baby are one, but Winnicott's claim about the absent mother still sets up the experience of death as the outcome of a future object-relation. This tallies but also contrasts with my suggestion that it is the toddler as subject, not the mother as object, who 'dies' in the sibling trauma.

Countervailing the traumatic 'death' experiences, Winnicott privileges the role of play. Play (with humour) is therapeutic because it is the child's natural way of coping with abuse, neglect, and lack of protection or too much frustration. Instead of having to deny what had gone wrong and

17 In the thesis presented here this could apply to the mother's insistence on reality.

develop a false, compliant personality, the child who is able to play can transform untenable reality into some everyday creative act and perception and through this make use of positive elements in its experience in order to come to terms with the traumatic elements. For Winnicott, the human importance of 'playing' as a state of mind and body was not to be interpreted as an association to problematic unconscious ways of thinking as it is by Melanie Klein but as an emanation of a person's self. There can be a playfulness between analyst and adult patient in the particular use of each of them within the clinical transference experience or as a practice from drawing 'squiggles' (see 'Sarah' below) to verbal communication. Play becomes what happens in the transitional space that develops between two people; in this location it comes to take on the status of the origin and reproduction of human culture – 'cultural experience begins with creative living first manifested in play' (p. 100).

Not only play but much more takes place in the transitional area which is initially between mother and baby. Winnicott wrote of what was to become this highly successful notion of a 'transitional' arena in a relatively early paper, 'The Deprived Child and how he can be Compensated for Loss of Family Life' (1950):

> ...one difficulty every child experiences is to relate the subjective reality to shared reality which can be objectively perceived. From waking to sleeping the child jumps from a perceived world to a self-created world. In between there is a need for all kinds of transitional phenomena – neutral territory. I would describe this precious object by saying that there is a tacit understanding that no one will claim that this real thing is a part of the world, or that it is created by the infant. It is understood that both these things are true: the infant created it and the world supplied it.[18]

At first then, psychically for the baby there can be no distinction between itself and its mother/environment. Reciprocally, the mother will be in a state of 'primary maternal preoccupation' – identified with her baby in a specific and necessary 'madness', an absence of boundaries. Through her identification she will recognize the different meanings of the baby's cries and other

---

18 D.W. Winnicott, 'The Deprived Child and How He Can Be Compensated for Loss of Family Life' (1950), in *The Family and Individual Development*, London: Tavistock Publications, 1965, pp. 143–4. As a concept this can be mapped over what will be seen as Pontalis' sense of 'dual reality' in which one can both see and not-see someone, but the tenor and therapeutic programme is very different. Parisian psychoanalysts as a generality are reputed to have admired British clinical work but scratched their heads about its theoretical thinking. This can be shorthand for the gap that separates Winnicott and Pontalis.

communications. If, instead, the mother either neglects to see and hear her baby for who it is in its specificity or intrudes into it her own vision of what she wants, the environment will fail to 'mirror' the baby and will produce a falseness in how it develops – as we will see, the patient with the split-off foreign object is a case in point. What then is such an object in Winnicott's case history and theoretical propositions?

Shortly before his death in 1972, Winnicott produced three radical propositions in separate talks and publications which thematically are in close proximity to each other and contain his theoretical thinking pertinent to the argument here. The first, 'Creativity and its Origins' (1968), used his patient with the split-off foreign object to produce a thesis about bisexuality as female 'being' and male 'doing' in both sexes; the importance of the 'unknown' early trauma is a focus of 'Use of an Object' (1969), which describes creative destructiveness, and 'Fear of Breakdown' is about a breakdown which has already occurred before it can be known about (1970; published 1974).[19] Winnicott saw these themes as important developments of a radical theory produced in complete conjunction with his equally radical clinical acumen. At the time of their delivery as lectures, they were controversial.[20] Today, very much accepted, they play a key role in 'relational' psychoanalysis but have a radicalism beyond this particular stance (see Chapter 2). They adhere within the prematurity-dependency framework because although there can be a transitional area between anyone, Winnicott privileges only the mother and baby.

The subtitle 'Split-off Male and Female Elements' comes capitalized in the chapter entitled 'Creativity and its Origins'; Winnicott takes creativity to be everyone's potential everyday creativity – 'creative living'. It is bound up with his notion of the 'environmental mother'; it is the baby's dependency and this environment mother that together produce the conditions of creative living or its failure. The first patient to be considered here is very much a case that highlights how the narcissistic-psychotic perspective is often concealed beneath analyses of neurosis: this patient, himself a doctor, had had years of such analyses and continued in the same neurotic mode with Winnicott until Winnicott surprised them both.

---

19  All these talks form the core of *Playing and Reality*, but 'Fear of Breakdown' (*International Review of Psycho-Analysis*, vol. 1, 1974, pp. 103–7) was not included in the publication. See below.

20  Since writing this there have been a number of publications which I would have used had they preceded my writing. Dianne Elise has written on Winnicott's erotic field theory in *Creativity and the Erotic Dimensions of the Analytic Field*, London and New York: Routledge, 2019. For this she is committed to giving Winnicott and bisexuality the maternal erotics of 'relational' psychoanalysis (see Chapter 2).

## The Little Girl as a 'Split-off' Traumatic 'Object'[21]

The analysis of a long-term, perhaps 'interminable', patient changed direction when Winnicott discovered that 'a little girl' was 'hidden' inside this male patient. She was an internal split-off traumatic presence from whom this patient had been completely dissociated. The case, which informs the whole chapter,[22] is the practice which unites the two dimensions of creativity and split-off gender in the theory and enables Winnicott to offer something new about bisexuality – a necessity for each sex to experience both female 'being' and male 'doing'.[23]

The (un-named) patient had had a series of therapies which had probably contributed to his professional and personal successes. He was married with a family and had a good job as a doctor, but something problematic had not been reached. The psychotic bedrock was untouched. One Friday session Winnicott realized his patient was expressing *penis envy*. He knew a change was on the cards when he found himself saying:

> I am listening to a girl. I know perfectly well that *you* are a man but I am listening to a girl, and I am talking to a girl. I am telling this girl: "*You* are talking about penis envy".
>
> (p. 73, my italics)

Winnicott thinks this interpretation broke into the 'vicious circle' of his patient's clinical stasis and tells us that this has nothing to do with homosexuality and that his verbal 'playing' with the patient was the opposite of indoctrination. After some comments both ways, the patient says that if he told anyone about this girl, he would be considered mad. Winnicott surprised himself with his response which 'clinched the matter': 'It was not

---

21 This chapter and several preceding lectures were finished some while before Nathalie Zilkha's essay, 'Stumbling Blocks of the Feminine, Stumbling Blocks of Psychic Bisexuality', in Perelberg (ed.), *Psychic Bisexuality*, op. cit., so I have not engaged with her analysis of this episode here.

22 Winnicott gives a long footnote citing a woman patient with a commensurate dissociated male element but comments that additional clinical references would distract from his argument – 'if my ideas are true and universal, then each reader will have personal cases illustrating the place of dissociation rather than of repression related to male and female elements in men and women' (ft. 2, p. 76).

23 We should remember that when a father wanted Freud to make his teenage homosexual daughter heterosexual, Freud declined, instead suggesting that she should regain her bisexuality and herself move as she wished from there ('The Psychogenesis of a Case of Homosexuality in a Woman', op. cit.). The structure of the whole chapter in Winnicott comes over as somewhat associative – in part this was his usual mode but on this occasion it was also due to the fact that he was fatally ill during both its composition and the verbal presentation from which it was posthumously published.

*you* who told this to anyone; it is *I* who see the girl and hear a girl talking, when actually there is a man on my couch. The mad person is *myself*' (p. 74, Winnicott's italics). This enables them to reach the madness of the mother 'by proxy' in the patient: 'This is like treating a child only to find that one is treating one or other parent by proxy' (p.77). Together they construct from a plethora of material that has come up in the transference that the mother had seen the girl she wanted in the boy she got.[24] The patient is moved and the analysis shifts. Winnicott is the mad mother, so they are working within a 'delusional transference' which 'puzzle[s] patients and analysts alike' (p. 75).

Winnicott tells his patient who has caught flu that his wife will now get it! We can appreciate the establishment of reality – 'really' flu. But the patient wants to understand his illness, which feels to him to be more and other than flu, in psychoanalytical terms. Winnicott explains that their work had freed him from the penis-envying girl so that he could have successful male sexual intercourse (as the patient had described) with his wife. But this male behaviour upset the 'little girl', so she herself became ill with a 'pregenital pregnancy' which made the man whom she inhabited feel ill in addition to the flu. Winnicott concludes: 'It had to do with identity. The pure female split-off element found a primary unity with me as analyst, and this gave the man a feeling of having started to live' (p. 77). Now the patient can become his creative male 'doing' self. The girl, then, no longer belongs to the patient in whom she resides but to the perception of the mad mother who invented her and whom Winnicott had become in his necessarily 'delusional' counter-transference.

In an 'Addendum' to the 'Clinical Section', Winnicott further observes: 'The split-off other sex part of the personality tends to remain one age, or to grow but slowly' (p. 77).[25] The whole depends on Winnicott's realization that in this patient the defence against something traumatic was almost total dissociation – an effective 'split' between two states that ought to be held together in the experience of our essential bisexuality. What is to be found from now on in the chapter is a re-thinking of 'bisexuality' as female 'being' (with no drive to it) and male 'doing' (with a drive) equally for both genders.

To take this somewhat further than Winnicott does, but only by deploying his terms: the patient could not *be* his female self, being one-and-the same as the mother who in her madness thought he was a girl. He could

---

24  D.W. Winnicott, 'Nothing at the Centre' (1959), in *Psychoanalytic Explorations*, Cambridge, MA: Harvard University Press, 1989, pp. 49–52. In an interesting account of this analysis N. Zilkha (op. cit.) considers Winnicott's description of the mother's treatment of the nappies is confused – this is wrong, Winnicott is right: terry towel nappies were folded and pinned differently for girls and boys at that time in the UK!

25  Winnicott says that truly imaginative figures in a person's inner psychic reality do mature but then instances a man who has endless young women sexually – the man grows old, but the girlfriends are unlikely to reach thirty years.

only *do* his male self – his apparently successful professional and marital life which because it could not rest on his female 'being' inevitably had something 'wrong' in it. The Little Girl, once she is recognized by Winnicott, becomes the crazy vision of the mother who had a 'mad' perception which Winnicott has allowed his deluded counter-transference to share – he *hears* a girl talking about penis-envy. In the context of the language used in the session, what the mother *saw* in her baby, Winnicott *hears* in his patient's talking. It is as though the girl has been re-owned by the mad mother and this frees the man to be a man. Presumably the male patient can now have a female experience of 'being' with Winnicott, who in a non-delusionary way stands in for the 'environment mother' on whom the patient can sufficiently depend.

'The Little Girl' as a 'foreign object', however, must be a formation created in response to trauma. In locating the trauma in the madness of the mother, has Winnicott removed the trauma? Is this possible? What has happened to the 'separation trauma' in this trauma of having a mad mother? Who is envying whom in the formation of the penis-envy which Winnicott hears? The questions will be held over while we consider another of Winnicott's cases – the trauma of teenage 'Sarah' whom Winnicott had seen for some consultations when as a toddler (called 'Phyllis') her sister's arrival had triggered a breakdown.

## 'She Screamed and Screamed and Screamed'[26]

Winnicott recounts a consultation with sixteen-year-old 'Sarah', who had 'screamed and screamed and screamed' on a recent incident at her boarding school. He also had notes of sessions when he had treated her at age two. On the birth of her younger brother (actually a sister), she had likewise 'screamed and screamed and screamed'.[27] For that treatment she was called 'Phyllis'. Of a patient who cannot scream Winnicott wrote that the scream is the last cry for help before either too rigid defences or some form of breakdown occur. As a two-year-old and as a sixteen-year-old alike, Sarah can scream and get help – from Winnicott and, with his assistance, from her mother. What would have been the trauma she was resisting?

Phyllis/Sarah provides and illustrates Winnicott's thesis: when she was one and three quarters, her six months' pregnant mother told her toddler that she would be going to stay with her grandmother while Mummy had a baby – a separation trauma:

26  D.W. Winnicott, 'Inter-relating apart from Instinctual Drive and in terms of Cross-identifications' *Playing and Reality*, Chapter 10.
27  He writes: 'I was in touch with Sarah's case then, and my notes made fourteen years previously covered the history given me at the time, so that I was sure of my ground' (p. 126).

Two days after being given this news (Phyllis) reacted with a week of refusal to take food, and she screamed incessantly. After this she settled down into being nervous and irritable and somewhat of a problem of management. *Thus did her illness start.*

(p. 138, my italics)

For Winnicott, relational interactions mostly replace the drive; these will be discussed later. For now, the trauma is our concern. Winnicott and Sarah start with the 'Squiggle Game': he draws a squiggle and his patient comments and draws one in response; the game proceeds until direct dialogue takes over:

Sarah said she liked school. Mother and father wanted her to come and see me but so did the school. She said: "I believe I came to see you when I was two, because I didn't like my brother [sister] being born, but I can't remember. I think I can just remember something of it"

(p. 121)

Sarah has great difficulty with one drawing, 'It's all cramped up, it's not free and spreading', and Winnicott notes in italics: '*This was to be the main communication*' (p. 122). But he asks about dreams. Most are frightening; in a recurrent one she is chased by a man (p. 144). In another 'squiggle' she draws her house from a sideways perspective. Winnicott footnotes that 'Sideways' may be a reference to her mother's later pregnancy (with a second sister) (p. 144, n3). On Winnicott's interpreting how this relates to her mother, Sarah replies that she was always, and still is, telling lies to her mother. Winnicott notes both Sarah's dissociation at this point and the possibility that she herself may have been lied to by her parents. They explore Sarah's lies and then in response to Winnicott's asking when menstruation started, Sarah says 'ages ago' and adds: "I can't explain. I feel as if I am sitting or standing on top of the spire of a church. There's nothing anywhere around to keep me from falling and I am helpless. I seem to be balancing, just" (p. 124). Winnicott considers this to be the nearest she comes to a statement of her position and re-constructs for her how she is unconscious of the fact that everything changed when, at age one and three quarters, her pregnant mother could no longer hold her as she had before.

However, instead of responding, Sarah reverts to the first dream: 'It's bigger than that. About whatever is chasing me, it's not a man chasing a girl, it's something chasing me. It's a matter of people behind me' (p. 143). Winnicott observes that at 'this point the character of the consultation altered and Sarah became a manifestly ill person displaying a psychiatric disorder of a paranoid type' (p. 145). Sarah talks of people on whom she has relied and who let her down – giving Winnicott his theme of her good mother who became bad: it is the good not the bad person she hates. The session concludes with Sarah confirming this by citing a boy who had loved her and acknowledging that she had spoilt the good relationship. Winnicott knows she cannot get in touch with her hatred of her betraying mother as yet, so he transfers it to her trust of a good Winnicott who is able to cure her of her problems but who will also be found a let-down and turn from good to bad in the transference relationship.

At the centre of the account of the session there is a school housekeeper whom Sarah passionately hates and whom Winnicott verifies is the same age as Sarah's mother and thus stands in for her. This forty-year-old house-mother may indeed stand for her mother and Winnicott, as is his wont, will have had to share the developing delusional transference as a second mater-nal substitute. But isn't there *also* a narcissistic attachment embedded here?

> She's got all the awful things that I feel most easily because I have got them all in myself. It's only herself she thinks of. She's self-centred and vain, and that's me again. And she's cold and hard and nasty. She's a housemother, looking after the laundry and biscuits and coffee and all that. She does not do her job. She sits and entertains all the young male members of the staff, drinking sherry and smoking black Russian cigarettes. And she does all this blatantly in what is really *our* sitting-room ... You see, inside *she* is as insecure as anyone else.
>
> (p. 126)

Winnicott takes up what is also Freud's thesis, that delusions defend against homosexuality –here that Sarah's forbidden object-love is for her same-sex mother. But we need also to ask: what about her love/hate for herself and her 'sister' mirror-image?[28] Sarah asserts that this woman is her own double with a bad side hidden behind the lies (e.g. Sarah threw a knife at the door but claimed that she was fixing a broken door handle!); the lies have the effect of turning *her* into the good girl (who tidies her room, works hard, etc.), which she isn't. This sounds like common enough teenage behaviour. However, Winnicott is able to help Sarah to express her madness freely.

> [Sarah] was not finished yet, and she was still very excited: 'And there I was wearing a cap of a certain kind ... and she came and she said, "Take off that ridiculous hat!" I said. "No, why should I?" She said: "Because I told you to. Take it off at once!" So then I screamed and screamed and screamed!!'
>
> (p. 126)

28  In his introductory paragraph Winnicott had noted the importance of a psychotherapist being the patient's mirror – presumably being the mother as mirror as in his other work.

The whole scene with the housemother is the energetic centre of Sarah's presentation and it is when the woman orders her to take off her 'ridiculous hat' that Sarah *screams*. What is the relationship between the toddler and teenager's screaming for help? 'Off with your hat'; 'off with her head'. An early essay by Klein recounts a school-child's difficulty with the lower-case 'I' – the '*ich*'; the little 'I' of 'who am I?' can 'lose its head' – go mad – be killed, the separated dot represented by the removable hat and later the castration complex.[29]

Winnicott introduces Sarah as at an 'early stage of adolescence'; as far as we know Sarah, with her menstrual periods well established, had no different external trauma at sixteen; it is puberty which is the new experience that revivifies the sibling trauma. The delusion, the madness, when the 'I' feels threatened with overwhelming sexuality and the danger of death – and goes mad – surely this is a repetition of the terrors, the 'who am I?' of the 'sibling trauma'? The incident with the housemother reactivates the initial sibling trauma; a substratum of Sarah's chronic insecurity about who she is in the newly reproductively sexual and binary gendered world of the teenager. Sarah's terror of being 'no-one', the renewed death of the self, leaps into psychosis – paranoia – when in the violent encounter she is commanded to take off her 'ridiculous' hat. Freud had this to say about hats:

> Experience in the analysis of dreams has sufficiently well established the hat as a symbol of the genital organ, most frequently the male organ ... It may be that the symbolic meaning of the hat is derived from that of the head, in so far as a hat can be regarded as a prolonged though detachable head.[30]

Is Sarah a phallic boy or a castrated girl? There is the prohibited male Oedipal incest *in both sexes* (Chapter 8) and there is also the new transition to reproductive sexuality which takes her back not only to the mother but also to someone like herself. This is the housemother flirting with men and smoking in 'our room' as well as Sarah's own several friends and boyfriends among the schoolboys whom she mentions throughout – the narcissism and excited lateral sexuality post puberty. If paranoia defends against homosexuality,[31] does Sarah desire the awful housemother who resembles herself and acts just as Sarah would like to? Is this a narcissistic love for her bad–good mirror-image – a recapitulation in adolescence of the narcissistic prelude to and a

29 Juliet Mitchell, Freud Memorial lecture. UCL and later as 'The letter "I"' *Sexual Difference*, vol. 8, nos. 1–2, 1986.

30 S. Freud, 'A Connection between a Symbol and a Symptom' (1916), *SE XIV*, pp. 399–40.

31 And as Herbert Rosenfeld added to Freud – homosexuality defends against paranoia. Homosexuality and heterosexuality are irrelevant terms for toddlers.

recovery from her infantile sibling trauma: 'who am I?'? Sarah is a teenager at a stage in life when the toddler saga can be compulsively repeated with the add-on of reproductive sex and its dangerous thrills. This is where Sarah stands but where Winnicott does not go.

## Trauma

'Phyllis' (who became 'Sarah') illustrated trauma in an article which encapsulates the meaning of the term for Winnicott: 'trauma is the destruction of the purity of individual experience by a too sudden or unpredictable intrusion of actual fact, and by the generation of hate in the individual, hate of the too good object'.[32] In his essay 'Neuroses and Psychoses' of 1926, Freud had contended that while the neuroses expressed a conflict between the ego and the id, the psychoses revealed one between the ego and the external world. Winnicott's work on trauma and the environment meets with this definition of the psychoses. He writes: 'The aetiology of these disorders takes us inevitably to stages that precede the three-body [the Oedipal] relationship. The strange corollary is that there is at the root of psychoses an external factor'.[33] This is something in the environment: 'trauma is that which breaks up an idealization of an object by the individual's hate reactions to that object's failure to perform its function' (ibid., p. 145). For Winnicott a trauma is an event or eventuality that impinges from outside into a baby's necessary omnipotence; the omnipotence may cope with the untenable, but if the untenable is stronger than the omnipotence, traumatization results.

This is the explanation of an inveterate developmentalist; there is no structural role for trauma, no conflictual linking between the two spheres of self and other – everything, such as play, me and not-me, the impingement of the traumatic and the location of culture, takes place in the transitional area, the space between individuals. Life in this interstitial space will be lived by all individuals, but the superstructural concept of prematurity and dependency confines it to a vertical hierarchy and in this it differs from the comparable understanding of a group theorist such as René Kaës (Chapter 3). Vertical helplessness underpins the traumatic and necessarily excludes the lateral.

Winnicott's favourite concept of a 'paradox' which must be sustained is a replacement for 'conflict'. Conflict with its production of symptoms can be deconstructed. In a paradox two ideas or situations which are apparently opposites can be held in balance with each other – this can lead to fruitful

32  D.W. Winnicott, 'The Concept of Trauma in Relation to the Development of the Individual within the Family' (1965), *The Collected Works, Volume 7*, op. cit., p. 186.

33  D.W. Winnicott, 'The Use of an Object' (1969), in *Psychoanalytic Explorations*, op. cit., p. 46.

thinking but not to a structural change in the way of thinking itself: untangling the symptom reveals the contradiction at the centre and forces one or other of the oppositional postulates to shift position and enter into a new contradiction with something else – this dialectical dynamic is present in the 'moving' work of the session. In classical psychoanalytic theory it is *conflict* which is active in the contradiction of desire and prohibition. In Winnicott's causative relationship of prematurity and dependency there is nowhere for the observation to go. The helpful and dependable good mother/analyst is hated until one can understand why she was hated – the trauma can be removed because it was only an excessive difficulty – what seemed at the time to be a 'z' experience (too much separation) can be re-modelled in therapy to produce a 'y' situation (reparable separation). The separation from the environment mother is mended in the therapy – no wonder that even at this practical level there is no room for an account of the sibling whose problematic presence elicits a quite feasible but forbidden murder.

## The Sibling Question

We need to return to the problematic questions which we left hanging with the little girl as the foreign object in the man patient. I think something shifted in Winnicott's work. Hearing the little girl was a breakthrough but assigning her to the mad mother, as his thinking had to do, was a collapse. Not necessarily untrue but uninteresting. What had the man patient done with the little girl? Winnicott tells us that he had to do a lot of work on his own counter-transference. He makes a general observation that seems pertinent:

> in a man patient the girl (hiding the pure girl element of earlier formation) may have girl characteristics, may be breast-proud, experience penis envy, become pregnant, be equipped with no male external genitalia and even possess female sexual equipment and enjoy female sexual experience.
>
> (p. 78)

Does a man who has only had a female being experience and no male doing experience grow up only 'being'? Does this make female sexual experience by definition lack doing? More importantly for us here, rather than the problem being the patient's deluded mad mother, are we instead in the terrain of both Winnicott's and his patient's transgender position – very much a lateral relationship demanding a quite different conceptualization than mad mothers?

Returning to the man's penis-envy, two features of Winnicott's account of the split-off little girl in his male patient can be used to suggest that what is also at stake is the laterality of the man and the girl: he addresses each of them as 'you' and his patient responds positively by saying he has felt that both parts of him are being addressed; Winnicott does not take this up. Further – although this sounds contradictory of the previous point – the man and the girl are different ages – as indeed toddler and baby are at the time of the sibling trauma. The girl is a very small child and Winnicott tells us that she does not grow up. The penis-envy which Winnicott hears her uttering, followed by his explanation of her 'pregenital pregnancy', would be the penis-envy and womb-envy in open and often joyful display between and amongst small children when left to themselves – the children who are still in Winnicott's narcissistic-psychotic developmental stage. In Chapter 8 we will see this recently described by psychoanalyst Rachel Chaplin as 'sexual difference denied' between lateral genders; Winnicott takes up only the mother and therefore the vertical axis.

When the boy-as-girl was about two years old, it would have been a bi-sexual toddler experiencing the mother separating from it together with 'the sibling trauma'; the bisexual child will have found the separation to be a Winnicottian trauma in which it hated the good mother for separating. The second would be a sibling trauma which would produce desires that must become unconscious. There may or may not have been another actual baby for the bisexual toddler to greet. If the future of the man is anything to go on, the girl the mother saw in her son stopped dead in her toddler tracks as she personifies the sibling trauma itself. She will become a foreign object internalized by the boy part who will become completely dissociated from her – she becomes the new sibling of his sibling trauma. By recognizing her, Winnicott looks after her, leaving his male patient able to have sex as a man. But the little girl is the man's twin and would like him to be the baby of her own sibling trauma while she got on with a toddler's belief that she can produce babies.

This complicated scenario is only an extreme version of a common oc-currence. Most first-time mothers expect their babies to be either a girl like themselves or a boy or girl like their own first sibling. Most adjust their illusion to a normative perception – some allow it to persist as a delusion such as this patient's mother apparently experienced. For Winnicott, the mad mother's misplaced gender ascription is a/the trauma. In the still usual course of events this should instead have been an at-birth gender assignment coincident with the customarily agreed biological sex as signified by the dominant genital; for the sibling trauma differently, there would have been a gradual subjective recognition that one is a gendered sister or a brother on the lateral, horizontal axis.

So, for Winnicott's theory the trauma he proposes must be two-fold: both separation and the addition from the mother of a mad gender ascription – the male toddler will be separating from the mother who thinks he is a girl and joining the world that 'correctly' considers him to be the biological boy which he is. He more-or-less makes the transition and acts the future man.

This mis-gendering by the mother would have been a traumatic invasion from the environment, but by taking the little girl away from his patient Winnicott can resolve the problem. The patient had had the mother's madness by proxy – Winnicott gives the madness back to the mother via his own transference persona. This entails finding the environment to be at fault. From the child's perspective or indeed from the mother's, there is nothing about gender which is intrinsic to the separation trauma. However, that the little girl becomes a 'foreign object' or 'foreign body' shifts the goal-posts. To use the clinical material to add the sibling trauma (whether or not there was an actual new baby) is to make further – but legitimate – demands of the theory.

The bisexual two-year-old will have been experiencing a sibling trauma – if resolved following the mother's law it would have meant becoming either a sister or a brother like the new or expected baby. This would have been a gender acquisition within the framework of its bisexual subjecthood; in other words, something internal to itself as a subject in the world and not the responsibility of the faulty environment. With a little girl self, the man patient is, as he himself says, 'mad' in this sense and Winnicott calling himself mad for seeing the man as a penis-envying girl is again as the patient says, just Winnicott's 'way of putting things'. Only a bisexual lateral relation, to which a gender distinction becomes an inevitable but secondary part of the sibling trauma, explains the 'foreign object'. A foreign object in fact is the very insignia of a dynamic trauma in which a desire with its prohibition rises to meet the external blow of the new baby, followed by the wish for murder and incest, whatever its gender.

Within his own theoretical framework, the mother-and-baby unity that Winnicott recreated in the transference was in itself the therapy that was needed. He was dissolving any necessity for there to be a psychotic defence mechanism: 'There is no possibility whatever for an infant to proceed from the pleasure principle to the reality principle or towards and beyond primary identification ... unless there is a good-enough mother' (p. 10). In other words, the normal psychotic phase will become a pathological defence mechanism if there is not a good enough mother available. Whether or not that is the case, the argument itself presents some problems for the unconscious processes at the heart of psychoanalytic work.

We need to take this issue somewhat further. The childhood to which psychoanalysis always refers is the very condensed time in which we acquire everything needed to make us social human beings: born into this constructed world, the constructions have to be taken on board; they are about what we can and cannot do. The child in all of us is the subject which it is, the embattled child negotiating society's strictures and contributing anew to its construction. In Winnicott's observation, punishments play a part, but they are local renditions, like being forbidden to thumb-suck. His 'environment' is a permanent, something always there, a given not a constructed social world. Whether it assists or abuses the individual child is up to the individual mother and her individual child – as he says: '*this* mother and *this* child' (p. 81. Winnicott's italics). This makes the unconscious processes of the patient descriptive rather than dynamic.

Winnicott's child is the object who receives the good or bad environment; the subject is the environment mother as understood through her effect on the child – thus Winnicott can become the mad mother by understanding what she did to her child and help to change that by standing in for the 'environment mother'. We are in the terrain of a neat distinction that Ilse Grubrich-Simitis makes about trauma, if we add 'emotionally' to 'sexually' and enlarge the numbers: 'Whereas the more conventional trauma model applied to the pathogenesis of a comparatively small number who had been sexually violated in childhood, the revolutionary drive model is concerned with the psychogenesis of everyone'.[34] Winnicott's trauma model is that of the children who had been abused in childhood. The psychoanalytic model of trauma, which the omnipresence of the human drive established, has shifted to the 'universalism' of the environment mother.

With his primary stress on the social conditions produced by human dependence, Winnicott is naturally always concerned with the vertical – those on whom the neonate and beyond can depend. There is quite simply no place in the explanatory framework for the siblings who play so rich a part in the clinical sessions. Yet the presence of these clinical accounts of the lateral is a near match to his theoretical emphasis on the vertical. Thus, in recounting twins in his war-time studies he first notes only the needs and difficulties of each individual twin with a parent. However, a particular adult patient was so 'identical' with her twin that she could recall that when her twin was picked up, she had wondered why she herself did not rise too. There is one moment when twins make Winnicott stand stock still in his thinking; following his somewhat negative review of Dorothy Burlingham's fascinating study[35] it occurred to him that a twin's lateral relation might co-exist or even pre-date the always-there environment mother. This would be to acknowledge that the unrecognized lateral relations on the horizontal axis were on a par with the vertical family.

In a way quite unlike anyone else, Winnicott gives us the evidence of the equation of the narcissistic-psychotic individual and the collective social world in its near personification as 'the environment'. In particular, through his extraordinary understanding of children and theirs of him as they came to his pediatric hospital practice, and in his work with evacuee children during World War II, Winnicott offers the pathology of the *socio*-psychically

---

34  I. Grubrich-Simitis, *Early Freud and Late Freud: Reading Anew Studies on Hysteria and Moses and Monotheism*, trans. P. Slotkin, New York: Routledge, 1997, p. 63.

35  Burlingham, *Twins*, op. cit.

ill – the anti-social child, the 'delinquent', 'the mal-adjusted', the habitual offender, shyness, nervous disorders, the wayward youth, homeless children, the aetiology of anti-social illnesses and what he called the male 'doing': the stealing, the knife-fighting of boys and the female 'being' of maiming, ano-rexia and 'cutting'. These accord very well with the notion of a 'socializing' – and its failures – of the sibling trauma after the Law of the Mother.

This is surely the point – lateral relations are always also part of the hu-man world and dependency is manifold and will involve a mirror self, an actual or imagined twin – who, whether positive or negative like Sarah's housemother, will always also be there to some degree. This contributes to a re-consideration of the narcissistic dimension of narcissistic-psychosis. In so far as the breast is of course the mother's, the baby experiencing itself as the breast is an illusory unit with the mother. But it must also be a single unit with itself; its 'me' as breast. And such a primal horizontal identification will spread to later narcissistic objects such as siblings, much as Jane Smiley describes her contemporary rendition of King Lear's daughters:

> My deepest-held habit was assuming that differences between Rose [her sister] and me were just on the surface, that beneath, beyond all that, we were more than too alike, that somehow we were each other's real selves, together forever on this thousand acres.[36]

It is often noted that Winnicott's mother suffered from depression. Here I would note that, by repute a gentle boy, Donald suddenly smashed to smith-ereens the face of 'Rosie', the favoured doll of his two close-to-each-other older sisters. Later he was sent to a boy's boarding school where (unlike Bion) he made lifetime friends – it had been thought by his family that he needed to separate from his female-dominated household. He went on to Cambridge University in October 1914. Planning to become a doctor, he was exempt from service but worked in the military hospitals into which a number of colleges had been converted, and in 1917, he left the University for the Navy to be stationed as a medical officer on a destroyer.

A quarter of his close school friends died on the killing-fields of France. Of his slaughtered contemporaries, he reflected that he had subsequently experienced his own life as part of a universal 'whole', the rest of which was composed of their deaths – rather he had to die, like the men of his generation, when he was still young at least in spirit. Feeling *their* death to be the meaning of *his* life, Winnicott memorialized child's play as what life can offer to its survivors. But his insistent playfulness in theory and practice

---

36 J. Smiley, *A Thousand Acres*, New York: Knopf, p. 307. Quoted in T. Apter, *The Sister Knot: Why We Fight, Why We're Jealous and Why We'll Love Each Other No Matter What*, London and New York: W.W. Norton, 2007.

may have been tinged with their death, a survivor's suicidality – as an aging man he cycled down Hampstead's hills with his feet on the handle-bars. He was embedded in a generation who died before or on the edge of adulthood. Their trauma was to be located in the beleaguered, dependent child of all times. Sisters and brothers were perhaps too important to be thought about intellectually, theoretically – instead he continued to play with them personally and clinically. Towards the end of his life, he started an unfinished autobiography in which he jotted down a prayer 'Oh God! May I be alive when I die' – as his shell-shattered brothers were not.

Winnicott's environment is as much the lateral siblings as the vertical mothers; it is his theory that excludes them. Here one cannot 'add' siblings as we will see that we can with the work of Bion – there is no place for them in the superstructure. Later, writing about Freud's *Moses and Monotheism* and clearly influenced by it, Winnicott speculates that an early punishing superego is like a set of polytheistic gods before there is the one God of monotheism. If we think of the pre-social mother's constant introduction of 'reality' through her endless 'nos and don'ts' this plural superego makes good sense. Inspiration for both Klein's and Winnicott's work can be traced to Freud's *Inhibitions, Symptoms and Anxiety*, which in turn was in part a response to Otto Rank's proposal of a birth trauma as determinate of psychic life. 'Helplessness' resulting from our prematurity is the pre-condition of the many conventional traumata of a baby's daily life. We cannot manage the tensions of our predicament and certainly we need – but may not get – a good-enough mother.

However, there is another necessary mother existing alongside and beyond the environment mother with her containment and small personal reprimands: the mother who represents the universal requirements of the social and from birth is introducing her baby, infant and small child continually and continuously to the reality of their separated condition. Within the 'universalism' of the human condition of dependency, Winnicott presented a portrait of the normal and abnormal state of narcissistic-psychosis which, although specific to individuals, can be used as a rich description of the background condition in which the sibling trauma and the social law of the mother operate.

# Chapter 6

# Using Wilfred Bion

## The Social and Its Models

### Toddler-Siblings: The Family and the Social Group

Although siblings are not mentioned within it, Wilfred Bion's work with groups provides a model for a reading of the unconscious processes that are in play on a horizontal axis of social relations. In *Experiences in Groups*, Bion made an absolute distinction between the family and the social, emphatically explaining that the one is not the other:

> When the group has come together in this way it has become something as real and as much a part of human life as a family, but it is in no way at all the same thing as a family. The leader of such a group is a far remove from being the father of a family...[1]

In a very different essay, 'A Theory of Thinking', he notes the profound sociability of humans:

> The emotional problems are associated with the fact that the human individual is a political animal and cannot find fulfilment outside a group and cannot satisfy any emotional drive without expression of its social component. His impulses, and I mean all impulses and not merely his sexual ones, are at the same time narcissistic. The problem is the resolution between narcissism and social-ism.[2]

Because siblings are in both the family and the group, holding them in tension with each other is crucial. In the family, siblings are daughters and sons on a vertical axis but their presence as lateral sisters and brothers is foundational

---

1   W. Bion, *Experiences in Groups and Other Papers*, London: Tavistock, 1961, p. 69. Hereafter, references to *Experiences in Groups* will be given in the text.
2   Wilfred Bion, 'A Theory of Thinking' first published, *IJPA*, vol. 43, 1962; here, W. Bion, *Second Thoughts: Selected Papers on Psychoanalysis*, London: Heinemann, 1967, p. 118.

DOI: 10.4324/9781003347125-9

for the social on the horizontal axis.[3] To amalgamate the family and the social group would be to fail to realize that our sociality in and of itself is a fundamental human characteristic: we are intrinsically and innately gregarious. As Bion forcefully maintained: 'for a man to lead a full life the group is essential ... the group is essential to the fulfilment of man's life' (p. 53). He describes the social group as always having both psychotic-like 'basic assumptions' and a drive to become a neurotic-like 'work group' which because it knows the distinction between reality and fantasy can use both appropriately to think and function with collective logic and rationality.

Using Bion to understand the toddler in its social group could be either to set up parallel pictures of his therapeutic work with adults and comparable psychic states in a child's history or instead to suggest the presence of a child still within the adult. In the main and initially, the former is selected here because the aim is to produce the child's trajectory in the social group in a way comparable to its well-known history within the family. Subsequently, referring to Bion's debt to Klein, the persistence of the toddler in all our psyches will be briefly reviewed.

When a new baby 'steals' its place as the one and only baby, the toddler becomes part of a social group as a striking alternative to, not a derivative of, the family. The human being is always social wherever it is but the resistant toddler wanting to stay in the family in the period of the sibling trauma can be matched with the resistant-to-change 'basic assumptions' in Bion's account of the social group. This stasis is a feature of the group of new social sibling friends and enemies; the small child is both reluctant and excited to go forward. In the vertical *family* the toddler will undergo a 'trauma of separation' from the mother (Winnicott; Chapter 5); it resists this separation forcefully by developing its pre-Oedipal attachment into an incestuous Oedipal love for her. This incestuous love is a way of holding on to the mother who is otherwise in danger of deserting the small child. On the horizontal the toddler has to take on the mother's law against murder and incest to become a child embarking on the early stages of an intra-childhood 'work group'. The same child who is the daughter or son in the family will then in its social self *as part of a group of children* start playing, then working together with its peers.[4]

---

3   This family/social differentiation is contrary to Freud's and most subsequent theses of individual psychoanalyses. Idiosyncratic and highly original, somewhere Bion always has Freud in mind even where the explicit reference is to the theories of Melanie Klein. This is never more so than with groups. It is as though there is within the huge respect and debt to Freud, also a creative challenge.

4   As mentioned in Chapter 5, this is the distinction that a middle-class Western mother knows between the child at home and the child at play-group, nursery, infant school. Elsewhere in the world or in different social classes maternal care devolves on an older sibling or grandparent until the child takes its share in collective work. I remember the first time

The toddlers own quite normal unconscious and conscious narcissistic-psychotic mental processes operate both in the vertical family and in the horizontal social group where these qualities are the psychic mark of its deliberate entry into forming its own small social group within the large social world in which it has always been embedded. These same narcissistic-psychotic perspectives are thereafter an intrinsic element of the unconscious and conscious psychology of human society in a way that differs from their progress in the family. When they are positively socialized on the horizontal axis, they suggest an essential benign and playful relationship to a shared social reality which has a characteristic fantastical or creative dimension to it; when the results are negative, it is the continuing effect of the 'sibling trauma' and the resistance to the mother's prohibitions with its group response as 'basic assumptions' as Bion propounds.

Bion formulates the *'basic assumptions'* of 'dependency', 'pairing' and 'fight and flight', and the shifting inter-relationship of these three assumptions offers a reading of the perpetual place of normative *psychosis* for the group that operates in social life. The development of a *work group mentality* is the growth of an equally *normative neurotic* triumph of a greater sense of reality.

Bion's theory of groups does not specify any family relation. The group is a homogeneous structure that is not divided into interacting activities engaged in by discrete entities such as family members or meaningfully specified gender relations. For Bion, although of course individuals speak and contribute in the clinical situation, the group so-to-speak obliterates these single identities and hence the interactive 'relationships' between them, as will be described later; in this, his contribution turns out to be in some respect unique. This emphasis probably emanates from the work he shared with his friend and colleague (and briefly his training analyst) John Rickman with psychically invalided soldiers in World War II.

Rickman, although a life-long Quaker and a conscientious objector in World War I, thought Nazism had to be opposed militarily in World War II. He mentioned siblings in order to note their absence in classical psychoanalytic theory:

> Another derivation of the analysis of the transference situation is a study of sibling rivalry as a side issue in the examination of the Oedipus complex. This branch is not very clearly developed as yet but there is just enough to warrant the establishment of the four-person psychology.[5]

---

I saw (in India) a grandfather teaching his toddler grandson to help him break and collect stones for a construction site. A nanny in the upper or upper-middle and colonial families such as Bion's protects the parents from encountering many or any difficulties.

5   J. Rickman, *Selected Contributions to Psycho-Analysis*, London: Karnac, 2003, p. 220; first published 1957, London: Hogarth Press.

The rivalrous sibling of popular imagination comes in as an extension, 'a side issue', a fourth person to the triad of mother, father and child of the Oedipus complex. However, in musing on a possible four-person psychology Rickman, certainly 'no ordinary psychoanalyst',[6] took up a revolutionary stance as he contemplated the implications:

> ...suppose a study of group dynamics shows us how we are more than the children of our time and generation, are indeed its slaves, that we are in fact ruled from without by group forces of which we are unaware, then our narcissism would get another nasty knock and flinching before the scattering of another illusion, we would pull round us the consoling blanket of incomprehension and keep our minds engaged within the cosy circle of the family and its simple social derivatives.[7]

Rickman was opening further vistas beyond Bion's elevation of the social group and relegation of the family into insignificance when faced by the circumambient social. Sadly, his premature death brought an end to his speculations.

## Multi-Person Possibilities and Siblings

Some psychoanalysts have been interested in the 'multi-person' or social perspective of the individual patient, but they have excluded the sibling who somewhere, they realized, should feature; these are 'symptomatic' omissions. Thus, in *Totem and Taboo* Freud, describing the psyche of the brothers when laterally they forged a social contract, called them 'sons', which they are on the vertical axis. As the contract-makers for whom he is arguing, they are not sons but lateral brothers. Before World War II, S.H. Foulkes, credited as the founder of Group Psychoanalysis, was Director of the Frankfurt Psychoanalytic Institute; this shared a building with the famous Institute of Sociology and thus provides an icon for the combination of psychoanalysis and sociology which is Foulkes' hallmark. Yet, a Vienna-trained psychoanalyst, Foulkes mentions siblings only once in his entire oeuvre! In the middle of an article on 'multi-person groups', Enid Balint has a bracketed aside: '(For the sake of simplicity I am leaving out for the time being the existence of siblings)'.[8] Although typically they appear in her case histories, in her theoretical excurses they disappear even from their bracketed status. Bion himself, probably under the influence of Klein, his second training analyst, reneged on his

---

6    J. Rickman, *No Ordinary Psychoanalyst: The Exceptional Contributions of John Rickman*, compiled and edited by Pearl King, London: Karnac, 2003.

7    Ibid., p. 112.

8    E. Balint, *Before I Was I*, op. cit., p. 68.

interest in groups. But before this, he had likened the experience of working with psychosis without a theoretical model to trying to talk about your father with your brother *when you have not got a brother* – his own situation. However, paradoxically this missing brother makes Bion's concept of the group as an undifferentiated totality particularly applicable to an account of siblings and the horizontal axis – that is, because of, rather than despite, their omission from his work. What we need from Bion is exactly an account of the group as a unit-structure which is not the family with its fixed position members.

As we will see, Bion's concept of the group offers something absolutely distinctive. A group exists when it is unformed, when it seems not to be there:

> The congregation of the group in a particular place at a particular time is, for ... mechanical reasons, important, but it has no significance for the production of group phenomena; the idea that it has springs from the impression that a thing must commence at the moment when its existence becomes demonstrable. *In fact no individual, however isolated in time and space, should be regarded as outside a group.*
>
> (*Experiences in Groups*, pp. 168–9)

This is everyone; siblings are no more important that anyone else; you, me, all of us are simultaneously individuals and group members. Although, on becoming a child, the sibling forms its own social group, it has also been conceived and born into a group no less than into a family. Often our single and social dimensions of ourselves do not get on together – Bion's contrast of 'narcissism and social-ism': 'Group culture is a function of the conflict between the individual's desires and the group mentality' (p. 66). The fact that the social and individual person can be self-conflicted does not mean that there is any distinction in the psychology itself: 'The apparent difference between group psychology and individual psychology is an illusion...' (p. 169).

What Bion wrote in distinguishing his work from other group theorists still applies: he is describing two different categories of mental activity co-existing in the same group (just as they do within the individual). A 'work group' in which the group has a normal-neurotic Oedipal knowledge of reality is one and the same group as a 'basic assumption' group which has only a psychotic grasp – the states of mind flow in and out of each other. For psychoanalysis, the focus is on the child because it is in childhood that the person attains the social in which it is already embedded – child's play is Bion's work.

## Siblings and *Experiences in Groups*

Bion's small therapeutic group is the material for understanding the world-wide, always-there social group as such. Here the ever-widening sibling group is paralleled to the small therapeutic group as a unit which stands for the larger social structures – 'the horizontal axis'. The horizontal axis is wider than the group. Its own small group is what the toddler forms as it enters the social world in which it has always resided. We can make use of the core assumptions which are the same for the group and the larger social world and thus use Bion's work for the horizontal axis. Although he is explicit and emphatic that his group work, whose task was to enable the men to return to fight, was not and could not be the open-ended practice of psychoanalysis, yet, as he also said, it is only as a psychoanalyst that he can work. What then are the unconscious processes of a group as he analyses it?

Bion lists the condition of the formation of the basic assumptions that underlie social life. But the wider framework for all social formation is his notion of 'valency'. Three 'basic assumptions' unconsciously operate within this framework.

### Valency

Born into a social world, everyone thinks and acts as a 'group animal'. Groups form automatically through a process for which Bion borrowed the useful notion of 'valency'. Of the human version of valency, he wrote:

> [In *Group Psychology*], Freud turns to discussion of something that crops up under a variety of names, such as 'suggestion', 'imitation', 'prestige of leaders', 'contagion'. I have used 'valency' partly because I would avoid the meanings that already adhere to the terms I have listed, partly because the term 'valency', as used in physics to denote the power of combination of atoms, carries with it the greatest penumbra of suggestiveness useful for my purpose. By it I mean the capacity of the individual for instantaneous combination with other individuals in an established pattern of behaviour – the basic assumptions.
>
> (p. 175)[9]

Valency was introduced into chemistry (not physics) in the late nineteenth century. An atom which has a positive charge attracts two electrons with a negative charge – together they occupy a 'shell'; there is room for more, and next six electrons join, then eight till a shell is at capacity. The term is used more generally to signify the way in which one element combines with other elements to form a chemical compound; the valency of an element explains

---

9   Bion credits physics with this concept from chemistry. The original notion offers a rich-ness which I think attracted Bion beyond his explicit use. The combination of inorganic and organic – which is also to be found in our physical bodies – is likewise an aspect of the social: the baby is born into a world of fascinating rocks and stones and buildings and railways as well as trees and other people.

the molecular structure of compounds which consist of the inorganic and the organic. As in linguistics where the term is also used, Bion's 'valency' is really a metaphor to account for an automatic combination or aggregation – an excellent description of spontaneous group formation. In other words, unlike the 'multi-person' society proposed by his colleagues, Bion's group is not a collection of individuals; it is a conception of a group as unitary – as though 'valency' might stand to the social as the metaphor 'blood' does to the family.

With valency's 'instantaneous combination', the group presents a collection of the 'basic assumptions' which come from one emotional source and are sometimes singular, sometimes combined; they endlessly change places, and it is in noting these shifts that understanding the group's normal psychosis takes place. The neotenic (or in utero) fears to which the toddler and small child regress arise when the basic assumptions are each and all expressions of a fear of death which if not 'contained' become, in Bion's nomenclature, a 'nameless dread'.[10] Seen from the sibling perspective, this generalized fear of death becomes focused on the new 'replacement' baby in the sibling trauma. The three basic social assumptions we all share are:

## Dependency

Dependency assumes that an external person or object exists whose sole function is to provide security. Such a leader is not a family parent. A leader is expected to do what is needed as if by magic: 'all facets of behaviour in the dependent group can be recognised as related if we suppose that in this group, power is believed to flow not from science but from magic' (p. 84). Revered as God-like, he may come crashing down from that eminence if, as often happens, it is felt that he has failed the group. Bion's 'he' is, I think, intended to be generic. If the leader seems to accept the reverence but, inevitably, does not provide the goods, another leader will be sought from out of the group itself: 'In its search for a leader the group finds a paranoid schizophrenic or malignant hysteric if possible: failing either of these a psychopathic personality with delinquent trends will do' (p. 123). Hitler haunts aspects of Bion's text.

However, dependency if it is within a neurotic work group can also acknowledge the importance of the group itself for its survival – it can usefully depend on the group or another individual within the group. Bion recalls one of the 'forgotten heroes' of D-Day, who had been left for dead amongst the bodies of his massacred fellow soldiers, answering a question about his 'impossible' survival with the words 'well I guess there is some Man up there

---

10 'Nameless dread' is not used in *Experiences.*

who must have helped'. Dependency not on God but a mate. Dependency can be – indeed must be – on each other for the small child as well as more obviously for the adult.[11]

### Pairing

Bion's 'pairing' repeats the love the toddler has for the baby when it thinks the baby is just an extension of its own baby-self. This can develop either into incestuous sibling desire or into the really loved 'best friends' of 'work group' children. There is an age of incessant questioning, in which the small child can for a while supply the answer from their own body fantastically conceived – for instance it contends that babies will come from their own tummies or anuses. But as a group it is soon evident that babies will not emerge from itself, so private fantasy turns instead to group play; among other pursuits, the group will enact the family of parents and children; the pair can really be in love. A friend of mine moved her two-year-old to another country – when the toddler was immediately reunited with her best friend but only visually online, they went crazy with their frustrated physio-emotional desire for each other. At three years old I similarly lost my daily companion – when we eventually re-met in adulthood we were as shy as lovers! Although Bion links it with sexuality, pairing as an ordinary occurrence should not surprise: pairs are the unit that, even in a large group, engages in pleasure or dispute – shaking hands, hitting out, etc. It is the child in us excited by its friend rather than, or at least as well as, the parental 'primal scene'. *Pairing* always implicates the sexual[12]:

> ...whether these two are man and woman, man and man, or woman and woman – it seems a basic assumption, held both by the group and the pair concerned that because it is only two people choosing each other the coupling implies a sexual interest. It is as if there could be no possible reason for two people's coming together except sex.
>
> (p. 62)

The sibling group is not necessarily unstable; it can indeed be a successful work/play group. But it can also regress, as did Bion's adult patients who assumed the 'basic assumption' of excited 'pairing', hetero- or homosexual coupling with imaginary reproduction in which the hoped-for wonder is

---

11  Compare Anna Freud's Bulldog Bank infants in Chapter 9.
12  This for me was very marked in the 'small group' part of my group analytic training. If the toddler is behind it, then incest would also subtend the everyday pairing. *Totem and Taboo* notes the inordinate lust of the brother for the sister which must be controlled. What of the sister's sexuality (Chapter 10)?

always 'unborn' – as of course is the fantasy baby of the toddler-child either alone or in its group play. Two people becoming a pair in a therapeutic group setting tend to talk excitedly and exclusively together about coincidences in their past and about their future, similarly coincidental, plans. Two are one – with a split-hair between to generate the minimal difference for sexual desire. 'Pairing' within the social group is the condition of always hoping, or rather, always being in a state of hope which is never realized – if realized, hope, of course, would end.

### Fight/flight

War or no war, as war-honoured and war-shattered Bion knew all too well, is the third basic assumption, of which he wrote: 'It is my contention that panic, flight and uncontrolled attack are really the same' (p. 179). However, the group has survival as its immediate necessity, which can be achieved either through aggression and hostility or by giving up and wasting time. Although valency produces 'combination', there is always inevitably, in lesser or greater measure, conflict (war) in groups – whether child or adult. A group will always have a (conscious) purpose or work objective, but it will also be driven by (unconscious) beliefs or assumptions of what is the best way to deal with a difficulty or a threat. 'Fight or flight' is the toddler's response to the sibling trauma in which it felt annihilated. An older child can hear as an auditory hallucination the critical voices of its peers – usually a temporary but not unusual 'decompensation' (see Chapter 2); it creates an enemy from its own lateral paranoia. Fight/flight can lead to regressive bullying and cruelties or to the necessary resilience and survival strategies of the work group.

  With the sibling group, dependency, pairing, flight and fight display themselves as psychotic processes but also as mental states that are normatively socialized towards consciousness with the positive survival qualities both of community-building and, depending on one's values, of legalized warfare which has the function of re-unifying a group when this is required. The basic assumptions shift and change places and as they always permeate the work groups this can be extended to see that they feature in the whole process of socialization that is undertaken in childhood. When basic assumptions of any kind prevail in an adult group, there are repetitions of common physical illnesses. But for 'pairing' there is more than this. Much as the dependent aspect of the group discovers its maddest member to elevate to leadership, so too it is not infrequent that a group member in the 'more-ill' period finds an ill partner with whom to fall in love and 'pair'.

  As we have seen, the group is defined by all these interlinked 'basic assumptions': 'dependency', 'pairing' and 'fight/flight'. Each basic assumption is transformed as the work group status is achieved. But equally the work group can collapse into or regress to any of the shifting modes of the basic assumptions at any time.

## The Sibling in the Group

Although the group leader is not a parent, if we are working on the horizontal axis we can make analogies to later group members – to siblings and their mother. The sibling uses its family members socially – the mother is depended on as a group leader will be. When the toddler transitions to its own group, it has found that the mother fails to do everything it wants magically so it turns its babyhood's joyful utter identification with her on its head, finding instead that she is now completely useless. It attacks her, and probably after an uncomfortable period of splitting and depersonalization, which Bion sees as linked with feelings of depression, it treats her as useless and stupid just like the baby she now tends; the toddler itself will be a magical substitute mother in her place. Thus, this rejection of the mother is repeated by the basic assumption group with the leader. But the new baby features more strongly still: when Bion gave interpretations that implied he knew more about groups than the group itself knew (as a toddler's mother might easily indicate), he became for the group a baby that had to be humoured by indulgence of its baby-ish grandiosity. He had become the new, wondrous baby only then to be keenly denigrated as 'little' and utterly unable to do anything at all – repeating the toddler's familiar tactic with its new sibling.

The group, like the distressed toddler, can really feel as helpless as a baby when it loses 'who it is'. If the group leader/mother fails in magic and becomes the useless baby, so too the sibling child group shuffles around looking for help. The good and bad mother on whom the toddler was dependent can be replaced by a 'leader' selected from amongst its group self while it is in the basic assumption mode. Children too can often find and create a bully leader. The most ill person in an adult group sums up in their being the infantile madness of everyone – they are truly representative of the dependent group's craziness and felt need for a magical rescue. The toddler who fears its own desperate questions about the presence of a foetus also experiences the pregnancy and birth of a baby as magic – as indeed may do the grown-ups around it! So the woman who produced the baby is a magician. This is the perspective of the toddler-small child group that can no longer use its mother but has not yet settled with an acceptable authority such as a teacher.

The toddler who must leave the family to the new mother–baby dyad has to go out all alone into what may feel like an enormous wilderness – however, both the acceptance and potential transformation of the prohibition on murder and incest and the natural force of valency turn this into the social act it must be. When the Law of the Mother transmutes the effects of the sibling trauma and her prohibitions into a rite of passage, the *proto*-social condition of valency becomes the movement of the social *pre*-group into the social group and the shift of valency's agglutination into sociality. The basic assumption group, like the toddler-becoming-a-child, changes its spots and forms a work group – needing a teacher in its social life. From

thinking it can give birth to babies 'from itself', it works out family relations and begins to grasp 'pretending'. This is a child's 'work group'. The
sudden efflorescence of infectious illnesses which is usually blamed on the
physical gregariousness of the group matches the protracted psychological-
emotional 'dis-ease', as Bion describes the increasing illness of a group when
it first starts to engage with the therapy. This too is the toddler's illness at the
sibling trauma[13] (as it is often at the start of individual therapy). However,
accepting the baby opens up the work mode and these same children recover
from their illnesses with happy and miraculous speed.

*Experiences in Groups* focuses on the pathology of psychotic processes,
stressing that 'even in the "stable" group the deep psychotic levels should
be demonstrated' (p. 165). Yet this can be understood and can change: 'I
believe that intellectual activity of a high order is possible in a group together with an awareness ... of the emotions of the basic assumption groups'
(p. 175). The toddler becomes the child who in its collective inter-child work
learns so much between leaving the family for its group until puberty. Bion's
concepts of 'valency', 'basic assumption' and 'work group' can be used for
young children by pointing to the obvious correlations.

\* \* \*

In an illustration from one of his groups, Bion emphasizes his contention
that where an individual analysis would highlight the psychic defence of
*repression*, an understanding of a group would emphasize *projective identification* (this will compare with Winnicott's selection of 'dissociation' – a
defence which Bion also mentions). An example he uses shows how through
the use of this defence, the group is achieving a complicated interplay of
superiority and inferiority. We can think of this, as Bion suggests, as an outcome of any group meeting in which we, all his readers, have been engaged.
However, initially this is also the toddler's attempt to be superior to the
inferior baby it jealously leaves behind in the family.

Because all groups have 'basic assumptions' which interfere with their intention to work, this describes the latent and normal narcissistic-psychotic
'toddler' who is ever-active in every adult. We are looking, therefore, at the
adult version of a toddler psyche, a perpetuation of the toddler's 'sibling
trauma' and the psychological effects of the 'Law of the Mother'. The adult
reproduces and inescapably echoes the 'toddler' who is always present within
us; the slippage between the two shows how each can be used to understand

---

13  D.W. Winnicott, 'A Note on Normality and Anxiety' (1931), in *Through Paediatrics to
Psycho-Analysis: Collected Papers*, London: Hogarth Press, 1975 (first published 1958),
pp. 3–4.

the other. If we read Bion's account of his experiences with groups through siblings, what is arcane becomes clear.

## Bion and Klein

In shifting his group material to siblings, it is important to note that Klein (on whom Bion rested an aspect of the theoretical case for his new material) proposed her theories of psychic babyhood from the clinical evidence of the psychological and behavioural regressions of the toddler and child patients whom she treated and observed – as we discussed in Chapter 3. For Klein this practice was analogous to how Freud had found the Oedipal child in the regressions of his adult patients. However, in moving this to groups we can ask what becomes of the toddlers and small children such as the youngest – her two and three-quarter-year-old patient, Rita – who gave Klein her theses: 'the effects of the primal scene showed plainly in her analysis. The occasion of the outbreak of her neurosis, however, was the birth of her little brother. Soon after this, still greater difficulties manifested themselves which rapidly increased'.[14] The subsequent explanation here and in all the other cases is a very early Oedipus and castration complex in which the patient wants to steal its sibling from the pregnant or parturant mother, thereby taking its father's place. There is no reason why this should not be the case – but what has happened to the toddler's experience of this sibling itself?

Klein has moved the timing of the Oedipus complex and forgotten what her patients are talking about at a simpler level. The toddler and small child both hated and adored not only the mother but also the intrusion of *the new baby* into what had been their old mother–baby dyad. Introducing siblings into the equation is to put on stage these toddler and child patients whose regressions are to the babyhoods they had traumatically lost to the new sibling. Klein's patients were ill exaggerations of every toddler who for a time demands to be carried, not speak and wear nappies. And whose demand for the total mother opens the door to later Oedipal love. For Bion, working with their adult versions, their 'toddler' characteristics are writ large through the extremities of pathology. He offers us the narcissistic-psychotic period in such observations as: 'the more disturbed the group...the more easily discernible [are] ... the primitive phantasies and mechanisms' (pp. 164–5). The biological and *social siblings* are the children to whom Bion's adult patients are regressing. As usual, adding siblings simplifies the issue.

When the toddler is de-throned by the next baby it crazily tries to become *both* the lost and magic mother *and* the magically arrived new baby. Its own unique, omnipotent baby-identity has been shattered; it tries to *get* all the

---

14  M. Klein, 'The Psychological Principles of Infant Analysis', op. cit., p. 27.

attention like the baby and to *give* all the attention like the mother. In the return of the identifications it has tried to project, it is itself as a baby and itself as a mother – the double and futile omnipotence makes it a fragile hero. The 'know' as in 'to *know* a woman' is not the vertical sexuality of knowing the mother incestuously but a primordial intellectual enquiry into the contents of the mother's body. As Bion notes: 'The attempt to make a rational investigation ... is perturbed by fears, and mechanisms for dealing with them, that are characteristic of the schizoid-paranoid position' (p. 162). The position is Klein's attribution to a tiny baby in the tiny world of the most nuclear family – Bion's is always the wide-open social world in which we flounder (p. 168). This dilemma can be transferred directly to the group's sibling originators. There needs, however, to be a continuity between the normative and the pathological.

For Bion, the group has ways of undoing individuality, which can be made to include the siblings proposed here. Bion is looking at how the condition of valency and the psychotic basic assumptions play out with groups of adults. These observations were based on the group therapy of his inter-war years at the Tavistock Clinic and then after the invalided soldiers in World War II, his return to a very different Tavistock Clinic and a training analysis with Melanie Klein. His groups have come together to work but the work needs a normal-neurotic contact with reality – which unlike Klein and other 'object relations' theorists, Freud had regarded as essential for therapy.

To Bion, neurotic work is always infiltrated by the groups' regressions to the more primitive psychotic states of mind which are always prevalent. What Bion is adding to Freud's account of the social as the normal-neurotic is the perpetual normal-psychotic expressed as 'basic assumptions'. This completely changes the group picture. In fact, as we will see, if we look from the perspective of siblings, there is a double regression – when the group talks, they talk like a two-year-old, when they fail to talk, they are regressing to the baby-status to which the toddler itself has regressed.

Bion describes a characteristic pattern which he considers crucial

> ...subsequent communications were in terms of short interjections, long silences, sighs of boredom, movements of discomfort. This state of affairs in a group deserves close attention. The group appears to be capable of enduring almost endless periods of such conversation, or none at all. There are protests, but endurance of this monotony appears to be a lesser evil than action to end it. It is impossible to give all my reasons for thinking this phase of group behaviour to be significant. *I shall content myself with saying that it is closely linked with ... splitting and depersonalization. I also believe it to be linked with feelings of depression probably in much the same way as maintenance of the schizoid position serves to suppress the depressive position.*
>
> (p. 185; my italics)

Again, we move from a reference to Klein's baby to Bion's own very different seeming group. Reading this group through the horizontal axis would suggest that what is going on in the broken speech and general discomfort is that each participant is shedding its own 'personalization' – its sense of itself as an individual, of who it is, in order that there can be only a group. It is a group 'negative therapeutic reaction' in which anything is better than changing the status quo. But also, if serial 'splitting' is added to general 'depersonalization', each can equally well be anyone as in a play, a novel, a dream – or as in the terror and nightmare of a threatened crowd when a football stand collapses or with one's soldier brothers on a defeated battleground. In this way, the resolution of knowing that hatred and love can be for one and the same person does not exist – there is, so-to-speak, no *one* person there. So the reverse happens and the basic assumptions trump the work group, as in the stasis of inarticulacy that must be preserved in the instance that Bion singles out above and which will be described in the context of the survivor in Chapter 10.

## Why *Experiences in Groups* Can Be Used for Siblings

How then can we insert what we know of the specificity of our siblings into this group that is only a group? The issue is over-determined but a brief answer to be considered here concerns the significance of both war and marriage. Although women are raped in war as much as men are killed[15] and although men marry no less than women, following puberty and into adolescence the gender distinction based on sister–sister, brother–brother comes into play. Here, although some cultures and customs witness behavioural separation of the sexes (and other divisions such as race), nothing suggests any intrinsic distinction at the level of unconsciousness. And yet sisters are subsumed under brothers. From aged about three until about ten or so, lateral relations would not seem to encounter any hiatus. Furthermore, after the Oedipus complex, the part of the child, the daughter or son, that has been engaged with family vertical relations largely leaves these to engage with its social self. The horizontal axis triumphs and though always persistently present, parents and their psychoanalyst successors are thrown into the psychological long grass of 'latency'.

Siblings on the horizontal axis are not primarily significant for their relationships – interesting as these are. They are all-important for the social

---

15 Sexual violence against women has very recently been recognized as the rape it always has been. See the case of 500 gymnastic victims; 'Nassar Abuse Survivors Reach a $30 Million Settlement', *New York Times* Dec. 14, 2021, https://www.nytimes.com/2021/12/13/sports/olympics/nassar-abuse-gymnasts-settlement.html.

unconscious because they are the specific bearers of a prohibition without which no-one can make their own entry into human society as they must do when they are children; they are adherents, successful or failed or both, to a prohibition which insists that there must be no intra-sibling murder or incest. When the prohibition is installed, murder is unconsciously displaced onto legitimate outlets, most notably warfare between one-time, some-time 'brothers' and incest which inverts itself – the illegal transposes itself to the legal – to become marriage. These socially required replacements have their own 'other sides' – rape and sex-trafficking, abusive violence and terrorism.

The degree as to how different in their effects are the identical prohibitions of parental and sibling incest and murder is evident from the different *allowances* of parenting and commanding on the lineal and of warfare and marriage on the lateral axis. Clearly, they are inter-connected – but they are not the same. To build or re-build a society through strengthening its endogamous structure, siblings may even be encouraged to marry and reproduce with each other; likewise, fraternal warfare is everywhere, somewhere – one must ensure one's survival by killing he who, repeating the new baby, would otherwise kill first. This of course applies to combatants on both sides and thereby contributes both to 'legal' war and to unacceptable internecine violence.

There is no doubt that although *Experiences* was not published until 1961, much of the originality and energy of the work comes from the groups with which Bion and Rickman had to engage during World War II. The soldiers had been surrounded by the shattered corpses and body fragments of their dead brothers. When alive, they had fraternized occasionally with the German and Austrian enemy (Freud's sons, friends and colleagues) – who, underneath, were brothers too. War makes the (male) world go round. Aged eighteen, Bion's heroic 'experience' on this lateral social plane in World War I was as a very young leader among brothers. Does no-one in the group, Bion himself included, want to think of the massacre of brothers – and therefore of brothers at all? The deaths can only be re-lived in nightmares. Actual war does not descend from the skies; it constructs or re-constructs human society. Was the pain of a brotherhood destroyed so great that the soldiers and their leader enacted it rather than thought about it? Was the brotherhood aspect of war trauma so overwhelming in World War I that the sibling became unmentionable – were they all so missing their brothers that brothers had to be missed out?

The two 'allowances' on the horizontal axis are gendered – war for men and marriage for women. Siblings can add to Bion's contribution to our thoughts on marriage by thinking further through the basic assumption of pairing; 'pairing' looks to the future sexual and social coupling. In his groups pairing is equally homo- or heterosocial and the pairs are always sexual. The basic assumption of 'dependency' is on the group rather than to the parents one is leaving, not simply replacing; 'fight and flight' is to the be-killed or kill of warfare. When he moves his argument to social institutions

Bion adds to Freud's classic analysis of the Army as a hierarchal family structure the basic assumption of 'fight/flight' and to the Christian Church as a fraternal democracy the basic assumption of 'dependency'.

Bion, as it were, casually makes some inexplicit references to social class. These sneak in with a surprise addition: 'The sub-group in a society most likely to have to deal with the manifestation of baP [basic assumption "pairing"] is the sub-group which attaches most importance to breeding, namely the aristocracy' (pp. 136–7). As a condition of perpetual hope, the wondrous hoped-for offspring has to be 'unborn'. Yet the over-riding hope is two-fold: the pair hope to give birth to the Messiah and at the same time that this Messiah (the heir who continues the line) will be just like their own ordinary selves:

> The aristocracy must inspire Messianic hope but at the same time con-fidence that the pairing group leader, if he materializes, will be born in a palace but be just like ourselves – democratic is probably the modern cant term for the desired quality.
>
> (p. 158)

What can siblings contribute to this bizarre-sounding assertion? Why the 'aristocracy'? The very term 'breeding' indicates a pinnacle status whether in horses or humans. Probably well beyond his own conscious intention, Bion is rightly letting us know that he (maybe 'we') live in a world in which social class inter-segmentalizing with sexism and racism dominates along with other inequities. A society ruled by wealth, prop-erty and elite education – an aristocracy in which we all hope (in vain) to participate – our 'democracy'. Siblings help us to understand the reality behind the doomed hope of pairing. With marriage, siblinghood becomes a social 'fraternity' revealing (like war) its generic origin – with of course 'exceptions'. We are expected to marry laterally within the same class, same colour, same nationality, ethnicity and religion. This thought, so pertinent in these days at the time of writing of the inequity of a pan-demic, takes us away from the pragmatics of the clinic into questions of the theory.

## Thinking Theory with Bion's Models; the Riddle of the Sphinx and the Tower of Babel

> [Communication] does also develop as a part of the social capacity of the individual. This development, of great importance in group dynam-ics, has received virtually no attention...[16]

---

16  W.R. Bion, 'A Theory of Thinking', op. cit., p. 118.

Thinking collectively is crucial and is for Bion instanced by scientific work. He is unusual in psychoanalysis and the social sciences more generally in thinking through models, as do hard scientists.[17] Models test hypotheses and predict information. Often they are inaccurate because not all the data is available. They must, by the definition of their task, be open to new material, which in its turn must be open to further experience and information, all of which may confirm or discount aspects or totalities of what has preceded. Bion's work on groups, indeed his way of proceeding more generally, is within the purview of model-building *en route* to a theoretical extension of what is known about unconscious thinking.[18] To reiterate a common saying: 'models are never right. But some models are helpful'. In using them is Bion himself an example of his observation that an individual can communicate ideas that emerge from social thinking?[19]

The stories of the Sphinx and the Tower of Babel are the two myths which provided the model that Bion proposed would encapsulate the psychotic 'basic assumptions' manifest in any social group:

> The model may be regarded as an abstraction from an emotional experience ... In the group the myth has some claim to be regarded as filling the same role in society as the model has in the scientific work of the individual.[20]

For Bion, the story of the Sphinx is one in which a confrontation with knowledge, science and 'ideas' elicits psychotic responses to the question she asks. For Bion, it is these, not sexuality, which must be fore fronted before Oedipus solves her rather easy riddle. There are many variations to the story of the Sphinx. It is Freud's Oedipal Sphinx that Bion clearly has in mind when he experiences himself as a Sphinx 'leader' in a group. What is Freud's Oedipal Sphinx up to? Oedipus answers 'man' to the riddle she

17 W.R. Bion, *Learning From Experience, in Seven Servants: Four Works by Wilfred R. Bion*, New York: Jason Aronson, 1977, p. 79.

18 It is important that models are tested as new data comes to light. Bion abandoned, for instance, his explanation of what he had experienced of a patient with an 'imaginary twin' as described in *Siblings*. op. cit. He likewise did not continue what he had discovered about the social unconscious of groups. He did not, however, as he did with the 'imaginary twin', offer a different explanation of groups. There are auto-critiques, changes of mind within the text itself, but subsequently it is rather as though he dropped not groups from his thinking but let the book *Experiences in Groups* fall by the wayside. In doing so, he left it for others to pick up, which they very much have done.

19 This could account for the difficulties of his thinking. It is here that not having a brother to talk with, after Rickman's relegation by Klein and then his death may have left Bion isolated despite the great importance of his marriage to Francesca.

20 Bion, *Learning From Experience*, op. cit., p. 79.

set: 'who goes on four legs, then two, then three?' Correctly answered, the Sphinx throws herself off a cliff. Freud comments:

> The ... great problem which exercises a child's mind ... is the question of the origin of babies.[21] *This is usually started by the unwelcome arrival of a small brother or sister. It is the oldest and most burning question that confronts immature humanity.* Those who understand how to interpret myths and legends can detect it in the riddle which the Theban Sphinx set to Oedipus.[22]

So what is this burning question? It turns out that it is Freud who, though also it seems without quite 'knowing' the full implications of his knowledge, offers us the siblings: 'faced with the great riddle of where babies came from, which is perhaps the first problem to engage a child's mental powers ... [Hans] therefore inferred that Hanna had been inside his mother's body...'.[23] These are the brothers and sisters on a horizontal axis whom Bion needs for his group.

Bion's work showed that the group dreads above all else asking the question which Klein's Rita had also feared to ask – what is happening in the mother's 'tummy'? The reason must be because the group itself is the answer: 'For the group approximates too closely, in the minds of the individuals composing it, to very primitive phantasies about the contents of the mother's body' (p. 162). The group like every old toddler and young child who has witnessed a mother's pregnancy asks the same question and comes up with the same answer: I or we can also have babies inside us. But instead of Freud's siblings, Bion answers that his 'basic assumption' adults are Kleinian three-month-olds imagining in schizoid-paranoid mode a 'primal scene' of their parents procreating them as a baby in their sexual intercourse. But, he argues, this is an individual fantasy. So we can suggest that if the group

21  Freud also was uncertain whether this or the difference between the sexes was the most burning question. As discussed in Part One the first question about gender difference arises with the new baby sister or brother.

22  S. Freud, 'The Sexual Enlightenment of Children' (1907), *SE IX*, p. 135. In all the half dozen references to the Sphinx which Freud made he explains a 'distorted version' of the Sphinx's riddle to be the arrival of the sibling. The Sphinx is first mentioned in *The Interpretation of Dreams* (1901) then his writings on children's sexual theories, his proxy study of a child – 'Little Hans' (1909) – to a section added to his introduction of infantile sexuality in the 'Three Essays' (1905/15), to his Autobiography of 1935. For Freud, failure to explain truthfully the new sibling baby's origin leaves the child in a state of near-total mistrust with potentially dire psychological consequences. It is in one of the contributions on the sexual theories of children where he cites the Sphinx that he notes that a child who was persistently misled and lied to, probably partly as a consequence, eventually descended into schizophrenia (see 'The Sexual Enlightenment of Children', p. 136).

23  S. Freud, 'Little Hans' (1909), *SE X*, p. 133.

is having a collective fantasy, then it will be of a collectivity – *more and more siblings*; an unstoppable flow, a series.

The 'Tower of Babel' is the second 'myth' which, along with 'the Riddle of the Sphinx', offers a model for Bion's theory of groups. Bion shows that the shifting interaction of the group's basic assumptions means that the group is not using 'language', which was for Freud the pinnacle of social achievement. We always have to remember the shift from Freud's unit-individual to Bion's unit-group. In a basic assumption group, speaking is used for the expression of sound and to act instead of to think or reflect and communicate, all of which can only be done in a work group. Basic assumption language has no vitality – it is not primitive but rather it is 'degenerate and debased'. The biblical myth of the Tower of Babel has

> the following components: a universal language; the building by the group of a tower which is felt by the Deity to be a menace to his position; hence a confounding of the universal language and a scattering abroad of the people on the face of the earth.
>
> (pp. 186–7)

Resting his complicated exposition on an observation of Melanie Klein's that some individuals cannot form symbols, Bion suggests 'extending this to include all individuals in their functions as members of the basic assumption group' (p. 187). In other words, the group is pre-symbolic. We can transpose this observation to siblings.

What is the language of the toddler and the social child it is becoming when it regresses to absorb the implications of the new baby? It tries a 'false' baby language which can sound 'debased' (as indeed it also can when adults practise it on babies). Or the toddler-small child can attempt to sound 'grown-up' in the unrealizable hope of being part of the Deity-adult's world. This pseudo-adult speaking uses language to get in on the universal grownup action. In response this Deity of adults destroys the idea of a universal language – children cannot join in adult conversation. In fact, it was only the individual family toddler who ever wanted to participate – as a group, toddlers do not try. But there is, as yet, before the socializing of Oedipus, no access to symbolism.[24]

Symbolism, within and beyond psychoanalytic thinking, is a vast topic. Here I will just relate it to the regressed toddler's obvious failure to grasp

---

24 However, although we can add siblings to Bion's work under the rubric of his myth of the Sphinx, the Tower of Babel goes in the contrary direction to offer something to siblings. What Bion understands about the nature of language in basic assumption groups is a useful indication of sibling speech when, because of the loss of the mother to the baby, its language for a time is not its own. It is also not yet metaphoric.

that something can 'represent' something – to the infant, the idea of the baby is the same as the baby itself, which is an example of what, in a rich analysis of the topic, the Kleinian analyst, Hannah Segal called 'symbolic equations'.[25] However, instead, if we look at the question in the context of the relationship to the lawful mother on the horizontal axis, the toddler's version is 'literal thinking' which it is using as it struggles to grasp the metaphorized world. It is also literal thinking in a metaphorized world as it tries to link up to the narrative story-telling of the becoming socialized child.

For the toddler on the march towards full sociability, this schismatic breakdown of a universal single language can turn into the different characters in a story. The story first creates the conditions whereby the raw emotions, the psychotic terrors, can be experienced by proxy as literary representations to replace the pre-metaphoric literal thinking – Pooh the bear instead of an actual bear. This is not achieved through the return of Oedipal repression but instead through the transformation of psychotic-narcissistic thinking, which Bion identifies as essential to the 'basic assumption' group – as it is to toddlers: 'The establishment internally of a projective-identification-and-rejecting-object means that instead of an understanding object the infant has a wilfully misunderstanding object – with which it is identified'.[26] With toddlers, however, all the earlier fragmented projections can be identified with as they turn into more and more endless characters in stories. It is the story that enables the child to move into its life on the horizontal axis where it will take its mother's or grandparents' vertical story-telling into the enacted stories of lateral play – its own first work group.

Bion does not propose the story, instead he elevates the concept of 'correlation'. In 'A Theory of Thinking' with its focus on mothers and babies, he notes the effects of the breakdown of the mother's ability for reverie on the baby's rudimentary consciousness are manifold but 'they are all in different degrees related to the function of correlation'.[27] If things go wrong, the baby's fear of dying is handed back to it as a 'nameless dread'. If the

---

25  In a post-Oedipal world only representations can become part of the 'repressed' unconscious so this regressed toddler state in which speaking is sound and action is not unconscious in the way which individual psychoanalysis can treat – but a psychoanalyst can understand it and treat it differently: 'If it is felt that the attempt to establish a group therapeutic procedure as a method for treating the individual is worthwhile, psycho-analysts would be well advised to find a new name for it. I cannot see that there is any scientific justification for describing the work of the kind I have attempted as psycho-analysis' (Bion, *Experiences in Groups*, p. 189). I think Bion meant group not individual treatment. He may not call his work with groups psychoanalysis but without doubt it is the production of a highly experienced psychoanalyst.

26  Bion, 'A Theory of Thinking', op. cit., p. 117. In this very different paper, Bion has babies and infants very much in mind.

27  Ibid., p. 116.

situation is favourable the mother can accept the emotional fragmentation which the traumatized baby experiences. The mother sees a whole baby and gives this sense of its survival back to the baby who will then have a sufficiently coherent sense of itself. The baby and the mother's experience are correlated. *Correlation* – how two or more variables are related to each other – can be given more specific meanings in different contexts. For Bion what is essential is that a correlation lies at the heart of communication and *if successful* gives it both its social and its truth-bearing character.[28]

Psychoanalysis demands a lot and for Bion it can only be maintained if what is experienced by the patient and the analyst can be correlated – which can only be achieved through signs and words – in other words, the Oedipal normal-neurotic work mode. The experiences are not the same – but they have an intrinsic relationship to each other. People come to therapeutic treatment expecting to talk about sex – but psychoanalytic practice is about knowledge and the capacity for the 'negative capability' or not knowing (Bion calls this 'minus K') so that the correlation between the two can be communicated:

> An important function of communication is to achieve correlation ... conceptions, thoughts and their verbalization are necessary to facilitate the conjunction of one set of sense-data with another. If the conjoined data harmonize a sense of truth is experienced and it is desirable that this sense should be given expression in a statement analogous to a truth-functional-statement.[29]

Such a correlation produces a 'truth-functional' statement which would mitigate the persecution that can otherwise prevail. For the rite of passage on the horizontal axis, Bion's individual baby and individual mother can become the story-telling mother and the metaphor-seeking toddler who can correlate their experiences and whether fiction or fact know a narrative that seems true from one that is false, that is just 'telling stories'.

Can we adapt Bion's suggestion for the clinical work to theoretical propositions and perhaps re-direct his proposal that in the social field a myth can stand as a model? A correlation or co-relation can be suggested between, on the one hand, the sibling trauma and the subsequent sibling formation of the social group and, on the other hand, Bion's theses about basic assumption and work groups. Can these produce not a 'symbolic' but a 'truth-functional' equation in the mother's narrative and her child's metaphorization? The question remains open – or does it?

---

28 Ibid., p. 118.
29 Ibid., p. 119.

After he had written *Experiments in Groups,* Bion was uninterested in what is still today his most popular and successful book. Knowing this, it has felt legitimate to divert its purpose to siblings – they need its knowledge and Bion's account of basic assumptions and work groups describes well the difficulties of this social group process. What siblings are is what they do – they repeat and initiate anew the social group for better or worse – they are us. Left aside or not, Bion has given us an inestimable account of how the social indelibly differs from the family.

# Chapter 7

# Questioning Fraternity

## J.-B. Pontalis – 'Death-Work' and *Brother of the Above*

### Brother of the Above[1]

To start with last things first: in his 2006 booklet, *Brother of the Above*, Jean-Bernard (J.-B.) Pontalis is looking for a general truth about *fraternity* to emerge from an examination of *pairs* of brothers. His booklet has at its centre his relationship with his own younger brother Jean François, his nearly four-year-older brother who had died a horrific death after a mostly appalling adult life:

> You loved me perhaps, and detested me certainly. And as for me, what can be said? Invoking ambivalence – the remarkable sturdiness of the alliance between love and hate – seems to me too facile, to all-purpose a response: what strong relationship – love, friendship – cannot be described as ambivalent? I want to go beyond that.
>
> (*Brother of the Above*, p. 9)

He goes beyond that in a study of pairs of brothers from stories of life and literature, personal history and clinical case references. The theme of *Brother of the Above* is wedged between the story of Cain and Abel and Pontalis' abiding question: 'Was this brother story of mine a war?' (p. 11) Rather than 'brotherhood' he favours the coinage: '*frèrocité*' (of *frère* – brother – and *férocité* – ferocity). Death, murder and war are centre stage, but the emotional thrust is the more underground self-analysis of the relationship between himself and his brother. He died himself seven years after its writing on his 89th birthday in 2013.[2] Their mother had called her two children J.-F. and J.-B. ('Jibi' a life-long nickname).

---

1 J.-B. Pontalis, *Brother of the Above*, trans. D. Nicholson-Smith, New York: Unconscious in Translation/International Psychoanalytic Books, 2012; 1st French ed., Paris: Gallimard, 2006. Hereafter, references to the New York edition of *Brother of the Above* will be given in the text.

2 In the year following the American translation into English.

DOI: 10.4324/9781003347125-10

Pontalis is only interested in 'pairs':

> I wanted to venture … into a continent quite obscure to me. But I was
> not the first person to take an interest in pairs of brothers. Pairs. I
> weighed the import of the word. Pairs of brothers – not wider fraterni-
> ties, nor brother-sister pairs. No, quite simply: two brothers.
>
> (p. 12)

When taken in conjunction with the insistent 'pairing' of Bion's 'basic assumptions', this makes the *pair* of the 'sibling trauma' a likely candidate for
the underlying trauma: 'When the second one was born, the first exclaimed
"How ugly he is!"' (p. 29). No longer a toddler, the nearly four-year-old J.-F.
responded to his sibling trauma of J.-B.'s arrival with a more sophisticated
dismissal. 'Pairs of opposites' is a psychoanalytic concept laying out the
conditions of conflict which produce the symptoms of a pathology. It is important here for the pair of hate and love in response to the sibling trauma.

The effort for Pontalis to produce this self-analysis was considerable but
also compulsive and compulsory: 'turning back was out of the question. It
was as though I was off to war: "It will be tough but we have to go!"' (p. 11).
He describes vividly both how he cannot face it and cannot stop it. Yet
its local implications are worldwide: re-reading the Bible, he realizes that
Cain the murderer – although cast out of Eden and into the wilderness – is
yet forever protected by the 'mark of Cain' on his forehead. The murderer
comes remarkably close to founding civilization itself – the city of *Henoch*
(or *Enoch*), named after Cain's eldest son.

We can see the serious life-long effects of sibling relations in the cameo
Pontalis offers of their childhood. As a child he himself became almost mute
as his brother seduced and then betrayed everyone who visited their home.
J.-F. ecstatically praised the academic successes of J.-B., then rapidly de-
bunked these to their mother and her friends – so that J.-B. was first ago-
nizingly embarrassed at the false praise then completely humiliated by the
'scoffing'. The effects of this spilled over into Pontalis' professional and social relations with teenage schoolfriends and adults. J.-B. internalized J.-F.
as an endlessly persecutory, scoffing, mocking 'superego' that was far more
tyrannical and over-present than a father. We could ask – is this different or
just a much more powerful variant of the common 'decomposition' of peers
mentioned previously?

In adulthood, J.-F., who had 'not uncourageously' chosen to undergo
treatment for his opium addiction, raged uncontrollably at everyone: 'Fury.
Pure hatred. Hell':

> For him this [detoxification] was shock treatment indeed, a trial of un-
> precedented violence, while for me it was a shattering moment: I no
> longer recognized my brother. I saw him screaming, showering everyone

who approached him with insults, and hurling abuse even at "Darling Mama" – the person he claimed to love more than anyone in the world; I saw him flailing wildly in every direction, as though thoroughly out of control as a madman fit to be tied.

(p. 131)

When dying, J.-F. refused contact with anyone. Appalled, J.-B. recounts how Hubert, a patient of his from long ago, reluctantly went to the funeral of Julien, his much-disliked brother, and recalled their childhood game of 'Puce and Zig'. On the edge of Julien's grave Hubert's voice says, 'Goodbye old Zig', and he breaks down in floods of tears. This association suggests what was probably J.-B.'s own collapse[3] – but there is no personal mourning within the book. Instead: 'I want to be free from a grimacing brother. To free myself from the image, to cure myself of it' (p. 132). But how, when J.-F. was J.-B.'s own 'scoffing' superego, could he cure himself – except by the deepest self-analysis?

Unable to mourn, J.-B. tries to counteract the horror with good memories:

I refuse to dwell on this image, preferring to call up other pictures from our childhood, from the time when we would play hide-and-seek, racing from one floor to the other in our tiny house ... or from the years of our youth, when we read the same books, played the same records all evening long. I try to alter the portrait, to replace the gaping mouth with a smile...

(pp. 131–2)

Wherever he looks at brother-pairs what seems like affection and love only masks hatred. An example: Marcel Proust loved to excess his younger brother, Robert, but discovered the way of perpetual childhood illnesses to get all their mother's attention and adoration for himself. When Robert, a doctor, tried to help Marcel on his deathbed, Marcel repudiated him with a virulence that was obviously long-standing.

If love cannot counteract hatred, will being completely different from each other do the trick? *Brother of the Above* opens with how utterly unalike are the Pontalis brothers as the heirs of their exalted ancestors. J.-F. proudly claims them, but J.-B. wants to disown their fame and pompous superiority: 'I know the last sentence of Sartre's *Les Mots* by heart: "A whole man, composed of all men, equal to any other, to whom any other is equal"' (pp. 7–8). He is proud only of the future through his children. Nothing on earth would

---

3  Confirmed by Pontalis' suggesting, as I have done elsewhere, that Freud is also talking about himself through the example of a patient in his essay on Goethe: 'A Childhood Recollection from *Dichtung und Wahrheit*' *SE.XVII*, p. 145.

have made him want to be anything other than Other, totally different from J.-F., his brother. But their entangled sameness becomes increasingly evident. Another Jean-François, the decipherer of the Rosetta Stone and his 'paired' younger brother, the archaeologist Jacques-Joseph Champollion, is anxiously cited: 'you have shown me that I am *you*' (p. 110). Is Jekyll also Hyde? Is Frankenstein's monster also his double? Is the 'uncanny' replica intrinsic to fraternal pairing? As is reiterated throughout this book, it is because a person is the same as oneself that they must be resisted – it is the person who is the *same* who takes one's place in the sibling trauma.

Pontalis' self-analysis challenges his egalitarian claims – he finds he too wants his mother for himself alone. He asks – was his endless quest for a true brother in fact for a mother, one who would simply be there to supply all his needs? When J.-F., an addict, was institutionalized, J.-B. had nearly daily phone-calls with her – he slips in a reference to this fact so that J.-F. will be jealous. The wish may be for an equal portion of a mother's love, but sharing is impossible – 'A mother cannot be divided up. She is mine not yours. Do jealous husbands really feel any differently?' (p. 88) Sartre's *bon mot* does not work. Although claiming to be no theorist, among Pontalis' theoretical try-outs is this about the impossibility of brotherhood: no brother can tolerate sharing a womb, a mother: 'At *the root of the conflict*: a mother who cannot be shared' (p. 94; my italics). In fact, more importantly, we can also see that in wanting the mother for himself alone, once again J.-B. is all too like J.-F.

One may well ask: can the terrible difficulty Pontalis had in bringing himself to write about brotherhood be anything other than the omnipresence in his mind and emotional life of his un-mourned older brother?[4] But that would not be a self-analysis – instead beneath the overt contention this has to be a painful booklet about himself. He finds out that in important ways he is the same as his brother. Like all psychoanalytical patients, he has to ask what was his own contribution? It surfaces in stray bits and pieces throughout which is a testimony to its permanent underlying presence. It is revealed in a self-image near the conclusion when he realizes with surprise his own addiction to listening to or reading about 'incomprehensible' horror crimes, 'all manner of infanticides, parricide, matricides' (p. 181), in fact largely family murders. This unstoppable identification with murderousness rounds off his self-analysis and he ends the account with muted relief.

4    Yet it is this particularly bad experience of an older brother that haunts not only this book, but also, I now suspect, the earlier essay on 'death work'. The contrast between the warmth and energetic optimism of collaboration that marks the *Vocabulaire de la Psychanalyse*, researched and written with Laplanche at the end of the fifties, and the critique of psychoanalysts at the end of 'Death-work', first given as a lecture in Paris in 1976, is notable.

Pairs of brothers originate in the toddler and its first baby sibling – brothers, not sisters, because as *Totem and Taboo* argues it is brothers who initiate society. Pontalis asks: if there had been a sister between himself and J.-F., would the sibling relationship have been different?[5] There may have been a pregnancy or birth of a dead sister in the nearly four years that separated him from J.-F.; a possible sister bears the weight of any hope there might be. Reminiscing about hope, Pontalis tells of his adolescent love and secret yearning for such a 'sister', embodied by 'Cathy' in Ernest Hemingway's *Farewell to Arms*. However, in recalling his love of the novel he seems not to notice that (as Cathy has foreseen) she and her first baby both die in childbirth.

A dead intervening sister as the trauma between the brothers would account for the raw two-year-old toddler so vividly present in the sophisticated terrorizing of the four-year-older J.-F. Although Pontalis wants the impossibility of sharing a mother as a final theory, instead it comes over as a *cul de sac*, a frequently asserted stopping-point in the booklet. This study is about brothers. In offering themselves to be killed and to destroy by killing those who are too alike, brothers leave the mother behind. The endemic warring of pairing brothers contributes an essential nucleus to the fact that somewhere the world is always at war. It is going to war which is the most persistent theme, from start – 'was this brother-story of mine a war?' (p. 11) – to finish in the work's concluding lines: 'Must war always have the upper hand? ... War never ends. War is everywhere' (p. 190).[6]

However, going beyond ambivalence as Pontalis specifies we can discover that there is something about brotherhood that makes its worst also its best; as well as the hatred there is the love even if it is utterly reduced as with J.-B. and J.-F. This may be the problem: hate and love, although always unevenly balanced, are a 'pair of opposites' in constant tension with each other at the very heart of brotherhood. Implicitly Pontalis knows this because he notes in what he names a 'Recess' that 'fraternization' – his own and collectively – occurs within the hating violent fraternities which he loathes. It feels as though his self-analysis has resolved something. He concludes that maybe this book is a 'fraternization' just as he and J.-F. as children and the English-German soldiers of World War I experienced: 'I think the soldier had it right who noted apropos of his fraternal enemies that "they are in the same muck

---

5   We should note, as Pontalis does not, that the Fates discussed in 'On Death-Work' are three *sisters*. To a man, a woman giving birth, marrying and helping him to die, is the sister become mother whom Pontalis wished for – Freud had too many sisters! The Three Fates towards whom Freud addresses his enquiries about death and a man's desires, are sisters. See S. Freud, 'The Theme of the Three Caskets' (1913), *SE XXII*.

6   This is a slight rearrangement from the original French edition which concludes: 'La passion de détruire, Mal triumpherant – ils toujours de l'amour fin? Du bonheur et de la douleur d'aimer?'

as us". In a word, human beings' (p. 184). Looking at the horizontal axis we have noted how the same prohibition on murder with its hatred allows for the legality of war with its brotherly love.

## 'Death-work' and the Death Drive

To go back nearly thirty years to this earlier essay, 'On Death-work', is to offer Pontalis' self-analysis in *Brother of the Above* the theory he reluctantly seeks there. There he states: *'In my view the theme of death is as basic to Freudian psychoanalysis as is the theme of sexuality. I even believe that the latter was largely accorded a more prominent role in order to conceal the former'* (my italics).[7]

As they come together the essay makes itself available for adding siblings and seeing the different effects of the horizontal axis on the psycho-sociality of us human beings 'who are all in the same muck'. In 'On Death-work' Pontalis shows how Freud's own avoidance of death privileged his new revolutionary understanding of infantile sexuality. Subsequently the *bête noire* for Pontalis became classical analysis with its insistence that as we have not actually died, death has to be unknown and can only be represented by the threat of castration, a focal point of Jacques Lacan's 'return to Freud'. Winnicott's work is firmly set against this. What Pontalis offers instead is an extremely radical theoretical exposition of the supreme importance of 'death', both overt in Freud's early adulthood and hidden within his later evasive conceptualizations of it. Finally, it forcefully struggles out as the all-important notion of a 'death-*drive*' of which Pontalis comments[8]:

> Lastly, what was throughout the most general definition of *Trieb,* the drive: a *constant demand for work* imposed on the psychical apparatus and the complex modalities of this apparatus's response to what constitutes a foreign body' to it, while compelling it to function –the very object of analysis.
>
> ('On Death-work', p. 184)

7   J.-B. Pontalis, *Frontiers of Psychoanalysis: Between Dream and Psychic Pain*, trans. C. Cullen and P. Cullen, London: Hogarth Press, 1981, p. 184; 1st French ed., Paris: Gallimard, 1977. The chapter was an expanded version of a talk at the Goethe Institute in 1976. Hereafter, references to 'On Death-work' will be given in the text.

8   This absence of discussion about this chapter was the case when I first lectured on this in 2006. Since then, John Fletcher took it up in 2013 and Adam Philips apparently focussed on it in some talks at the University of York in 2017 which I have not been able to trace. As my purpose is different, I have not incorporated Fletcher's theses, which focus more fully on the work of Laplanche. The English *SE* translation of 'instinct' for 'drive' can be confusing in this chapter. Pontalis is talking about the drive (*trieb*).

The concept of a 'death drive' bringing in its train the notion of a 'life drive' importantly affected the theory of the drives; the death drive provides the model for the drive. But first of all, it can be used pragmatically as an energetic force without which we could neither die nor live.[9]

The working term 'death-work' is Pontalis' neologism in analogy with 'dream-work': *'Dream-work* ... transforms quite diverse raw materials "delivered" by the body, by thoughts, by the day's "residues", so as to manufacture as a product a series of images tending towards a narrative form...' ('On Death-work', p. 184). The argument is that 'death-work' will do the same for the existence of death in the psyche both in the clinical encounter and in the theory. Pontalis is 'interpreting' the mechanisms that 'death-worked' in the various manifestations through which Freud's life and work was driven.

With World War I as an insistent foreground, Freud's formulation of a death drive arose in particular from his clinical observations of the so-called 'negative therapeutic reaction', wherein patients appear to be driven not to get well at any cost and also of the 'compulsion to repeat' a traumatic experience.[10] As set out earlier, a 'Death drive' is an oppositional force that goes *'beyond'* the psychic dominance of the avoidance of unpleasure in the 'pleasure principle'; it drives us back to the inorganic of death. 'Visible' when turned inwards as in melancholia, it brought the proposition of a 'Life drive' incorporating sexuality and self-preservation in tow as an equally important force. The Life drive, or Eros, tries to bind chaotic forces, producing ever greater unities; the Death drive strives to undo and destroy them. As well as opposing each other as conflictual forces, the drives fuse and, for instance, the libido of the Life drive will join with the Death drive to make it turn outwards in aggression and destructiveness – the simultaneous enemy-hate and brother-love of warfare. Going up to the boundary with the biological, where it leaves further enquiry to biologists, psychoanalysis merely points out that the opposition of death and life can be mapped over 'repulsion' and 'attraction' in the inorganic.

For Pontalis, it was death's overwhelming importance for Freud, its extreme personal meaning, which explains his denial of it, and which therefore stood in the way of its theorization. He proposes that Freud's thinking on death can be elucidated by examining the three stages that Freud himself went through in his personal relation to death. Putting Freud on the couch – 'the man and the thinker were singularly linked, as should be the case with all psychoanalysts' (p. 185). The suggestion is that tracing Freud's

9 See Freud, *The Interpretation of Dreams*, Part 1 (1900), *SE IV*, pp. 178–80.
10 It was Lacan who argued for the change of terminology to 'repetition automatism'. The Lacanian term captures well the sense of something apparently beyond any mental control.

personal – emotional and intellectual – trajectory can be used to bring death into its proper eminence. First, Freud suffered an 'actual' neurosis (a term we used for the sibling trauma), indicating that its problems were not in some infantile past but in the excessive trials, tribulations and trauma of the present-day. Pontalis' account does not originate at the historical point of a foundational trauma in childhood, when the child became socialized by accepting society's prohibitions – the present actual neurosis has no past aetiology.

While working more than full-time with an extended family to support financially as well as socially, Freud was endlessly ill in his body. Pontalis lists terrible head and heart pains, 'great cardiac disturbances', migraines, fatigue, intestinal chaos, nasal discharges; death had Freud's body in its grip. He had insistent images of dead people, terrified superstitions of death-evoking names and numbers and psychical depression as well as his usual hyperactivity. As a way of being in control of this actual neurosis Freud engaged obsessively in 'necrological bookkeeping',[11] plotting the likely day of his own death. He had difficulty in confronting the topic of death because death was *too* present: 'He felt himself under its gaze' (p. 186). It was not that death did not matter but that it mattered too much. This first phase of death-work was when a death-disturbed body ruled the psyche; 'the soma takes charge of everything' (p. 187).

Looking at our horizontal axis: in the first stage of the 'actual neurosis' when death is expressed in the body, the *soma* is a *presentation* (not a representation) of death. There is no metaphoric relationship between the psyche and the body; one does not stand in for the other. The identification of toddler-and-baby in the sibling trauma gives us access to Freud's 'actual' illness. The toddler has felt the baby must be more of itself – the family's baby and future couplings bear the mark of this seminal relationship. At the time of his 'actual' neurosis Freud was entwined in a confused intimacy with his beloved and then repudiated friend, the wacky Berlin otolaryngologist, Wilhelm Fliess, just *two years* Freud's junior.[12] Pontalis comments: '(Freud) was ill with Fliess, by Fliess, for him, from him' (p. 187). In *Brother of the Above*, he depicts Fliess in a verbal description and with a photo-portrait as Freud's so look-alike younger brother. And as though he knew it without knowing it, Freud called his troublesome bowels 'Conrad', the name of

---

11  Pontalis attributes his borrowed phrase to Michel de M'Uzan. There are no bibliographical references in this chapter fourteen of *Frontiers of Psychoanalysis*.

12  In his biography of Freud, Ernest Jones sees Fliess as a father figure – but, two years younger than Freud, he was surely a brother? In *Brother of the Above*, Pontalis includes a photo in which Freud and Fliess are indistinguishable. Through Fliess, Freud discovered his hostility to his father – reminiscent of Bion wanting an older brother with whom to discuss his father. Pontalis whose father died when he was thirteen could not find him through his older brother.

Fliess's two-year-old son. For us here, this is the anal-stage toddler muddled up in its mind and body with the new baby of the sibling trauma.

Pontalis does not specify the trauma – but we can ponder that the wild intimacy with Fliess followed on Freud's embedment in a group of same-age male friends whom he had recently relinquished on the death of his father. We can wonder: did his father's death thrust him back to his sibling-traumatic love–hate with Fliess in the persona of a follow-on sibling, whom he then left behind as he joined the social group which he hoped to create around himself with *The Interpretation of Dreams*? More particularly it will have been his trauma when his two-year-younger brother, his first sibling, was born to replace him – but then died.

The 'actual' body cannot be symbolized – neither Freud's nor that of the toddler in all of us – but Pontalis sees Freud as trying to get hold of his un-controllable body and mind with its death obsessions and psychosomatic outbursts by first creating a picture of them. Rather as dream-work makes a picture from all the apparently incoherent elements that underlie the for-mation of a dream, so death-work makes a picture of death – it becomes something we can see in the way that it can be depicted in a painting; a skull pertinently placed or a picture's unifying wholeness ready to be de-scribed.[13] This actual neurosis was succeeded by Freud's discovery of how to understand dreams, which led to the central tenets of psychoanalysis. Finding the repressed sexuality of the hysterical patient to be all-present in his own dreams, Freud's theorizing of it was, one might say, the death-knell of death-work for psychoanalysis. Death-work becomes primarily the *work* of mourning because it is in the process of mourning that death is thought about and *re*-presented: 'Death ceases to have a direct grip over the body. It is internalized. It spreads out, losing impact. In changing space, it changes meaning' (p. 188). Instead of being an external threat from outside which the body-psyche must handle, death becomes a desire from within – simply a wish to get rid of the father as a rival in the love for the mother – 'to kill the dead' – so as to replace him. Freud became psychically the father of his family and of psychoanalysis. Triumphant paternity (Lacan's 'Law of the Father') led to the concept of an Oedipus Complex and from there to the no-tion that as we haven't experienced death (we are after all alive), it can only be *represented* by the castration which the father threatens. 'Representation' becomes the buzz word.

At the time of publication, Freud recognized that his understanding of dreams was a once-in-a-lifetime achievement. There came other nodal

---

13 His intense friendship with the cranky Wilhelm Fliess had been a part of this first 'actual' stage with creative but wild fantasies and worrying physical clinical mishaps. The end of the friendship was fraught with complications, but the transformation of the actual neu-rosis will have played its part in enabling Freud, on his side, to leave Fliess.

moments, but though they were re-investigated, dreams retained their significance. But for Pontalis, what follows their interpretation is the central problem: in the relaxed conditions of sleep dreams are a way in which we enjoy the desires that are prohibited in waking life, they offer the 'wish fulfilment' of otherwise forbidden sexual pleasures. Sexuality gains the upper hand over death. The lengthy *Interpretation of Dreams* is saturated with pictures of death, but it is the sexuality hidden in dreams that are the purpose and theory of the book – dreams are what Freud claimed as the 'royal road' to the unconscious. Yet however important, to Pontalis this is all a denial of death which Freud knows very well through his sensitive literary references and his own life as well as through his understanding of narcissism, annihilation, negativity and his own 'actual' neurosis.

In this dispute about 'death' there is still without doubt an alternative place here for the Freud whom Pontalis is addressing, but there is no place at all for the subtext of Jacques Lacan whom I believe Pontalis also has in mind but does not overtly mention. Indeed, as a former adherent, his later opposition to Lacan's notorious 'return to Freud', which emphasized language and highlighted Freud's contention that the castration complex is death's only representation, often seems to make Lacan a ghost in the text.[14]

After *Beyond the Pleasure Principle* in 1920, Freud was emphatically and increasingly committed to the existence of a death drive while at the same time retaining castration as death's only representation. This quasi-contradiction gave Pontalis his profoundly creative moment as he described Freud's move from his first picture of actual death, through to the unfortunate second-stage drama of dreams and sexuality and then to giving a new meaning to 'actuality' in the third stage. The 'death drive' is a return to the actuality of the inorganic – death. This third stage is Freud's response to World War I where death-work forced him to *think* the enormity of actual death; the result is the richly associative text of *Beyond the Pleasure Principle*. This time around, Freud, rather than himself experiencing an actual present-day neurosis of his own disordered body, reconsidered the implications of 'actuality' for traumatized combatants – the many massacred millions and his own people. Freud thought their death and death anxiety through the symptoms of the clinic. As Pontalis so usefully but complexly formulates it, *death-work* came back into action over actual death and

---

14  Pontalis had had his 'training analysis' with Lacan in the 1950s but had not joined Lacan's subsequent break-away group. In addition to a known critique by Lacan of an un-named Pontalis (see Roudinesco), the way in which Pontalis disagrees with Freud seems tinged with this silent confrontation with Lacan – his quondam analyst. In *Brother of the Above* (2006) again Lacan is not mentioned but as with any self-analysis what has been missing or mistaken in the therapy will emerge – it could not be a continuing analysis if it did not do so; what for Pontalis is so at fault with brotherhood extends to all lateral male relationships – colleagues, friends and Lacan.

produced the theoretical concept of a death drive: 'Third Stage: Death as enacted or, better, as acting in the depth of being in what I would call the "psychical body", as a recurrence of elementary processes which look organic' (p. 185).

All drives drive one to work – for the Life drive one can say the main aims are to unite elements and to avoid unpleasure – but the death drive entails something beyond this: it is as though the drive to death sets up the physical or actual presence of death not as something the body enacts but as an alien 'foreign body' within the psyche. To try and tease this out: for all our pleasure in living there is within us also the presence of an urge to be dead. The all-determined survivor – a refugee on the high seas – knows well the risk of this urge to give up and die. We are always a 'body-I' – but the death drive repeats in a different, reverse modality the actual neurosis. Instead of the psyche being in the body, the body is in the psyche. The actuality of death is restored as a factor which is external to the sufferer and experienced psychically not as inner distress, as with mourning, but as something from outside which resides in the always aging body.[15] As in stage one, death is an outside event but instead of being acted out it becomes an always present 'other' part of oneself. A 'foreign body'; the unconscious produced as a way of thinking by the foundational trauma.

This 'psychical body' is key to the future which psychoanalysis needs to grasp. The psychical relation to the biology of death can be witnessed (as always) most easily in pathologies. Pontalis gives the example of 'organic-seeming' depression which today is sometimes called 'biological depression'; the condition is not a representation – it is a deadness of the body emplaced in the mind.[16] Perhaps Pontalis' concept of a psychical body can be envisaged as death's presence as a lodestone in the core of our being – a presence that in turn makes us think and speculate. But Pontalis claims that no sooner had Freud achieved this knowledge of the implications of his hypothesis of the death drive than he simultaneously reneged on its revolu-

15 Perhaps it is relevant that when friends and colleagues explained Freud's hypothesis of a death drive as a response to his daughter Sophie's death, he was insistent that he conceived the notion before she died of the Spanish flu. However, I would suggest that with Sophie and even more with the death of her second child, Heinerle, Freud certainly experienced not only their tragic deaths but the feeling of his own 'psychical' dying. His wife and daughter could grieve, but he felt his own narcissism was impeding his mourning. Was something else also going on? A certain 'giving up'? (see Chapter 10). Pontalis points out that those many psychoanalysts who dispute the death drive make the same mistakes as those who endorse it – they see it too simply as a synonym for destruction or, to the contrary, as 'nirvana' and its derivatives. Thus, they miss its foundational, its radical '-over-turning' nature. This also affects its role in reorienting the metapsychology and the nature of the clinical practice.

16 Personal discussion about her work with Felicitas Rost, University College, London University.

tionary potential in order to preserve the triumph and single centrality of the sexuality of the Oedipus complex and the death-representing role of the castration complex.

From the viewpoint of the omitted siblings and the horizontal axis, it is important that Pontalis' stance necessitates that he not only emphasize the death which is what the toddler experiences with the sibling trauma, the identical body illnesses of Freud and the toddler-child but also that perforce he must discuss *pre-social* as well as social (or as he specifies 'transindividual') unconscious defences – narcissistic-psychotic and borderline rather than neurotic conditions. But we also need to remember that death as a 'foreign object' in the death drive is a traumatic object – what then of the 'primal repression' of a foundational trauma?

In the 1970s, Pontalis does not mention 'primal repression' by name in 'On Death-work'. Because repression relates to the Oedipus and castration complexes which are known as sites of 'secondary repression', 'repression' of any sort might have queered the pitch of his argument. Primary repression in Freud is both a hypothesis and – in *Totem and Taboo* – the speculation of a pre-historic murder of the father. Here it has been located on the horizontal axis as what happens to the obliterated sibling trauma – which Pontalis does not encompass. However, some ten years earlier he and Laplanche had given an excellent account of 'primary repression' in the *Language of Psycho-Analysis*.[17] To take 'On Death-work' forward for our purposes necessitates the concept. Laplanche and Pontalis note its importance in the case of Daniel Paul Schreiber but also its conceptual uncertainty. The meaning of the 'primal repression' which is implicit in 'On Death-work' accords with how it can be deployed for siblings on the horizontal axis – the close relation of the death drive to trauma.

## Trauma and Primal Repression

In the practice and theory, the centrality of trauma returns to the psychoanalytic corpus after World War I; 'primary repression' is the most suggestive explanation of how a foundational trauma which resonates through a lifetime is dealt with. We bring a blurred consciousness–unconsciousness with us when on birth we come crying hither; but what we need for the distinction of these states of mind is that an attachment to a prohibition is *repressed* to form a dynamic unconscious deeply within us. With the 'secondary repression' of the Oedipus complex the prohibited desires always strive to become conscious possibilities. This is not exactly the case with 'primal repression'.

17 Op. cit. Particularly for Laplanche it was an important concept. Quoting Freud extensively it features in the *Vocabulaire* of 1967 but is not in the index to the Standard Edition (*SE*) of Freud's works.

It is usually seen as underlying the later 'proper' secondary repression. But it must also underpin the several other earlier psychic defences such as splitting, dissociation, projective identification and the rest if they are to be unconscious.

In the secondary repression of the Oedipus complex the new breach that the external trauma has made in the psychic protective barrier is met by the unconscious prohibition of old Oedipal desires – a pull-me push-me movement. With 'primal repression' there can be nothing prior to itself, no internal prohibition to exercise the all-powerful pull. For its operation it needs the further notion of 'anti-cathexis' – which has to do a double job. Laplanche and Pontalis cite Freud's idea of 'anti-cathexis', defining it as an attachment to whatever can impede the entry to consciousness, and comment:

> Lastly Freud invokes the idea, in connection to the organism's relationship to the environment, to account for the defensive reactions to an inflow of external energy which has broken through the protective shield (pain, trauma). In such an event the organism sets internal energy in motion at the expense of its own activities ... in order to create a sort of barrier for staunching or reducing the influx of external excitations.[18]

In 1915 Freud had written 'Anti-cathexis is the sole mechanism of primal repression', and in 1926: 'It is highly probable that the immediate precipitating causes of primal repressions are quantitative factors such as an excessive degree of excitation and the breaking through of the protective shield against stimuli'.[19] All this would seem to be latent in the formulations of 'On Death-work' which, I argue, needs to be *re-read* through the concept of 'primal repression'.[20]

The death drive is here working against the unity for which the life drive aims. Using the sibling trauma as an exemplary instance, it is clear that the trauma is *not* the death drive – it, so to speak, uses and exemplifies it. The

---

18  Laplanche and Pontalis, *The Language of Psycho-Analysis*, op. cit., p. 37.

19  Freud, 'The Unconscious' (1915), *SE XIV*, p. 181, and *Inhibitions, Symptoms and Anxiety* (1926), *SE XX*, p. 94.

20  Pontalis writes: 'the death instinct asserts itself in a radical unbinding process, a process of enclosure that has no aim but its own accomplishment and whose repetitive nature is the sign of its instinctivity. This is a process that no longer has anything to do with conscious death anxiety, but which mimics death in the being's very nucleus, and this led Freud to assign it to the cell, the nucleus of the living being. Then the psyche is no longer a substitutive representation of the body. It is the body ... The unconscious can no longer be deciphered through its formulations, in a mobile and articulable logic of "signifiers", it is realized and immobilized in the logic of the psychical body. This process of functioning has a secondary effect on reality, provoking splitting in the object, in the ego, in every individual or group agency which claims to achieve an ever increasingly embracing unity'; ibid., p. 191. See too S. Freud on 'Splitting'.

new baby breaks up the wholeness of the toddler's ego which feels shattered and in pieces. The anti-cathexis attaches itself in opposition to the trauma as a spurious wholeness which is cast faraway but also retained as an image of itself in the 'traumatized toddler', a terrified manikin, a 'foreign body' within. It feels like a kind of lump (an enclosure) which will always stay inside, awakened and responsive to any new terror. In this response it adds itself as the mad bit to 'secondary repression'. The anti-cathexis accompanies the trauma rather as one might hurl away a cluster bomb that one is left holding as it is blowing one up, it also lands elsewhere as the rages (and worse) with anyone and everyone who matters. Pontalis' brother, J.-F., exemplifies both processes throughout his life and *in extremis* when withdrawing from an opium addiction.

Primal repression sets up the trauma that is 'death' as an enclosed, encapsulated 'foreign body', which will be everybody's individual history – terrifying or relatively benign – of the generic 'sibling trauma'. The unconscious traumatic experience, the 'death', is stuck there, becoming 'fixated'. Or to use a term popularized by Abraham and Torok, the unconscious expression of the trauma is *'encrypted'* in the invaded psyche. But it is also violently expelled. 'Primal repression' is thus the process that underpins all unconscious defences against trauma. As Pontalis states: 'Death is no longer localized in the consciousness or the unconscious, it is at the very roots of the unconscious' (p. 189). Death-life is encapsulated as the 'foreign *body*' where the drives contend and co-operate, unbind and bind the energies to make it survive and live, be dead and die.

We have seen how such a traumatic 'foreign body' acts as an insistent little girl located in an adult male patient of Donald Winnicott's all-important observation when he himself was dying. Pontalis' death drive wraps itself over a definition of trauma which is primally repressed – both entrapped and hurled away – but where, as a *drive*, it is also in opposition to and in union with the life drive which binds the chaotic emotions unleashed by trauma. This is the hypothesis which Pontalis claims that Freud increasingly could not avoid: 'a double drive against nature and the law, in that inconceivable concept, unless it be the one to conceive us – the death instinct' (p. 189).[21] 'Death' which opposes the social and the natural drive to live is with us, also social and natural, as our unconscious from the outset and forever.

The toddler who has felt annihilated, 'dead', when a new baby takes over its identity, does not actually die. However, as Pontalis puts it, this death inhabits it in the form of an imitation of itself as a nucleus of some innermost 'cell' of the being's body-ego. What has happened is that our 'body-ego', in which an actual neurosis is temporarily enacted, has become a permanent

---

21 For 'instinct' read 'drive'.

'psychical body' which is inhabited by the death drive – we live with death. The ego is perhaps the most argued over, complex and complicated concept in psychoanalysis. The emphasis here has been on its origin in the body because this is so evident in the toddler. Freud wrote 'The ego is first and foremost a bodily ego; it is not merely a surface entity but is itself a projection of a surface…[T]he ego is ultimately derived from body sensations…'.[22] This aspect is largely forgotten – as though it has gone missing from the main corpus of psychoanalytic work along with the toddler who exemplifies it?

Because some residual body-ego is always there – and always has been– the psyche-body 'knows' without remembering – amnesia rules the roost. In utero and at birth, the baby (and the mother) could die – like Cathy – or live. When we live, the ever-present inorganic continues to exist in us alongside the organic. 'The instinctual forces which seek to conduct life into death may also be operating in protozoa from the first' (ibid.[23]). This, however, is death as stasis. Something else is added – the processes of 'binding'. Binding and unbinding are notions which Freud used long term, but they were given new meanings with the death drive in *Beyond the Pleasure Principle*. Both socially and in the individual, the death drive is a principle of discord – a drive that disunites, that prompts splitting; it is negativity opposing life's positivity.[24] There is here the overlap between the death drive and trauma; the death drive and trauma are completely interrelated but not identical.

In concluding his chapter, Pontalis writes:

> If the psychoanalyst seeks to specify the present social forms assumed by the death instinct [drive], he is at first glance confronted … by the burden of choice … The analyst today, at grips with narcissism, the narcissism of his patients, of his colleagues and himself, sometimes has the feeling … that the clamour of the world … is but the echo of what he hears in his seemingly padded office.
>
> (pp. 192–8)

In seeing, I think, narcissism in its colloquial sense of anti-social selfishness, Pontalis is not mentioning or just forgetting that narcissism is also essential for survival. The toddler must re-assemble its battered narcissism in order to survive the sibling trauma. As Pontalis writes: 'The term "survivor" comes

---

22 S. Freud, *The Ego and the Id* (1923), *SE XIX*, p. 26.
23 This was explained to me by the much-grieved late Christopher Dobson, St John's College, Cambridge.
24 This singling out of 'splitting' foresees Freud's final unfinished thesis wherein he considers 'splitting' as a new concept different from its origin fifty years previously. Today 'negativity' is a popular concept, heralded by Herbert Rosenfeld's 'negative narcissism' and as a centrepiece in the work of André Green.

up repeatedly in his writings: Freud was a survivor, his place was between two deaths' (p. 186).[25] Freud's father had died but there was also his dead younger brother when he himself was a toddler. Of Julius (named from their mother's very recently deceased brother), Pontalis writes on behalf of Freud:

> little Julius, who died, if I may say so, right on time, when chance or fate intervened and answered the agonizing questions: "How can he be banished? Where did he spring from? Why not throw him out? How can I get rid of him?" (p. 174)

So J.-B. knew what J.-F. experienced when perhaps a sister died as Julius died for Freud. Instead, like Freud's sister Anna, J.-B. himself came along somewhat late – and primal repression took over for J.-F. J.-F.'s initially quite normal death-wishes on the birth of J.-B. turned to a horrible 'foreign object' of himself within him and to a cast away violence towards the world surrounding him.

For Pontalis, Freud's concept of a death drive acts as the catalyst for him to make a major intellectual 'reversal into the opposite' of death for sexuality. For siblings with two foundational traumas, the sibling and the Oedipal, we have two places for death. The *prohibition on incest with the mother* leaves the 'male' individual of either sex (although subjectively bisexual) universally dreading castration as a representative of death. But beneath this, the sibling trauma with the so-alike sibling has its experience of death transformed by the prohibition on murder. Murder can be understood as death when through the law of the mother it can be applied to other people. This 'death' confirms the death drive. This is the 'transindividual reality' of which, as Pontalis says, Freud was always thinking and writing (p. 184).

Clinically, the death drive of the third stage addresses not the Oedipal problematic of classical (or Lacanian) psychoanalysis but today's prevalent narcissistic-personalities and borderline cases. However, Pontalis does not just move forward from this position; instead, he completely shifts perspective and re-configures how the omnipresence of the death drive, which sets up the structural dis-ease at the heart of all civilization, is made more manifest than ever in his own twentieth century and by extension our twenty-first century. He lists our collective and individual fragmentation, the end

---

25 I don't know to which two deaths Pontalis is referring in this passage. He writes of the relationship of Freud's self-analysis and therefore psychoanalysis to the death of his father and to the longevity of his mother, notable because Freud felt certain he could not die before she did. Had she had too many salient deaths? To these might we also add the death of Freud's grandfather Shlomo just before his birth, and, much more likely, of his baby brother, Julius when he was a toddler. His pregnant mother had just lost her own brother Julius, the new dead baby's namesake.

of communication and creativity, our narcissism and the atom bomb as an image of all our nuclear fission. His own identification as man and thinker explodes to all but fill the last two pages of this dense ten-page chapter.

There is without doubt a crucial connection between the early emphasis on the importance of death and the compulsive but reluctant focus on fraternity. *Brother of the Above* allows us to see that what Pontalis wrote in 'On Death-work', where siblings are never mentioned, is in fact a latent manifesto for a horizontal axis with characteristics provided by the sibling trajectory. Thirty years before his self-analysis of his own 'frerocity' in fratriarchy, his thinking was inevitably marked by its unconscious insistence in his life. 'The personal is the psychoanalytical'. Both texts can be re-read to take forward the need for psychoanalysis fully to register that 'we are lived by death' – as well as life:

> The question 'By what are we, as individuals, lived?' which Freud answered in various ways although always through transindividual reality, might find its immediate implicit answer in a phrase like 'we are lived by death'.
>
> (p. 185)

For siblings and the horizontal axis of social relations, to grasp the psychology of the experience of death and the concept of a death-drive is mandatory: '...death is insidiously present behind the most diverse masks, often silent, sometimes noisy, but always active along the paths of existence' (p. 184). Pontalis' condensed references indicate that he thinks that Freud, like the toddler, knew very well about the experience of death.

Referring to Freud's essay on the three caskets (*The Merchant of Venice*) he noted that 'there lay the encounter with the uncanny, in those "caskets" where the secret of Freud remains hidden' (p. 188) – and to quote Freud: 'But if the third of the *sisters* is the Goddess of Death, the sisters are known to us. They are the Fates, the Moerae, the Parcae or the Norns, the third of whom is called Antropos, the inexorable'.[26] With *Brother of the Above*, Pontalis, himself turning eighty, may also have felt the need to confront this most 'secret' hurdle of his own death in his self-analysis. After a prefatory note to his dead brother, he opened: 'No hesitation over the title. It imposed itself right away: *Brother of the Above...*' (p. 11). J.-F. (who wrote nothing) claimed one should only publish posthumously but also openly saw himself in this position – *below* his highly and variously successful younger brother – J.-B./Jibi. As he was dying, J-F. yelled 'No' at everyone in range – 'To what or whom was that "No!" directed, the only word that you uttered...? To death

---

26 S. Freud, 'The Theme of the Three Caskets', op. cit., p. 296; my italics.

who was to be your next visitor, or to life? And to what do I say yes? To life, despite everything?' (p. 9) He did, but death was on his mind.

Although Pontalis certainly chose life, this painful working through from the specificity of his own awful fraternal relationship to the pervasive destructiveness of brotherhood and fratriarchy in general may explain why he says (just one line, without explication) that its worst result was that it deprived him of a childhood: 'There is no good solution [to brotherhood]. But there is something worse. To have been robbed of one's childhood' (p. 33). This completely isolated and unelaborated statement resonates and makes sense. When he was sixty, he published his autobiography, *Love of Beginnings*[27]; it was a-developmental – as in *Brother of the Above* he asks, when does one stop growing up? Here in the earlier autobiography, there was no growing up. However, *Brother of the Above* is about endings not beginnings – for endings one needs old age and dying; for an analysis, a self-analysis, one needs to have had a childhood to recall. Indeed, is old age about letting one's personal generic past replace the present as a preparation for death? Pontalis would have liked to start his life again, at least after the death of his father when he was left with his older brother and the mother this brother monopolized.

Pontalis' father died when he was thirteen years old. Despite great perceptive and intelligent kindness from an uncle and cousins, he says that he never emotionally replaced his father. The awfulness of his older brother filled the absence. It would seem that instead of a dream couple, his mother and favoured older brother were dedicated to being the nightmare pair who never resolved J.-F.'s 'sibling trauma'. Which is a different way of explaining what Pontalis considers to be the universal fact of brotherhood: that a mother cannot be shared. Pontalis' suggestion, as we will see, perhaps reveals that as younger, abused brother to J.-F., he too, though a last child, had been through his own toddler trauma of a potential sibling who did not arrive but the very thought of whom showed he too would not share a mother. This would have been near impossible to know except by its effects because it would have suffered the process of primal repression.

The new baby makes the toddler into an old baby – so it is the toddler who has to change identity and become a child: a small girl or a boy, a sister or brother. Freud's personal history, which Pontalis recounts, bears witness to the *actuality* of the outcome which this sets in train. Pontalis selects features which have their origin with the not yet symbolizing toddler: 'the existence in the present of the conflict and its actualization in the soma, its non-symbolization...' ('On Death-work', p. 187). Freud affectionately giving his bowels a name can be credited with introducing the verbal metaphoric mastery and incipient story-telling that is so needed to turn the latent into

27 J.-B. Pontalis, *Love of Beginnings*, trans. J. Greene, London: Free Association Books, 1993. The book was much acclaimed and received the Prix Femina.

the manifest; so too all the psychic defence mechanisms Pontalis describes belong not to the neurosis of Oedipus but to the narcissistic-psychotic phase of the toddler on the edge of grasping a metaphorized world. Here we are only on the road to telling a story, a narrative. In *Brother of the Above*, the achievement of metaphor as an adult in the mad world of warring brothers is Pontalis' explicit salvation: 'Metaphor ... frees us from mortal repetition, from imprisonment. It animates and transfigures everything it touches. It is metaphor that opens up the world and opens me up to that world' (p. 126). Surely the toddler when it grasps the metaphorical nature of the world, that metaphor is in the world around it, must also feel like that?

## Metaphor and Its Reality

Understanding the implications of the death of others introduces the meaning of death; it also involves the cognizance that others are both alike and unalike ourselves. This perception depends on metaphor, as metaphor depends on it. In this respect the importance of metaphor for toddlers is underpinned by Pontalis' own trajectory – his childhood memory describes metaphor and reality in a way which helps us with the toddler's own needs and triumphs. It explains the stage of pre-neurotic reality in which metaphor is embedded not in how one is looking but in what one is looking at – this is a condition of creativity:

> For me reality was dual. The visible and invisible were one ... At bottom what I was discovering by conflating a cobblestone with a face, or a passer-by with a bird, was the power of poetry, the metaphor implicit in our perception of an object. Not just in that perception, not just in our vision, but in the thing itself. Yes, it must have been this ... that made me declare myself a metaphysician...
>
> (p. 125)

The association is to a bracelet his father had given him; he had inscribed on it his aspirational identity – a 'metaphysician' – someone who can go beyond a limited concept of reality. Interestingly and sadly, it would seem that an actual death – his father's in his childhood – plays a part in this triad of metaphysician, metaphor and creative reality: it was real that his dead father was both visible in his mind's eye and, being dead, invisible. Believing is seeing – the issue haunts all our mourning, all our personal losses. Freud's grandson of the fort/da game as with any infant or even baby is at pain to work out that disappearance need not mean death. Death is differently 'real' for the adult who has died (Pontalis' father) than for the son left behind (Jibi). At the heart of biological depression is an absence of metaphor: 'a wall is a wall...death is in life and, just like death, life *says* nothing. Dead language, speech silenced. Nothing...' (p. 126).

The most important of sibling defences, 'reversal into the opposite', in which hate becomes love and love becomes hate, a defence mechanism that the narcissistic-psychotic toddler takes into the social world, attacks as well as endorses metaphor. This can most clearly be grasped in pathologies where instead of living with metaphor and the story, the sufferer uses hatred to reverse the metaphor and insist on 'literality' – acting an actual 'a slap in the face'. The psychical body is abandoned in favour of the preceding 'actual' physical body; the mother's 'law' is rejected to enable a return to the actuality of the sibling trauma. Pontalis describes how his mother has her 'feet on the ground' and nowhere else – he cannot tolerate those who like her are literal-minded: 'a table is a table; a wall is a wall, closing off the whole horizon; an ashtray is an ashtray, its function being to receive ash...' (p. 126).

## From Metaphysician to Metapsychologist

In *Brother of the Above* the equation of pairs of brothers and war exceeds the autobiographical fact of Pontalis' personal family of origin with its just two boys – J.-B. and J.-F. If the 'pair' underlying all these real and fictional adults is 'originally' the toddler-new baby of the primarily repressed 'sibling trauma', then J.-B. Pontalis was the recipient of J.-F. Pontalis' sibling trauma: 'he hated me certainly'. J.-B was the new baby who was the initially innocent cause of this murderous hatred. But he too will have gone on to have his own sibling trauma as a toddler for whom no other sibling arrived; this would have been deeply unconscious – but he too must have found himself unwilling to share a mother. This dynamic can only be latent in the thesis Pontalis favours.

Is this new baby to J.-B. a non-arriving 'sister' like the one whom he thinks may have actually preceded him as a death or a miscarriage? 'Before' may have become 'afterwards' and her non-arrival left him consciously fantasizing instead, as we have seen, a literary, perfectly loving couple (with unrecognized death at the centre) – 'Cathy' in *A Farewell to Arms*. This recurrent benign fantasy morphed into its diametric apparent opposite in his adult passion for reading accounts of familial sexual murders – which gives us a clue to what might have been his own 'sibling trauma' with an absent wished-for sister – whom he would have simultaneously adored and wanted to sexually murder. Ambivalence pales beside 'reversal into the opposite'.

'On Death-work' has the insistent energy of urging people to embrace its argument for the importance of death[28]; *Brother of the Above* is about

---

28 On the death drive in *Beyond the Pleasure Principle*, Freud's writing is 'sustained throughout by a demand for thought, analogous to a desire that irrepressibly seeks out the path of truth: "It's as though I'm obliged to believe it"' (p. 190).

an enormous resistance to writing it at all – in addition to the obvious horrors of Pontalis' personal story, is it that incest and murder is unconsciously implicated for each pair of brothers which he describes? In *Brother of the Above*, the personal experience is overt but sometimes given on the oblique – Pontalis has experienced for himself what another pair of brothers – in life or literature – has also felt. We can put this another way: *Brother of the Above* provides through its self-analysis the *empirical material* of a nuclear relationship on the horizontal axis for which 'On Death-work' offered a potential *metapsychology* instigated by the difficulty of relating the psychology of death to its biological fact. These are much worked over questions but the interest here is particular: it suggests that the unique combination of death and the death drive with brothers and war necessitates as a framework a particular reading of Freud on both metapsychology and clinical work and their relation to each other.

In 'On Death-work' the intellectual theme – the importance of the 'actual' *experience* of death – is impregnated with how intensely Pontalis *experiences* the subject of his argument – the death drive. Pontalis' thematic focus, as we have seen, explains how decades after his actual neurosis Freud produced the hypothesis of a 'death drive' which, if theorized in the way Pontalis suggests, explains how the 'actual' experience is always also transformed. The interaction of the two texts – one on death and the death drive and the other on hating pairs of brothers – is the hallmark of Pontalis' originality. We often have one or other theme considered – outstandingly the one needs the other as is realized here.

If we look at this through the relationship with Fliess embedded in Freud's actual neurosis, rather than at its psycho-physical manifestations, something different emerges. Pontalis specifies their extraordinary closeness during the enactment of Freud's actual neurosis so that they can be felt as the near identical pair of social brothers which they become in *Brother of the Above*: this intimacy within a pair may be the condition of the production of a metapsychology.[29] It was not only in the amazingly rich letters to Fliess that Freud let his trained imagination run into the speculations of a

---

29 S. Freud:

> It seems to me that the theory of wish-fulfilment has brought only the psychological solution and not the biological – or, rather, metaphysical – one. (I am going to ask you seriously, by the way, whether I may use the name metapsychology for my psychology that leads behind consciousness.) Biologically, dream life seems to me to derive entirely from the residues of the prehistoric period of life (between the ages of one and three) – the same period which is the source of the unconscious and alone contains the etiology of all the psychoneuroses, the period normally characterized by an amnesia analogous to hysterical amnesia.
>
> J. M. Masson (ed. and trans.), *The Complete Letters of Sigmund Freud to Wilhelm Fliess, 1887–1904*, Cambridge, MA: Belknap Press, 1985, pp. 301-2.

metapsychology, but later also as a pair with Sandor Ferenczi up to and into World War I with its actuality of killing, though thereafter their ways began to separate.

World War I and its aftermath challenged previous theories and brought forth the magnificent strangeness of *Beyond the Pleasure Principle* (1920), with its all-important postulate of a death drive; this was a resurgence of Freud at his metapsychological height but increasingly without a partner to share his flights of transcendent, sometimes refreshingly 'mad' imagination. Although both Freud and Pontalis are dead, the latter's intense personal involvement in his subject, his teenage aspiration, and his wide-ranging abilities make Pontalis into a latter-day partner or 'pair' to Freud. He knows that Freud never gave up on the death drive but also that it was not what Freud handed down to his followers – it is this that the living work of the pair – Pontalis and Freud – can do. Siblings and the horizontal axis have gained access to both a metapsychological overview and the clinical effects of the sibling trauma of brotherhoods – frerocity, fraternity.

# The Social Child's World
## Latency and No-Latency

'Latency' is the title that Freud gave to the peculiarly human characteristic of divided, biphasic sexuality – a long lull – following the demolition of the Oedipus complex at roughly five–six years old and the onset of puberty when sexuality comes back in full force with prospective reproduction.[1] There can be no dispute as to its importance; but there is room for something else beside it, indeed almost for its opposite on the horizontal axis. Groups of children continue the Law of the Mother and socialize their own sexuality, their sibling incestuousness into intimate relationships. From the child's viewpoint this task extends unbroken from about three to ten years old; after the demolition or repression of Oedipus, more-or-less the whole child is social. The side-lining of parents from whom the concept of latency is seen to devolve, is crucial. What happens in this in-between age?

## The Toddler Becomes a Child

From the toddler's viewpoint, the next baby's arrival – actual or possible – makes the family unit into an unwelcome foursome; it is this knowledge of four that it takes into its same-age group where the four which defines a group will immediately extend into more. Its rivalrous wished-for threesome will persist in the family until after the Oedipus complex and from then until the shock of puberty repeats the 'who am I?' of the sibling trauma.

Thus, at the same time as the pre-Oedipal is operating as a threesome in the family, in the social there is plenty of peer group interaction, the beginning of social play and learning about others. Around ages three and four, children kiss and cuddle each other affectionately; with sibling incest forbidden, love can flourish between peers. However, if the prohibitions have not been adhered to, sibling incest can become endemic or displaced, persisting as disapproved of mutual masturbation; hatred can be either a

---

1   It is always said that Freud acknowledged that he got the term from Fliess – the attribution but not the letter is extant.

DOI: 10.4324/9781003347125-11

temporary explosion for a loved friend or a murderous enmity that has not been banished as an effect of the sibling trauma.

From age three to puberty, a child's sexuality is directed in various ways towards another. Transposing Bion's terms for his basic assumptions of groups onto small children, we can see the dependency on each other which has developed since its earliest expressions at a few months of age, and the social development of flight and fight which would seem to have a generic biological basis now becomes an essential interactive psychological process in friendship and enmity. Perhaps above all there is the tendency to pairing which can be expressed sexually or as love – based on finding an 'alikeness' – both same sex and other sex. The 'reversal into the opposite' of love and hate for the same person is still being negotiated.

Freud was always clear that what seemed like an absence of sexuality in post-Oedipal latency was in fact only a re-direction of it. Although obvious, this definition is often ignored. As an example of diversity which is still extant, the Trobriand islanders (who, as mentioned, occasioned an important anthropological-psychoanalytical debate in the 1920s) had a 'republic of childhood' with free sexual play for all children over the age of seven – except siblings. Latency, where lateral socialization takes place, far from being uninteresting, is dynamic and vivid. It is where the socializing of the subject's fundamental inter-subjectivity most fully occurs. Bion's concept of 'valency' is transformed into the organized social. The agonizing jealousy following the sibling trauma at this time can become competitiveness; envy can transmute to emulation; shame into a concern for others. It is a time when an explosion of thinking about everything is the product of an energetic defence against the traumatic, a time of loving and hating peers, of 'best friends' and bullies, of inventing, reflecting and learning, of despairing; of reading and writing, of creating and the beginnings of contributing to the world's art and culture or because of the vast stringencies of social deprivation, failing to do so.

There can be danger and utter wretchedness too in these lateral encounters. Bion himself, exiled from home and country, gives a vivid retrospective picture of the awfulness of this time. In addition to the horrors of the colonized, the penalties of Empire-building were visited on children of an aspirant upper-middle-class – mainly boys. The eldest child of a missionary family in North-East India, the racist but stimulating miscegenation of his childhood upbringing came to an abrupt halt when at eight, typical of his class, he was sent alone to a minor private 'public' school and to live with strangers in England. He developed an 'intolerable exo-skeleton of misery'.[2]

---

2   W.R. Bion, *The Long Week-End 1897–1919, Part of a Life*, ed. F. Bion, London and New York: Routledge, 2018 (first published 1982), p. 54.

Similarly placed, Alan Turing said that the only good thing that could be said about his schooling was that nothing so awful could ever happen again.

Whether good or bad, far from a gap, social childhood is full and nowhere latent. It is where children are trying out 'reality' through play, pleasurable and un-pleasurable, between themselves. Between children it is one of the most creatively intense learning periods. Listened to as a group among themselves, so-called latency children are fascinating. They play together and make up plays. Asked in a radio interview why she had placed Harry Potter in such an elitist, upper-class setting as a boarding school, J. K. Rowling answered that children of Harry's age are only interesting when they are among themselves, away from their families – boarding school was simply a device to ensure that.

## Parents and Psychoanalysts

The psychoanalyst inherits this parental redundancy. Latency is understandably uninviting for the parent and analyst, for it is indeed a repudiation of parents: the social child does not want any parent to get in the way of its excited explorations, its wondrous epistemophilic drive nor, indeed, its bullying, violent opposite. So, against any appreciation of the richness of the period from the analyst as transference-parent we tend to have the dismissal of the latency child. Winnicott, having unusually cited Klein with approval, continued:

> Unlike the small child whose lively imagination and acute anxiety enable us to gain an easier insight into its unconscious and make contact there, [latency children] have a very limited imaginative life, in accordance with the strong tendency to repression which is characteristic of their age....[3]

However, Anna Freud, less dependent on having only a parental transference role, greatly appreciated this child's 'drive-to-know'.

Latency child psychoanalysis tries to fit a lateral child–child psyche into lineal parent–child bottles and then goes on to bemoan the psychological poverty of the latency child-in-the-vertical parental family. Such a perspective is also tantamount to saying psychoanalysis should ignore the individual as a social person. Winnicott's concept of 'an environment mother' attaches to the vertical mother everything positive that the lateral environment can lay claim to. We can pillory Winnicott here but the same holds good in general. But it is the fault of psychoanalysis not of the child, who may well be

---

3   Klein 1932/1975, p. 58; quoted in Winnicott 1958/1965, p. 118.

keen to keep anyone who represents grown-ups and the family firmly out of the way. Work group children who can also be utterly miserable are notoriously resistant to parental and therefore to psychoanalytic help. Teachers who may be *in loco parentis* have to make sure they are also importantly something other than parents; that is therefore something the transference-counter-transference of the psychoanalyst has to face.

However, the work group is also different from the underlying and countervailing basic assumptions. It has been described as 'an arena for transformations'.[4] Truth and lies become distinguished, reality and its 'principle' are no longer the injunction of the mother but instead the need of the child and the children; there is space for the individual and for the newly acquired creativity of group thinking. A transformation of the child takes place in the various groups which make up the social when, for the child, the family is on the backburner.

Abuse may be enacted on both the vertical and horizontal axis, for instance when a near pubertal brother has sex with a younger brother or sister as is quite widely recorded, or the institutionalized intra- and inter-age cruelty that Bion recalls. Basic assumptions continue with children within their work groups.

The children outside my front door are luckier. As I sit upstairs at my computer, a noisy, exuberant gang from age five to ten years play together as always after school in the street and mid-town common beneath my window. Thinking about 'latency' I scribble down what they are shouting loudly in intense conversation to each other. With slight distress but even more determination in her voice, a girl protests: 'you are sabotaging my plan to sabotage'. They all stop racing round and a placating, kind but strong voice of a somewhat smaller boy states: 'Ok, I will be the imposter'. Pleased, several of the group plan their further plot in excited broken unison: 'and we can kill those who are in the Chinese emergency meeting'. Is this the language of privileged Cambridge, UK, or of more widely spread computer games where 'imposter' and 'sabotage' are frequent? Such games, in any case, are worldwide. Feeling fond, they make me smile as their aliveness transforms the sadness of the Covid pandemic. They also help me: why is 'latency' – the in-between period of biphasic human sexuality – so different if one looks at child–child interaction along a horizontal axis? These are latency children – but all is up-front, nothing is latent between them. How does one write about something that is not there? Latency – the apparent gap, the absence of sexuality between its wide-ranging florescence in our infancy and its explosion at puberty. Although not anti-adults, this is a time when children increasingly want less and less truck with parents. This gang

---

4   D. Armstrong, 'Names, Thoughts and Lies: The Relevance of Bion's Later Writing for Understanding Experiences in Groups', *Free Associations*, vol. 3, no. 26, 1992, pp. 261–80.

from different local state primary schools and one private college school – all close neighbours – are surprisingly nice to me (not a parent) because I can wolf-whistle (arduously self-taught when I was their age). However, had I opened the front door and stood among them for one single moment mid-play, they would all magically and instantly have vanished into thin air. *Their very noisy games are entirely private.*

# Part 3

# Fratriarchy

## Tomorrow, Today and Yesterday

I cannot express it; but surely you and everyone have a notion that there is, or should be, an existence of yours beyond you? What were the use of my creation if I were entirely contained here?....Nelly I *am* Heathcliff – he's always, always in my mind –not as a pleasure any more than I am always a pleasure to myself – but as my own being...[1]

Is this statement a portrait of bisexuality at its nodal point? An interpenetrating childhood and adolescent sister–brother dynamic could be said to underlie all of Emily Brontë's *Wuthering Heights.* In the novel, parenting is benign, evil or ordinarily flawed, but whichever, it is rapidly absented from the dramatic presentation of the sibling scene. Although Charlotte Brontë tried to explain and excuse her younger sister's extremities, the outstanding novel offers a rich portrait of the psycho-sociality of the horizontal axis. Psychic bisexuality is a fundamental human characteristic; fratriarchy cannot be grasped without an awareness of its underlying presence.

As the plays of Shakespeare exemplify, nothing in the social world makes sense without the concept of psychic bisexuality: 'I am all the *daughters* of my father's house and all the *brothers* too' (*Twelfth Night*, my italics). However, a question that implicates bisexuality underlies this final section: does the girl – a *daughter* – exist in the patriarchy, while the boy with his *brothers* creates the fratriarchy? Shakespeare had a second daughter, Judith, and through her he seems to have felt that he also had extant her deceased twin, his only son Hamnet, who had died when the twins were nine years old. Of the twins Viola and Sebastian in *Twelfth Night*, his character Antonio

---

1  Emily Bronte, 1847 *Wuthering Heights*. Harmondsworth: Penguin Classics, 1985, p. 122. See Rod Mengham, 1988. Emily Brontë, *Wuthering Heights* Penguin Books and Juliet Mitchell in *Women the Longest Revolution and Other Essays*, Penguin Books, 1982). For Shakespeare, the boy is the acting subject – his object is the girl he plays. But something stronger transforms this: at least in our Western times, Viola the woman (like Rosalind in *AYLI*) is the most important and powerful character.

DOI: 10.4324/9781003347125-12

claimed: 'an apple cleft in twain is not more twin...'. Here Shakespeare turned grief into the richest portrait of the bisexual subject available to us. Boy actors acting girls playing boys is a feature throughout his work and is particularly noteworthy in the high comedies.

So, wandering through my mind, like wine through water, is also the example of great artists whose art is the bringing of the unconscious to consciousness, of shifting trauma into the pleasure of the aesthetic, for whom subjective 'bisexuality' must be a *sine qua non* for any true art practice. Of her compulsively heterosexual father, Maya Picasso wrote: 'In my opinion my father was, in a sense, "bisexual" from his birth, or rather since his debut as an artist...'. Here we might say that Picasso's art portrays why exuberant but utterly diffuse love and penetration enabled him physically to experience Maya's mother's pregnancy before her mother knew of it.[2] The overwhelming wealth of works and writings about bisexuality by Louise Bourgeois (the artist most highly attuned to psychoanalysis) make her its portraitist and spokesperson today. She would address with puzzled preoccupation her own *Janus Fleuri* – 'we are all male/female', a looking-two-way sculpture of mixed genitalia. It is both portrait and self-portrait and thus an example of Pontalis' claim that the aesthetic is lodged in the object, not in the eye of the beholder or the creator.

Bisexuality is a crucial tenet of psychoanalysis that first came to prominence in Freud's excited friendship with Wilhelm Fliess and was still emphasized in his last writings, where his failure to link it with the drives – after 1920 the life and death drives – continued to nag at him but which, as we will see, can be helped by thinking laterally. Freud's introduction of a 'drive' (*trieb*) enabled his revolutionary concept of the multifarious nature of human sexuality. Because of our prematurity, we are without the strength of mammalian instincts, which make directly for the objects they want. He introduced perversions and inversion to explain his contention that we are driven to get sexual satisfaction through very various means and objects[3]; what Freud needed was to add 'bisexuality' as the foundation of these. He never gave up on the certainty of our bisexual disposition, and any subsequent difference between the psyche of women and men was constructed on its unilateral basis. But how can we reconcile the observation that we are all bisexual with the tenet that women and men are psychically different?

When the wild creative frisson of the relationship with Fliess was heading for the rocks, it was the origin and meaning of 'bisexuality' which was the

2   Maya Picasso in W. Spies (ed.), *Picasso's World of Children*, Munich: Prestel Verlag, 1996, p. 57.
3   S. Freud (1905), *Three Essays* op. cit.

focus of its tumultuous end.[4] For Pontalis, Freud and Fliess were 'brothers'. Lateral relations constitute 'gender' – how does sibling bisexuality contribute to 'gender' on the horizontal axis, where the drives will also welcome it differently from the constraints of the Oedipus-castration complex? With siblings the series overrides the binary – as it may do with transgender.

The hypothesis of a 'death drive' took ever firmer hold of Freud but a way to reconcile these two postulates of bisexuality and a death drive was elusive and this bothered him. Looking from a social axis, it would seem that the life drive, which works for union and reproduction and subsumes sexuality, would involve a difference between the sexes which are then brought together from their different standpoints for the aim of reproduction. But this would not hold true for the death drive.

Women die in childbirth and men in fighting, but death in and of itself is not gender differentiated. We need to think this through the questions of both vertical 'sexual difference' and of horizontal 'gender' with its privileging of bisexuality. In these enmeshed issues there are two underlying tasks: we have to examine the construction of 'sexual difference' as a contribution to a patriarchal 'oppression' of women and ask whether a gender difference makes its own contribution to fratriarchal discrimination and oppression. In order to ask this, we have to establish gender as a useful psychoanalytical category. Does it differ from vertical sexual difference in relation to privileging the death drive over the sexuality of the life drive? Is there likewise a distinction as regards the over-arching apparently shared concept of bisexuality? Involving a brief excursus into 'bisexuality' as a primary category, Chapter 8 will examine the understanding of Oedipal 'sexual difference' within the meaning of bisexuality. Chapter 9 will then focus on the contribution of 'gender' and its lateral, social axis in order to start to unwind this tangled web. Chapter nine will then bring us to an end with sisterhood which is above all a new beginning.[5]

4   Fliess considered that Freud had leaked his idea of bisexuality through a patient to Otto Weininger who gained notoriety through 'introducing' it to the 'world'. Freud, who acknowledged Fliess as its originator, in fact had given it a distinctive meaning – in his view he had made it his own. Which version was 'stealing' is a moot point as it was the notion as a slogan for object choice alone that became current and that then entered some psychoanalytic thinking where it does not make sense. Does 'everyone' start off with an unacknowledged 'theft' – and what counts is how dynamically and creatively one continues... or not.

5   See Juliet Mitchell, Shakespeare: *Siblings and Sisters*. Op. cit.

# Chapter 8

# Oedipal Sexual Difference

A sexual distinction ('sexual difference') defines patriarchy where 'gender' characterizes fratriarchy. The implications of this claim extend far beyond what is at first apparent and, unsurprisingly, they involve a varied place for bisexuality. We will start with the implications for patriarchy.

Freud emphatically establishes what he designates 'sexual difference' as the result of the castration complex; for the girl and woman its outstanding expression is 'penis-envy'. To grasp the import of this we can turn to his notorious text, the *New Introductory Lecture*, 'Femininity' of 1932/33,[1] which sets out the position more fully and forcibly than anywhere else.

The essay 'Femininity' has for the most part been negatively seminal in the history of psychoanalysis and feminism. It is by any count a strange lecture. The *New Introductory Lectures* were not delivered but were written to allay the financial difficulties of the psychoanalytic press. They are presented as supplements to the earlier series of Introductory Lectures (1916/17). It is as though this essay – 'Womanliness'/'Femininity' – initially gets caught up with, but then becomes a flagship, for Freud's general irritability at writing these pecuniary lectures for an imaginary uninformed general public. As his general preface to the volume puts it, this absent but inclusive public always demonstrates 'mankind's constitutional unfitness for scientific research' and 'demands of psychology, not progress in knowledge, but satisfactions of some other sort; every unsolved problem, every admitted uncertainty is made into a reproach against it'.[2]

Freud opens 'Femininity' with the statement: 'All the while I am preparing to talk to you I am struggling with an internal difficulty. I feel uncertain,

---

1  S. Freud, 'Femininity', op. cit. 'Femininity' is an unfortunate translation. See: 'die weiblichkeit' S.Freud Neue Folge der Vorlesungen zur Einfuehrung in die Psichanalyse XXXIII Forlesung p. 119. in S Freud Gesammelte Werke vol XV (1969) Frankfurt Fisher Verlag.
2  S. Freud, 'Preface', *New Introductory Lectures on Psychoanalysis* (1933), *SE XXII*, p. 6.

DOI: 10.4324/9781003347125-13

so to speak, of the extent of my license'.[3] Today as yesterday his imagined audience would be entitled to think he was referring to the fact that as a man, he is not in a position to talk about women – but this is not it. Instead, we have a very long justification, defensive to his colleagues, aggressive to the general public, for the entire book of seven lectures before he gets to the particular topic of 'womanliness'; when he does, he can only mention 'two things to recommend [the essay]. It brings forward nothing but observed facts, almost without any speculative additions, and it deals with a subject which has a claim on your interest second almost to no other' (p. 113). Freud is eschewing exactly what we so urgently need for the topic of women – a place for it in a 'speculative' metapsychology.

A metapsychology which describes the theory was his general aim and had been a focus of his 'wild thoughts' at the outset with Fliess and much later with Ferenczi. As though in lieu of 'speculation', for women Freud supports the platitude that 'the riddle of the nature of femininity' is age old by quoting some lines from his favourite poet Heinrich Heine. An echo of the poem and a brief quotation make it sound like a displacement of the missing metapsychology which would have addressed the question of the relationship of bisexuality and the death drive. Freud assumes his unknown audience is fully aware of the intense Nazi hatred of Heine with whom Freud is publicly proclaiming his total identification. A very few months after the writing of this lecture, Heine's books (along with Freud's) were burned in Berlin's public square by the Hitler Youth. Paradoxically this appalling lecture is a very brave one.

Thus, although Freud's critique of popular receptions of psychoanalysis will hold good in other times and contexts including today, 1932–33 had, indeed, a terrifying particularity into which we must set 'Femininity'. This would also be a context in the mind of circumcised Jews and 'castrated' women. Planned for 1935, an exchange lecture on female sexuality to explain the differences between British and German-Austrian psychoanalysis was cancelled. Instead, Freud's earlier 'Femininity', and with it what he considers the awful perpetual knowability and unknowability of 'womanliness', carry the weight of the horrifying times.

'Fragen' or 'Questions', the Heine poem cited by Freud, is in fact not about being perplexed by women as Freud suggests, but much more widely by mankind in general. It is with this despairing unknowability of what mankind is, and therefore what mankind may do, that Freud expresses his all too pertinent fears – for Jews and mankind – of Hitler himself and of Nazism's ascendancy. In revered tradition Heine's young man is asking ('fragen') to 'solve the/riddle of life', 'what does man mean?'

---

3   Freud, 'Femininity', ibid., p. 112. Subsequent references to this essay will be given in the text.

There would seem to be a slippage between Freud's identification with the conscious *riddle* about mankind and an unconscious association that refers this *riddle* specifically to women by only actually and otherwise rather oddly quoting just four lines about hats:

> Heads in Hieroglyphic bonnets,
> Heads in turbans and black birettas,
> Heads in wigs and thousand other
> Wretched, sweating heads of humans[4]

There is no explanation of these hats which suit men rather than to women and there are other parts of the lyric he could have quoted. In Heine's poem, the line that precedes the previous statement is 'What some/Heads have already pondered', and what follows is 'Tell me what/does man mean?' However, as we have seen previously, Freud has made it clear that these removable hats indicate 'off with your head', a synonym for castration – but also murder.

Is it that woman being castrated is mankind's problem – the 'excruciatingly ancient *riddle*' for which 'the fool is/waiting for an answer' (Heine)? Has the awfulness of the times become confused with the awfulness of being a woman, the awfulness of women? We could almost stop here. For us as women everything else feels like padding; for us as psychoanalysts the thesis is all too well sustained: because castration would certainly be awful for men, therefore as 'already castrated' the woman *is* that awfulness. Freud seems to think so – following his citation of Heine with the statement: 'Nor will you have escaped worrying over this problem – those of you who are men; to those of you who are women this will not apply – you are yourself the problem' (p. 113). Having disqualified women from being interested in asking, he makes the entire psychoanalytic project itself the terrified question which men ask. As in some sense it is – for Freud castration is the only signifier of death and as we have seen with Pontalis, death is what Freud would avoid – diverting it to mourning – until his proposition of the death drive in 1920. By 1932/33, death and a death drive can feel appallingly portentous of the future death of more than six million children, women and men in the death camps.

However, Freud is too much a psychoanalyst not to throw difficulties in the way of his own path. With, like Heine, 'a chest full of melancholy and a head full of doubts', he considers that first anatomy and then psychology are very uncertain of the distinction which we think we can so easily make between male and female. This takes three pages and seems to let him put

---

4   H. Heine, *Nordsee* [Second Cycle, VII i, 'Fragen'].

aside for the moment his all-too accurate political fears and come up with an excellent formulation of the proper psychoanalytic approach to femininity:

> In conformity with its peculiar nature, psychoanalysis does not try to describe what a woman is – that would be a task it could scarcely perform – but sets about enquiring how *she comes into being from a child with a bisexual disposition.*
>
> (p. 116. my italics)

The remainder of Freud's essay tries, but drastically fails, to hold onto this stance.

Immediately following the observation which should be our mantra, Freud mentions the work of 'excellent women colleagues in analysis' and then spoils it by rebuffing other women analysts who have accused male analysts of prejudice. He offers the excellent colleagues the 'courtesy' that 'on this point [they] are more masculine than feminine' – which, of course, establishes male superiority. When in concluding he mentions them by name and title – Dr. Ruth Mack Brunswick, Dr. Lampl-de Groot, and Dr. Helene Deutsch – they are three women who have been in a training analysis with him where the critics of male analysts have not had that privilege. It is interesting that when he makes his psychoanalytical observation of how to approach the psyche of women, Freud brings in an actual audience – his female colleagues and critics. However, when he has no actual audience in mind, he is freed for a more abstract presentation which is a male perspective and as such representative of patriarchy. But because he had his finger on the pulse of the times, dread of castration encapsulates both women all-time through all time and perpetual antisemitism, truly terrifying once again in the 1930s.

The first five or so pages of this roughly twenty-five-page 'lecture' are immersed in making sure his imagined audience know that we are all simply ignorant (which is the diametric opposite of what he means by 'uncertainty' in science). Six pages in, we get down to business with two general (and important) warnings – as usual the constitution will only adapt itself to its function with a struggle and everything that matters will happen before puberty – an assertion he had questioned previously with the case of the un-named non-neurotic 'Female Homosexual' whom he had treated some fifteen or so years earlier. The women psychoanalysts whom he has praised turn out to be interested in the psyche of babies – which he is not – so instead a description follows which is about boys as much or more than girls. Finally, we have a new, strident conclusion of a very popular extreme certitude about what women are like, indeed about how awful we are. Although Freud continued to assert the importance of 'sexual difference' in the years remaining to him, and although his thesis about castration as the cause and penis-envy as its symptom remained dominant, most of what surrounds this all-important certitude was never further explored. So what supports his main thesis here in this text?

Freud sets out behavioural differences in the two sexes as small children with a very even hand; any differences, he asserts, can be disregarded. The girl's libidinal development has been the same as the boy's until and into the phallic phase around three-to-four years old. Yet tellingly and all-importantly, while they are *the same*, 'the little girl is a little man'! It is in the phallic phase that she is set 'two extra tasks' in order to become 'a normal woman'. First, the girl who has used her clitoris for masturbation will have to hand over, wholly or in part, its sensitivity to the vagina when it is discovered.[5] Second, the girl must change from incestuously loving her mother as the boy does to instead actively desiring to passively receive love from her active father – her own very different Oedipus complex. We are familiar with these requirements but must ask some questions at their source in Freud's essay.

In the pre-Oedipal period (discovered by women analysts) the girl's attachment to her mother is – like the boy's – profound. So before her attachment changes to her father – in other words, prior to her own Oedipus complex – can everything of psychic importance happen to the girl and her psychic development take place when she is 'a little man'? What Freud is describing through the girl who is the subject of this essay are the narcissistic-psychotic defences against forbidden wishes – 'for instance, we discover ... the core of paranoic illness' (p. 120). If they can be treated in the girl (as in the work of Ruth Mack Brunswick), then they must be treatable in the boy.[6] This means that despite the girl's subsequent extra tasks this must be in the boy's pre-Oedipal phallic stage too:

> These wishes represent active as well as passive impulses; if we relate them to the differentiation of the sexes *which is to appear later* – though we should avoid doing so as far as possible – we may call them masculine and feminine.
>
> (p. 120, my italics)

As already noted, we can either avoid the terms 'masculinity' and 'femininity' or, if we use them, then they are only popular terms without specific psychoanalytic heritage or new meaning. Of course, what comes later affects what comes before. Symptomatically, Freud now adds to his long-abandoned

---

5   Freud discounts early vaginal sensations – which leaves a puzzle: everything is supposed to happen before puberty – so when is the vagina discovered?

6   Ruth Mack Brunswick whom Freud greatly respected, treated psychoses as here – in women! – even though Freud eschewed the use of psychoanalysis for narcissistic-psychotic conditions. In British psychoanalysis at least it is now commonplace to include them.

seduction theory of hysteria that while women at the outset of psychoanalysis had wrongly claimed to have been seduced by their fathers, they had in reality been seduced by their mother's physical-sexual care.[7] As his male patients had also told him of such a seduction by the father, had they also been actually seduced by their mothers? We hear only of the boy's active (incestuous) love.

As described in 'Femininity', this pre-Oedipal love for the mother is the axis on which the girl's turn to the father has to take place – she reverses her love to often violent hate of her mother (while the 'more fortunate' boy continues his love directly into the Oedipus complex which according to the logic of this essay is uniquely his). The girl hates the mother because she holds her responsible for not giving her a penis (p. 128). (We must remember this hatred overlays the earlier hatred for the mother who had abandoned her toddler for the new baby.) Hereafter the girl's desire for and envy of the penis is heavily emphasized by Freud; indeed, as in his later and last word on 'the repudiation of femininity',[8] her 'penis-envy' of men, provoked by sharing her mother's similarly penis-deprived status rather than her condition of being castrated, is the more noted mark of femininity. The logic of the argument hitherto has been that it is the boy's terror of losing his penis which makes the girl want something that is apparently so valuable. Although most minds will unnecessarily go to Melanie Klein, we will need to ask – what in this context is the status of the concept of 'envy'?

The girl turns to the father to be given the penis and thus transitions from the shared pre-Oedipal to the uniquely feminine Oedipus complex – which Freud now describes in detail. The different consequences for girl and boy are profound and pervasive: realizing the consequences if he resists the prohibition on incest makes the boy demolish and repress his Oedipus complex; '[w]hat happens with a girl is almost the opposite' (p. 129). This 'opposite' is 'sexual difference'. Obeying the prohibition on maternal incest, the boy develops a superego modelled initially on an identification with the father but now incorporating the power of his threat. So not only will patriarchal heritage be established but it will depend on the awfulness of the castrated woman.

The girl's pre-Oedipal 'prehistory' in the phallic phase debouches into her female Oedipal 'history' with gaining her father's desire for her. 'Sexual difference' on the vertical in this lecture is not just about a difference between the sexes in which one cannot be the other – it makes the sexes into psychological opposites. Despite the indistinction and bisexuality noted at

---

7   In fact, as noted earlier, when he had initially believed in paternal seduction as the source of hysteria, he had recalled it in himself and discovered it in male patients such as 'E'. *The Complete Letters of Sigmund Freud to Wilhelm Fliess*, op. cit.

8   S. Freud, *An Outline of Psycho-Analysis* (1938), Chapter VII, SE XXIII.

the outset between male and female, now anatomy must set its mark: 'After all, the anatomical distinction must express itself in psychical consequences' (p. 124). Why must it? A root and moot question, which is one Freud certainly asks – but not here. Instead, he moves on to a description of women in their sexual difference – or should we say their sexual 'opposite-ness' from men?

Although there are some cautionary preliminaries, the following is Freud's list of the 'psychical peculiarities' that mark mature womanhood (I will not repeat the reasons for them, most rest on the girl's ever-persistent penis-envy). The woman is more narcissistic, needs more to be loved than loving, is more physically vain, has more shame, more envy and jealousy, is more psychically rigid and unchangeable, has less interest in social issues, less capacity for sublimating drives, makes few contributions to the discoveries and inventions of civilization and has little sense of justice. The woman is happy if she can make her husband into her baby and if this baby is a son, then mother-and-son is 'the most perfect of all human relations' (p. 133). This overwhelming joy of a son aside, we are indeed dreadful! Freud concludes 'Femininity' with the statement: 'One gets the impression that a man's love and a woman's are a phase apart psychologically' (p. 134). He writes:

> Her libido has taken up final positions and seems incapable of exchanging them for others. There are no paths open to further development; it is as though the whole process had already run its course and remains thenceforward insusceptible to influence – as though, indeed, the difficult development to femininity had exhausted the possibilities of the person concerned.
>
> (p. 135)

Well, of course the lives are a stage apart. There is no way a girl or woman could move forward from the stasis which must set in with her own Oedipal complex. When the boy demolishes his Oedipus complex, what is left of his phallic pre-Oedipal desires will go down into unconsciousness with it. Not so for the girl who instead of repressing her 'male' incestuous desires must use their energy for the exhausting task of winning her father's love. The girl's pre-Oedipus stage and female Oedipus complex are mingled together; the two stages make up what it is to be feminine. For the man, normality and pathology are on a continuum, a bit more of one than the other. The girl's Oedipus complex, into which her pre-Oedipus must merge, being only a wish to be actively desired and – as we will see – all importantly having no prohibition and thus no conflict attached to it, can only have pathology or normality thrust upon it from outside – extrinsically. Yet underlying Freud's argument, even as he becomes sure of his ground of 'sexual difference' as opposition, is the vacillation in his reference to Heine's *'Fragen'* – are we talking about mankind or about women having to contain all that awful-ness? A feature of any oppressed group, unsurprisingly, is envy – here it takes the form of penis-envy. And penis-envy claims both the popular and psychoanalytic limelight. My question is: can it be made into the psychoan-alytic concept to which it lays claim?

Nowhere else does Freud refer to the constitution and biology (as 'anatomy') as being the determinants so much as in this, his essay on 'Femininity'. Psychoanalysis, as has been argued previously, goes up to the biological, to which it refers but leaves to its own field of knowledge. Only with girls and 'womanliness' does Freud fall back on the 'biological fact' of two sexes which he was initially challenging: 'for the psychical field, the bi-ological field does in fact play the part of the underlying bedrock. The *repu-diation of femininity* can be nothing else than a biological fact, a part of the great *riddle* of sex' (*Outline* p. 252 my italics). The perplexing paradox – or is it more than this? – is that no concept could be further from the biological than 'the castration complex' which establishes sexual difference – and are female elephants really envious of males?

### 'How to be Both by not being Both': Achieving Bisexuality by Accepting Sexual Difference

In a recent collection of essays on bisexuality, the British psychoanalyst Rachel Chaplin saves the day for Freud's account of 'Femininity' and 'sexual difference'.[9] Her essay, which breaks new ground, can stand as the very best we have on the contribution of bisexuality specifically to vertical 'sexual difference' and vice-versa. Chaplin's innovation is crucial; psycho-logical bisexuality is not only innate but also for both participants it has to be a construct, an achievement which if not present can take place through psychoanalytic work:

> We are born bisexual and yet we have to acquire bisexuality ... [this involves] the renunciation of phallic bisexuality to genital bisexuality in which sexual difference is accepted and interiorized. This is the transi-tion from bisexuality as defence to bisexuality as resource.
>
> (p. 224)

'How to be Both by not being Both' takes up the challenge in a way that gives us a radically extended and new perspective.[10] Instead of the popular

---

9  R. Chaplin (2018), 'How To Be Both, By Not Being Both. The Articulation of Psychic Bi-sexuality within the Analytic Session', in R.J. Perelberg (ed.), *Psychic Bisexuality*, op. cit., pp. 207–26. Subsequent references to this essay will be given in the text.

10  Interestingly, in none of the sensitive and detailed accounts of Chaplin's sessions with Christa does 'penis-envy' feature.

and too frequent psychoanalytic understanding of bisexuality as an 'object choice' of either sex person, Chaplin re-writes it through a nuanced psychoanalytic understanding of both a given and an achieved subjective stance – being bisexual.

In brief, Chaplin's discovery of 'genital bisexuality' is a new proposition within the theory which she arrives at through her subtitle: 'The articulation of psychic bisexuality within the analytic session'. Her engagement with Freud's work is an original reading of subjective bisexuality as the basis of symbolization and of the capacity to think: 'an active capacity for representation and thought, derived, I suggest from an underlying psychic bisexuality' (p. 209). Patient and analyst go in and out of psychic stages until, with phallic bisexuality overcome, a newly achieved bisexuality is the basis of 'sexual difference'.

'Genital' in psychoanalytic thinking refers to the achievement of different reproductive stances of female and male at puberty entailing different psychological states – one ready for motherhood, the other for fatherhood. Does genital bisexuality mean the playing psychically over these two states rather than the internalization of 'being castrated'/'fearing castration'? It seems rather that Chaplin intends 'genital bisexuality' with its capacity for symbolization to refer to the possibility of both genders acknowledging the difference between being castrated and fearing castration. She writes:

> First there is a complete immersion in the archaic maternal universe, a kind of undifferentiated and amalgamated fusion ... Second there is a form of primary homosexuality ... The mother ... is cathected as a narcissistic double ... her identity is assumed to be the same as the infant's ... Third there is a form of phallic bisexuality in which sexual difference and castration are known but refused. And finally, there is a form of genital bisexuality in which difference predicated on castration is both known and used. We could characterize these four positions in relation to sexual difference as identical, similar, different but denied. And different and used.
>
> (p. 212)

'Different and used' if it is to enable symbolization will refer to the Law of the Father. And this brings in the parenting behind 'genitality' which, as Chaplin shows, can only be achieved through having the patient's father and mother in at least a minimal union. This is what the therapy must achieve. So 'genital bisexuality' is both knowing castrated/castration terror and some union of fatherhood and motherhood within.

The single patient of Chaplin's subtitle whom she calls Christa presents her with a problem – Christa appears to think 'normally' but in fact has not reached a capacity to think with metaphors, she 'awaits analytic metaphorization' (p. 211). Thus, for Christa the analytical clinical situation is not *analogous* to a sexual encounter but is itself a sexual scene. Christa is like the toddler whom Bion described as literally 'keeping an eye on the baby' (Chapter 4) – the analyst has every reason to believe that as her patient can talk she can think – but it turns out she can do so only in so far as not yet understanding metaphors. As we saw also with Pontalis, the analytic encounter is itself 'metaphoric' – presumably a feature of the transference. Without having reached this stage, Christa, like a toddler, is immersed in the analysis while being unable to 'think' about it; the sexual is not 'integrated in her mind' (p. 211).

Christa, who comes over as a highly competent middle-aged woman, describes her teenage derring-do with her brothers as though she and Chaplin were actually present in these scenes. Chaplin comments on the brothers as 'the boys and men'. 'Men' is Chaplin's own accidental addition – Christa is shattered by this comment and after some self-analysis of her seemingly ordinary remark Chaplin realizes that it caused Christa to experience 'sexual difference as trauma'; the words 'boys and men' had been a rape: 'I seemed to have misread my patient's sexual identification and to have unwittingly committed raping violence and a stabbing penetration' (p. 212). The 'films' which they seemed to be watching of Christa's presentation of her exciting and frightening teenage wildness with her brothers had reached a moment when they were all racing for a bus. Why did Chaplin bring in 'men' – men would not have raced for a bus? Although a mistake, introducing men made Chaplin realize the importance of the missing father and in time the parents: 'Christa is caught in a panicked oscillation between two dangerous parents and can only make fleeting contact with each object in her mind before running off in "the opposite direction"' (p. 217). However, a trace of the union of these dangerous parents comes to the surface and leads eventually to an internalization of the primal scene of these parents who had to be together in some way for her patient's conception. The united parents can join the flow of castrated/fear of castration so that the innate bisexuality can produce a new genital bisexuality which provides the capacity for symbolization.

Chaplin argues that in order for this new successful Oedipal 'genital bisexual' 'being both' to be acquired, the 'phallic bisexuality' of 'being both' must become a 'not being both' which entails an acceptance of castration. The dominant psychoanalytic contention is that in the phallic stage of childhood before the Oedipus complex only the power of the penis is acknowledged by both sexes and the smaller clitoris produces penis-envy in the girl and an awareness that she is 'castrated' before the castration complex. It is this that Chaplin specifies as 'sexual difference denied'. However, this must be a denial of the future 'sexual difference' as it is understood in the castration complex.

Freud was adamant about the phallic dominance and penis-envying inferiority of this phase. In 'Femininity' he noted, as quoted above, of the phallic child:

These wishes represent active as well as passive impulses; if we relate them to *the differentiation of the sexes which is to appear later – though we should avoid doing so as far as possible – we may call them masculine and feminine.*

(my italics)

Based on the sexual difference of parents this can come as the interplay of passive activity and active passivity. In a manner reminiscent of Freud's certainty based on uncertainty, Chaplin's title – alluding to Ali Smith's novel *How to be Both* –[11] questions her thesis. She states that we have to 'hear the "woman-manly" and "man-womanly" stories, the coterminous temporalities of psychic bisexuality' (p. 225), and as well 'we have to hear the story of the patient's psychosexuality "more than one way at once"' (ibid).

Ali Smith's novel (referenced in Chaplin's thesis) has two interlocked stories, each of which can be read in either order. In one a child/teenager discovers a strange and wondrous fifteenth-century painting and their own bisexuality, and in the other story the renaissance child/young adult artist creates the amazing painting through using its own bisexuality. In the novel there is no 'not being both', just as there is not in the phallic phase if we turn to considering it on the social horizontal axis which is the province of Christa and her lateral brothers and sisters. Indeed, rather than denial the interactive social child achieves another 'being both' – this is the clitoral and penile bisexuality enjoyable as genital achievement. This was an important focus of second-wave feminism.

In the same paragraph wherein she returns to Ali Smith, Chaplin gives us licence to retain 'more than one way': 'But as Christa moved dreamily around in her mind one day, she thought of a photograph of a woman in a wedding dress, then one of a latency boy. Her brother? Her?' (p. 225). For vertical parenting, acquired bisexuality may need the knowledge that one cannot be both sexes; for horizontal siblings it would seem that one can experience bisexual gender fluidity.

At the heart of the problem that raises its head again in Chaplin's proposal is the girl's Oedipus complex which on the vertical makes her always and ever a mother. The girl is only and ever a sister in so far as she is the more bisexual sex; here the sad irony is that bisexuality therewith shifts into becoming a negative tribute – all-present as the condition of hysteria. This negative status is entirely against the intentions of its proclaimed all-time positive importance. Indeed, it is a double negative because hysteria – the founding condition of psychoanalysis – is still associated with femininity and through this world-long female association it is denied its significance as we will see in Chapter 10.

---

11  Ali Smith, *How To Be Both*, London: Hamish Hamilton, 2014.

## The Girl's Oedipus Complex

The Freudian thesis is all about the conditions that are needed for boys to have mothers in the future. If there is any penis-envy present in the phallic phase and her pre-femininity, a girl must proceed to her own Oedipus complex where mature womanhood equals motherhood bestowed by her father's desire which enables her eventually to be a mother on loan to the patriarchal world of sons and heirs. Women can be equal so long as they are male or masculine. But the implications of such a prescribed situation in the world at large are serious. The psychological handing-over of the sexual sensitivity of the girl's clitoris to her vagina may be assisted practically by its physical excision and the stitching up of her remaining genitals to be raped on compulsory and dictated marriage.

What, however, needs to be further emphasized is that *there is no prohibition on the girl's desire* to win her father's desire for her (and hence both threat and punishment are beside the point). Because there is no prohibition on her desires – indeed her desire for her father's desire is a patriarchal psycho-social requirement – the girl has no need of repression. A girl's own different Oedipus complex, to which no law is attached, accounts for the psychological source of women's oppression – her status is defined as 'outside society'.

That all societies, however variously, prohibit what is known as 'incest' and 'murder' has been a fundamental postulate of the thesis here. It is this prohibition which – at a psychological level – enables entry into human society. *Only a universal prohibition would allow the girl psychically to enter society.* Her own Oedipus complex instead entails her encouraging her father's desire for her which then at best can be *in*hibited but never *pro*hibited. This is the background to the prevalence of father–daughter incest.

No society can exist without some sexuality and some killing being outlawed; every prohibition entails allowances as its other side. The girl has to get her father to change places: he must want incest with her but then hopefully – but maybe not – inhibit the execution of this desire. For the girl, having to want and not having is a condition of permanent titillation; the father can use his absences to prove he is not having incest with the daughter he is supposed to desire. If there is incest, then the girl's earlier 'maleness' makes her guilty of abusing a prohibition which as a female does not apply to her. We can grasp the perplexity if we contemplate our straightforward response to son–father incest. We can also envisage a difference is we transfer from the vertical to the horizontal, where a bisexual boy or girl can each actively desire a same-sex lateral relationship.

The overriding concern here then is that *as future 'woman', without a prohibition after her Oedipus complex, the girl within vertical sexual difference is 'forever' psychically outside of society.* Given this, what woman in her right mind – or anyone who receives the opprobrium of being called 'feminine' as do most members of oppressed groups – would not try to 'repudiate femininity'? The phallus is the insignia of inhabiting the patriarchal social world. Displacement onto having the father's penis (in fantasy or reality) together with a baby as a penis substitute – however pleasurable and important – does not get round this absence of a prohibition.

The feminist mantra of 'the private is the political' – turning the private family world assigned to women into a social world which has hitherto been claimed by men – would create a universal political world. In other words, to validate rather than abandon femininity is a perspicacious attempt to up-end this situation; women as over half that universal with their very different life-histories have something of their own to contribute. The demand must be social, to be defined by a private world is to be defined by the desire for the father's desire with no place for a social relation to women and men as a collective. The private woman monopolizes the status of the feminine but she is all alone in her privacy.

What the girl must do is generically prescribed but thereafter she drops out of the general picture and must get on with being a future woman on her own or in competition with other girls. Where what boys must do is bound up with being all boys together – brothers – for girls it is a matter of an individual girl attracting her own father's singular desire and fighting off other girls for every other father. Being excluded from the father's prohibition and thus being outside the psychology of the social world means that there can be no collectivity in the experience – a generic demand to all girls is entirely dependent on the individuals concerned. Sisterhood as a parallel to brotherhood does not get a look in.

The differentiation between the sexes is effected through the 'universality' of the castration complex, which ends the boy's Oedipus complex and introduces the girl to hers. Except for when she is psychically 'male', the 'opposite' way in which the prohibition of incest with the mother and murder of the father impact on the girl and the boy is responsible for the complete psychic differentiation whereby the girl becomes the future mother in the family and the boy a future patriarch in the world. Where the boy has to be *like* his father so that he can in time take over the Law of the Father, the girl has to become the *same* as her mother. On the vertical family axis this 'being the same' is central for the construction of 'the woman'. As is popularly said: 'Women are the same the world over'; men are not. The girl struggles to be different from her mother, but on the vertical axis she must fail because she is the same in her definitional exclusion from society – a situation she repudiates at the cost of being her female self.

For psychoanalysis as it stands without the mother's law, unconsciously complying with the castration complex creates everyone's normative being; gainsaying it underlies our pathologies. Although normality and pathology may be unevenly distributed between the sexes, neither sex is exempt from pathology nor has the monopoly of normality. Untangling the situation: both sexes would seem to have the same Oedipal desire for the mother.

However, at the moment of the essential prohibition on maternal incest, the girl, as woman, not receiving this prohibition, is put on hold; she is psychically stuck in the gateway where she is induced or seduced into her own very different Oedipus complex to which no prohibition is attached. To paraphrase: do women come through the gate as part of *man*kind while as 'the woman' they are forever halted? The all-importance of castration so relegates her to the excluded 'second sex', what Simone de Beauvoir designated the original 'Other', that this seems likely.

The woman is definitionally excluded in a way which casts its all-pervasive shadow. Hers is the umbrella oppression which would be why 'femininity' is the Scylla and Charybdis which can trap all other oppressions. And this is why she has been compared to every other also-excluded social group. For de Beauvoir, only woman is distinguished by never having had another status *before* oppression as is the case with other oppressed ethnicities and races. No free past, no free future. I suggest, differently, that despite oppression and the absence of the father's prohibition, woman, as woman, is also *included* in society.

The Law of the Father against parental incest and murder on the vertical axis is matched by the prohibition proclaimed by the Law of the Mother against sibling murder and incest – here is the prohibition the girl needs in order to become included not as a would-be man but as an objectively gendered and subjectively bisexual girl and woman, a sister in a social world.

# Chapter 9

# Horizontal 'Gender' and Bisexuality

## 'Gender'

'Gender' refers both to a lateral distinction between girls and boys, women and men, as well as, all-importantly, to their 'indistinction' as psychologically bisexual and transgender *subjects* – not whom one chooses as a partner, but who one is as a person. Recently, the leading psychoanalyst, Rosine Perelberg, has argued that 'gender' is not a concept that can be used in psychoanalysis.[1] This is, I think, to mistake the nature of the concept. Gender is social as opposed to biological sex – how we feel and enact our lesbian, gay, bisexual, transgender, female, male sex rather than how biology or anatomy prescribes it. Perelberg argues that sexuality in all its permutations is the subject matter of psychoanalysis. However, it is not sexuality with which 'Gender' must be compared and contrasted, as Perelberg maintains, but with 'sexual difference' between girls and boys, women and men. 'Sexual Difference' is psychologically established as an unpassable distinction between the sexes at the castration complex.

Furthermore, although sexuality is bound to implicate the sexes, the all-presence of death in our lives is also the subject of psychoanalysis; this changes the terrain. Death in and of itself has no truck with this distinction. Gender, death and lateral relations – fratriarchy not patriarchy – are bound together as the neglected or ejected subject matter of psychoanalysis. And 'Fratriarchy', the institution of brotherhood, of course raises the question of the individual sister in a social sisterhood.

The history of 'gender' as a concept for feminism began with the psychoanalyst Robert Stoller's establishment of a Gender Clinic in Los Angeles in the 1960s. Stoller's writings were taken up and very successfully deployed and popularized by feminism in the 1970s with a largely sociological

1  R.J. Perelberg, *Sexuality, Excess and Representation: A Psychoanalytic Clinical and Theoretical Perspective*, Abingdon, Oxon and New York: Routledge, 2020.

DOI: 10.4324/9781003347125-14

implication.[2] Gender is a wide category within which different sexualities play an important part. Even though the word 'gender' has still to be translated as 'social sex' in some languages, I think the concept it represents has come to stay. Even if it hasn't, the social sexuality which it describes has unconscious determinants which need a place in psychoanalysis – our horizontal axis. The time therefore is ripe for creating a use of 'gender' which can join the important and strong psychoanalytical concepts of 'bisexuality' on the one hand and, on the other hand, be compared and contrasted with the Oedipal-castration constraint of 'sexual difference'. Vertical sexual difference, the *irreducible* psychological distinction between female and male, is described as 'femininity' and 'masculinity'. Freud is clear – femininity and masculinity are popular terms which unfortunately psychoanalysis cannot avoid using – they are not psychoanalytic concepts as they purport to give contents to a distinction which is only a distinction and should be nothing more.

Because of the ever-present universality of unconscious processes, there is always a proximity of psychoanalysis to the everyday. This is the case also with 'Gender'. It is the task not of the everyday but of psychoanalysis to forge and clarify the distinctions. The popular, everyday and widespread deployment of 'gender' is mostly but haphazardly used for what turn out to be lateral relations such as sister and brother; within psychoanalytic thinking I have long suggested confining the concept to the horizontal axis in what will need to be as rigorous a way as possible. 'Sexual difference' is an absolute distinction which references the biological female and male, although it is certainly not their equivalent; it is simply that if you are one you cannot be the other which, as we have seen, distorts bisexuality and, as we will come to see, oppresses transgender. It refers only to the prohibition on incest with the mother and murder of the father; it produces the *unconscious psyche* for the different parenting on a vertical axis. 'Gender' is for social siblings and their lateral heirs, their pairings, marriages and their warfare, their gender differences and their gender samenesses; there is no absolute distinction between genders; you may be one, but you could be the other. However, as we will consider further, if you are a sister, you cannot be a brother, nor, if a brother, a sister.

The sibling trauma and its subsequent Law of the Mother mark the transition from infancy to childhood in the formation of a social group. At puberty, key elements such as the 'who am I?' that characterize any major transition are repeated in the new context of reproductive genitality. Lateral forbidden incest and lateral enjoined marriage, together with lateral internecine murder and ever-present legal warfare, are the focus this time around. Still, as at birth, 'gender', sister and brother, a reference to the

---

2   For the UK, see A. Oakley, *Sex, Gender and Society*, Aldershot: Ashgate, 1972.

biologically sexed genitalia, now features 'on top' of their bisexual psychic identity so that what was a possibility in childhood may become a likelihood in adolescence: for teenage girls the social group may become one of all girls together and for boys it may well become a mainly male gang. Being in love and partnering, unlike in childhood, may be expected to be heterosexual. But this division is culturally and historically various rather than a universal determined and determining requirement. Except for the distinction of sister/brother, none of these are universal absolutes; sister and brother signify primarily social relations even if they originate in the biological.

Despite these social possibilities, as a widely used concept 'Gender' had a particular provenance which acts as a useful reminder of what has been largely overlooked. As a concept it arose from and is embedded in the 'sisterhood' of feminism – the sister is both a desiring subject and a prohibited object in lateral incest and murder. Prescribed in marriage and in wartime rape on the horizontal axis, the sister's place along with 'gender' is missing from psychoanalysis. The struggle against what feminism designated as women's *oppression* makes the feminist struggle 'the longest revolution'.[3] As we saw in Chapter 8, the construction of a girl's specific Oedipus complex means that 'sexual difference' must take a major responsibility for women being by definition oppressed. Although 'gender' too must take a share, the bisexual subjecthood of the social child, from birth to puberty, glimpses, even if remotely, a different future.

## From Childhood to Puberty

After infancy, the social world of the peer group increasingly becomes as important as, or more important than, the crucial parents for social formation, yet the interaction with parents, as usual, has monopolized psychoanalytic accounts. On the horizontal axis latency has to be shifted from the parent–child focus to intensive child–child interaction – and with teenagers, if anything, it is yet more mandatory to make the shift. As for the threatened toddler, life and death feels, and for the teenager too often actually is, at stake. Behind the urge for a new life is the threat of death. As with the toddler, so even more starkly with the adolescent, sexuality and death are intrinsically intermingled.

### Sexuality

Earlier we asked of the female Oedipus complex: if the vagina is said to be unknown in childhood, when does the girl's move from clitoral to vaginal

---

3   J. Mitchell, 'Women: The Longest Revolution', *New Left Review*, vol. 1, no. 40, 1966, pp. 11–37.

excitability take place? Are we talking about the *significance* of the vagina which would plausibly be with the advent of reproductive potential at puberty – the vertical axis? And what of the alternation – clitoris surpassing vagina – on the horizontal axis? Following the sexual revolution of the early 1960s, this became a major politico-practical concern for feminism and a major feature of its hostile confrontation with Freud.

Much ink has been – and continues to be – spilled on arguing whether or not vaginal sensations are felt or observed in childhood. This persistent interest could be an unacknowledged response to the problem posed by Freud's own insistence that Oedipally the girl must change her sexual zone. Although this is a question of logic rather than experience, Freud too urgently needed to reconcile processes: the formation of the 'repressed unconscious' had to take place in childhood and yet he needed biphasic human sexuality to wait until the meaning of reproduction within the body-ego could be available in puberty. This quandary is present in the decision to bring sexuality into a 'life drive', with its prospects of creating new unities exemplified in particular by procreation in *Beyond the Pleasure Principle* (1920).

As they *play* on the horizontal axis at being fathers and mothers or such-like, both 'non-latency' boys and girls in their persisting bisexuality may imagine an inner space that could receive penetration and hold a baby and, passive or active, will continue as polymorphously perverse – a melee of oral, anal, possibly vaginal sexuality; this can be sole or mutual masturbation or sublimated as penetrating questions and penetrated observations in this time of great learning potential. Clitoral pleasures which extend throughout the vulva are as pleasurable as penile joys; is the vagina a tummy to hold the baby? Collectively in child–child interaction this period cannot be described as 'phallic' – it is genital and mutual masturbation and milder sexual play is widely practised and widely discouraged, becoming thus increasingly secret. Puberty inherits this lateral pre-pubertal varied sexuality and its sublimations. Its experiences are of necessity hard for adults to get hold of except in their pathological disturbances. Vertically, parenting is a new possibility at puberty so the child's incestuous desires and its Oedipus complex will be re-worked in adolescence. But so too will sibling incest and its lateral relationships have to be re-negotiated with marriage or partnering as a socially prescribed prerequisite. The vertical and the horizontal can be complimentary or conflictual tasks. Where vertically teenagers are *en route* to forming new families, horizontally they will become lateral couples. Horizontally they must form communities and work and fight for these.

### Puberty

As with the sibling trauma, we need to read puberty through death as well as sexuality. The tantrums and social behavioural maladies that involve the deserting mother and the terrified toddler return in adolescence in updated versions: there are eating disorders, depression, self-harming, suicidality, gang violence and knife or gun crime. Psychologically these enactments are accompanied by renewed narcissistic-psychotic defences such as schizoid splitting, projection, dissociation and denial. Along with potential reproduction there are changes in genitalia, the commencement of secondary sex characteristics, different voices, menstruation and ejaculation, and vastly increased thrusts of libido which affect lateral relations.

Spermatozoa and uterine and vaginal possibilities will be discovered with their sexual meaning in relation to incest and murder vertically with parents, but probably more particularly with siblings and their social substitutes. The task in adolescence (as in toddlerdom) is for the psychically always important parents to be left behind and for siblings to advance towards their future, here they will establish their binary relationship in the privacy of marriage and their serial formation of endless siblings (as we used Bion to describe) in the public sociality of work, leisure and warfare (see below). This demands an emphasis on puberty both for itself, as a key repetition of the toddler experience of siblings, and as a different re-edition with a completely new gender distinction.

Freud's apparent failure with his analysis of the *petite hystérie* of 'Dora' became a *cause célèbre* of feminism – he had missed Dora's love for her father's lover, 'Frau K'. He was handed this problem on a plate some twenty years later with another father's request, this time that he 'cure' his daughter of her homosexuality. The analytic result was very different. In Freud's essay on these sessions, 'The Psychogenesis of a Case of Homosexuality in a Woman' (1920), the teenager has been betrayed by the loving father and the mother's new pregnancy and has transferred her repeated Oedipal desires to a substitute – another Frau K. But it is hard to see a mother in the 'unsuitable' sexually promiscuous lady for whom the teenager attempts suicide. And indeed, Freud recommends that the girl be allowed to explore her bisexuality in which its object choice might go one way or the other – as it had done with his own daughters. However, here a footnote to the observation is most pertinent:

> The displacements of the libido here described are doubtless familiar to every analyst from investigation of the anamneses of neurotics. With the latter they occur in early childhood, at the time of the efflorescence of erotic life; *with our patient, who was in no way neurotic, they took place in the first year following puberty, though, incidentally, they were just as completely unconscious. Perhaps one day this temporal factor may turn out to be of great importance.*[4]

> (my italics)

---

4   S. Freud, 'The Psychogenesis of a Case of Homosexuality in a Woman', op. cit., p. 158, ft. 2.

With the horizontal axis, that day has arrived – indeed Freud is describing a lateral, social female homosexuality. Adolescence is currently receiving increased attention,[5] but all we can consider here is the way in which the sibling trauma rises to meet the new conditions of adolescence and the importance of these new conditions for the development of a gender distinction.

Puberty repeats both the pathologies and the socialization of the toddler. To introduce again classics which current work rests on, renews and resists, Edith Buxbaum, the popular psychoanalytic author of *Your Child makes Sense* (1949) and *Troubled Children in Troubled Times* (1990), also wrote of the enormous importance of the social group for teenagers: 'In adolescence the youngster's desire to be part of a group is imperative; when he cannot find a group in school he will try elsewhere, but he is determined to find it'.[6] As with the toddler transitioning to the small child, the teenagers' group is a necessity. Buxbaum relates the two: 'Whereas the young child finds in the group support for his new-found physical independence from mother, the adolescent finds reassurance for his moral independence from home' (Buxbaum, p. 363).

With the sexual influx at puberty, the group will be managing its libidinal overflow and the mother will probably repudiate her Oedipal girl's competitive sexuality for the father/husband as she does with the young woman sent to Freud. It is not (as is commonly argued) that social groups in their sex and violence regress to infancy – it is that the trauma of infancy comes up again and is repeated in the very different context of puberty. Buxbaum again: 'The group which the individual has joined ... revives in him the old situation in which he found consolation and reassurance for his infantile anxieties' (Buxbaum, p. 365). The toddler's excitement about metaphor and stories is transformed in the teenager's yesteryear novel-reading and present-day inhabitation of social media. But where the toddler and its mother tried to establish a distinction between reality and fantasy by these means, the process can be put into reverse and the adolescent (and adult) is creating untruth as truth. A story becomes 'a story'. The danger in this is that the fusion and de-fusion of fantasy and reality which is so positive a feature of storytelling becomes confusion so that the former is taken for the latter and what has been called the 'big lie' is mistaken for the real world.

5   M. Waddell, *On Adolescence: Inside Stories*, London and New York: Routledge, 2018, and *Inside Lives: Psychoanalysis and the Growth of the Personality*, rev. ed., London: Karnac Books, 2002.

6   E. Buxbaum, 'Transference and Group Formation in Children and Adolescents', *Psychoanalysis of the Child*, vol. 1., p. 357, 1945; subsequent references to this article will be given in the text. Following a suggestion in Freud's *Group Psychology and the Analysis of the Ego*, Buxbaum considered the group to give satisfactions which the child can get nowhere else.

Although Anna Freud's work on adolescence focuses on the usual Oedipal configurations, her material makes her concerned with the earlier narcissistic-psychotic processes of the social siblings. What follows is taken from her timeless work in *The Ego and the Mechanisms of Defence*[7] but is set within the framework and expressions of the horizontal axis. To cope with the lateral as well as the vertical incestuous implications of the huge libidinal increase which can be seen trying to break out of unconsciousness, the adolescent withdraws from loving and hating his family of origin.[8] This withdrawal of family object-love replenishes in abundance the definitional narcissism of the adolescent: 'Adolescents are excessively egoistic' (A. Freud, p. 137). As with the toddler, the narcissism is needed to overcome the shock to the system of losing the old childhood and having to become a new person.

Adolescents endorse and then reverse the process of infancy, this time from sociality to narcissism but end up in the same necessary self-obsessed stance. Identifications or mimesis prevail, and the adolescent is an 'as if' person not only hovering between psychosis and neurosis but also with what Winnicott called 'a false self'. Once again, they often feel like the traumatized toddlers, empty of themselves and taking on the colours and voices of other people. Where the emerging small child tries to adjust to the loss of its identity with the new baby through a phony grown-up voice (Chapter 3), adolescents will make dramatic brief sorties into a try-out vocabulary of 'being in love'; the love object like the quondam new baby is largely endowed with the lover's projected narcissism.

Anna Freud often designated the normal psychic state of this period as 'psychotic'. To deal with the overwhelming strength of the once more incestuous sexual drive she considered that a defence stronger than repression is needed. She suggested not repression but the *repudiation* of the sexual drive; this may well match the anti-cathectic 'primal repression' proposed for the original sibling trauma. This concept of 'repudiation' is manifest in two new defences – 'asceticism' which re-establishes the full force of the prohibition on incest, and 'intellectualization' which hopes to transpose what is prohibited to an entirely conscious and manageable field of enquiry. Does this resemble the small child's first use of metaphor and its later sublimations in intense learning? Does this treatment apply to the prohibition of murder as well as incest as the mother's law demands? One only has to think of *Romeo and Juliet* to see the implication of its failure.

---

7  A. Freud, *The Ego and the Mechanisms of Defence*, London: Hogarth Press, 1966. I am mainly using Chapters 11 and 12 of this book.
8  The probably repeated decline of the mother's protection (as with Lady Capulet in *Romeo and Juliet*) and the resurgence of sister–brother incest, as shown in the works of many writers should be added; for the latter we can single out Freud's friend – Thomas Mann's *The Blood of the Walsungs* (1905).

Anna Freud was the proclaimed originator of the major concept of the 'identification with the aggressor'[9]; in this, an early stage of the formation of a superego, the sufferer of hostile criticism or aggression identifies with it and makes it their own. Typically, this is an assimilation into the personality of a vertical authority figure – but we could usefully also consider it interactively within a lateral group. The decomposition whereby a child feels internally attacked and criticized by its erstwhile friends is not unusual in adolescence – the teenager will identify and act elsewhere the aggressive persona. This, perhaps, thereby establishes what Theodor Adorno contended was not overt violence but a mode of passive aggressive socio-political conformity. Whether internalized in this way or externalized in gang crime or Mercutio's murder in *Romeo and Juliet*, as Buxbaum observes, surely rightly: 'Adolescence is known for the violence as well as for the inconsistency of its emotions' (Buxbaum, p. 357). Violence is also well known to exist at the heart of what is socialized as peaceful, most evidently marriage – underlying the fact that wishes for incest and murder are always proximate.

Historically in the West and in many cultures today, marriage is often imposed on girls in adolescence; it is siblings and lateral relations which are at stake. As infancy returns in adolescence, so adolescence haunts our adult future. Rachel Chaplin saw her patient Christa, married and a mother of a teenage daughter, as needing to work through her own earlier adolescence to find the trace of two parents who both separately and together had been cruelly unavailable to her. But Christa's adolescence was overloaded with sibling dynamics and they too persisted. Winnicott's patient Sarah was an adolescent. Is adolescence distinctive in that for the sister actual or imagined rape encapsulates the annihilation of itself which likewise the toddler felt? Death is in prospect for both genders: in the future as their brothers are killed, sisters are raped. Rape – a survived death? – brings together the forbidden incest and murder which the toddler wanted to enact on the baby. Once again, does the girl come to occupy the place of the attacked pre-social baby and boys the toddlers whose attacks are socialized?

On the horizontal axis, the psychic bisexuality of the subject is itself serial – the sisters and/or brothers who may already be there and who anyway can also always come along as Bion's basic assumption groups feared. Although there is binary marriage and marital-type relations, social siblings and peers and lateral sexual abuse as in sex-trafficking and rape are serial matters to which the evidence all around us bears witness. Likewise, there are fraternal pairs, but the serial basis of omnipresent warring is obvious; as

---

9   Actually acknowledged first as a concept of Ferenczi. 'Repudiation' is the term Freud notoriously used for the utter rejection of the feminine. It has been argued that Anna Freud's originality would not have been possible without Wilhelm Reich's account of Character Armour. Anna Freud initially respected then utterly rejected Reich's work.

well as making use of brotherhood, it replenishes and creates the fratriarchy anew:

> We few, we happy few, we band of brothers;
> For he to-day that sheds his blood with me
> Shall be my brother; be he ne'er so vile,
> This day shall gentle his condition;
> And gentlemen in England now-a-bed
> Shall think themselves accurs'd they were not here,
> And hold their manhoods cheap whiles any speaks
> That fought upon Saint Crispin's day.
>
> (*Henry V*, IV.iii.62–9)

## Marriage and Warfare

It is not that an already established society prescribes marriage and warfare; it is that on the socio-psychological plane, *marriage and warfare construct society*. Both marriage and warfare are the 'allowances' which are the required other side of the prohibited incest and murder: with the inversion (a more conscious 'reversion into its opposite') of those forbidden desires (which otherwise one has to continue repressing), one should instead marry and fight. They are the conscious and pre-conscious desiderata which match the unconscious wish for forbidden incest and murder on the horizontal axis.

That prohibition and allowance are two supposedly opposite sides of the same force suggests that it is inevitable they will get entangled: sex-trafficking and marriage, terrorism and warfare, marrying and abusing, fighting and torturing. It is the interpenetration of unconscious aspects from the repressed desire for incest and murder and the socialized psychic defences of these allowances that make psychoanalysis useful for grasping their import. The allowances may be an aspect of the 'reality' which the mother always induces; although always infiltrated by the prohibited desires, these belong to the category of 'rules and regulations', not 'laws' as this term has been used for the Laws of the Mother and of the Father.

Whatever the role of future mothers and fathers, women are given away and men command; nevertheless, marriage and warfare as generic activities belong fundamentally to lateral relations. Where the new reproductive potential of eggs and sperm will be the physical insignia on the vertical axis of parenting, on the lateral axis the surge in libido will define sex and violence between peers. Although social customs will continue to differentiate binary gender as they did on birth by reference to different genitals, there is no commensurate gender distinction as an effect of the law of the mother. Is the oppression of women as severe on this axis as it is on the vertical – is it differently and hopefully changeably so? Freud proposed that to introduce the social axis, the brothers bonded as a homosocial group.[10] There is no discussion of the fact that this necessarily excluded the sister as an agent. Although oppression would seem to be borrowed from the vertical patriarchy, the horizontal fratriarchy cannot be entirely exempt and thus we need to follow something of the trajectory of the *sister* through her female Oedipus complex.

There is marked disagreement as to whether or not there is *unconscious* psychological gender difference before puberty. Our concern is only a structural difference revolving around the prohibitions that make one psychically social. Both girls and boys sublimate violence and sexuality into excited and aggressive curiosity and both can bully and terrorize. On the horizontal axis within their bisexual subjectivity, the girl stays 'male' until puberty just as the boy stays 'female' with his desire for parthenogenic babies – although this is well-recorded it is rarely discussed. What this really means is that both sexes are psychically both. Jeanne Lampl-de Groot (one of the women analysts recognized favourably by Freud) wrote against the grain of the boy's pre-Oedipal identifications and his discontents with the mother. She was perhaps concerned that the success of women analysts in putting the marginalized girl into the pre-Oedipus context had resulted in it sounding as though the boy's path was relatively problem-free pre-Oedipally as well as in the Oedipus complex. Lampl-de-Groot showed that, to the contrary, the lateral boy's childhood history was very similar to the girl's, particularly in relation to the mother. Once again, where on the vertical axis everything changes for girls with the Oedipus complex, on the horizontal axis it is roughly plain sailing for subjective gender equity.

## Serial Sexuality and Adultery

Despite ideological and a degree of empirical change, men must be able to go to war; women, in order to become acceptable mothers, should first be married. If the prohibition on incest underlies marriage, it also encompasses its companion – adultery. Until the high comedies of the turn of the seventeenth century, *As You Like It*, *Twelfth Night*, and the later 'problem' play *Measure for Measure*, Shakespeare's comedies ended with a jig. The prospect of a happy marriage completed the play, but a final jig performed by the clown and his associates set out what happened after the play was over.[11] With the tragedies

---

10  S. Freud, *Group Psychology and the Analysis of the Ego*, op. cit., p. 124 and ft. 1.
11  J. Shapiro, *A Year in the Life of William Shakespeare: 1599*, London: Faber & Faber, 2005, p. 47.

> If comedies were about love, jigs were about what happened after marriage – adultery, deception and irrepressible sexual desire. Jigs – anarchic and libidinal – were wildly popular ... the extraordinary vitality ... the explosive energy ... the high-spirited singing, the spectacular leaping, the titillating groping....

to which the high comedies led, Shakespeare took this extraneous feature into the internal structure of the play – adultery becomes part and parcel of the fabric of the play as it is endemic to marriage. Adultery must be added to marriage as the social definition of a gender distinction; both sexes marry, both sexes are adulterous, yet it is a customary differentiation on top of the prohibition as it is akin to incest in women and yet is ego-syntonic in men.

The fact that men on the horizontal axis can far more rarely be raped and receive violence is a small-time confirmation that we are within the pur-lieus of sibling relations in which the genders are so much the same – when men in oppressed groups are raped it is as though they were also women. For women, whether or not they are actual mothers, those raped are not raped as mainly the mothers which they are or represent: they are sisters. As sisters, one in four lateral wives and not husbands over a lifetime are wounded or killed in domestic violence.[12] The Nobel prize-winning econo-mist, Amartya Sen, famously asked: where are the hundred million missing women in India?[13] Now we learn that the same proportion of children are stolen and sex-trafficked. How many girl babies disappeared in the one-child policy of China? Girl neonates are left exposed not because, as with Oedipus, it is foreseen they will kill their fathers, 'but simply because they are girls'.[14] A participant in the 'Me Too' movement suggested that rape was not a side-issue of making movies, making movies was a side-issue of rape.[15]

The endemic, extreme physical violence against women makes the fear of it a perpetual, permanent and taken-for-granted feature of all female ex-istence signalled by a recent feminist protest against men: 'the rapist: that is you'.[16] That rape is now registered as an abuse of Human Rights and a 'war-crime' on the one hand is significant progress but it makes it particular

---

12 Figures are not yet available for the marked increase under the conditions of Covid-19. As I correct this book for submission to the press on 1 June 2022 this comes up on my screen: The UK is facing an 'epidemic' of violence against women and girls (VAWG). Figures re-leased by the Office for National Statistics (ONS) show that for the year ending September 2021, sexual offences recorded by the police were the highest on record, a 12% increase from the previous year, whilst a survey in June 2021 revealed that 32% of women over six-teen had experienced at least one form of harassment in the previous twelve months. The outpouring of testimonies in the wake of the murder of Sarah Everard, sparked calls for urgent change, starting a conversation which was galvanized by further killings, including those of Sabina Nessa and Gracie Spinks. Issues of institutionalized misogyny and declin-ing conviction rates have left women and girls feeling unsafe in public spaces, with 89% of those who had experienced harassment reporting feeling 'very or fairly unsafe' walking on their own after dark.
13 A. Sen, 'More Than 100 Million Women Are Missing', *New York Review of Books*, Dec. 20, 1990.
14 S. Pinker, *Better Angels of our Nature*, op. cit.
15 BBC World Service, Jun. 6, 2020.
16 From Valparaiso Chile, '100 years of Women'. BBC World Service, Nov. 27, 2020.

and thus misses the point of its generality. In warfare, rape is as normative as killing yet killing in war could not be a war-crime or an abuse of Human Rights. As there has never been a war in which killing and raping are not commensurate, warfare is both killing and raping.[17]

## A Gender Distinction

The psychological rapid rise in libido at puberty is accompanied by an equal increase in the power of destructiveness. On the horizontal, siblings and their heirs have always fought, it is a condition of the degree of their same-ness and difference, but as with incest, murder will seem nearer than ever with puberty; death features as fully as sex in the psychology of adolescence. The problem is that women's proclaimed exclusion from fighting has meant that they are also largely excluded from analyses of war. Does war construct gender difference as part of its creation of civilization?

Women are considered excluded from warfare for the very reason that they are women, not because they cannot or do not want to fight. Indeed women fight in wars, but their fighting gets written out of history so that today 99.9% of officially recognized combat troops are men.[18] In his book, *Better Angels of Our Nature*,[19] in which he tries to persuade us that we are be-coming ever less violent, the cognitive psychologist Steven Pinker comments

---

17 Except that they are also distinct: war despite its many abuses is a 'legal' allowance; the status of rape is uncertain, sometimes subsumed under sex-trafficking or prostitution: the United Nation's position on prostitution can illustrate this prevarication:

> It is important to note that when the Trafficking In Persons Protocol was negotiated, Member States decided to keep the issue of prostitution within the domain of national competence - that is, as a question of national policy for the discretion of States.

Effectively rape is the equivalent of a prohibited 'murder' which the raped person has probably physically survived as people sometimes survive attempted murder. The failed murderer/successful rapist will try to plead '[wo]manslaughter'; whatever happens to the victim, someone who rapes is likely to rape again so all women are always in danger.

18 I am omitting the previously mentioned very gender-differentiated inclusion of women in the Israeli military and the very deliberately egalitarian place of women in the Kurdish struggle against ISIS and many historical precedents.

19 S. Pinker, *Better Angels of our Nature*, op. cit. Elsewhere in his book, Pinker records re-search that indicates that in fact it is not young men or even adolescents who can claim this privilege; it is toddlers in what he describes as the 'aptly named "terrible twos"' (p. 483); see Chapter 4. A psychoanalytic perspective resolves Pinker's puzzle: humans are histor-ical persons with a future; not only are all of us still psychically the toddlers we all once were but young men repeat their toddlerdom with the huge additions of puberty and thus become humankind's most violent group. Although we develop from past to present, if we are to argue that war is endemic to human society and thereby constructs a gender differ-ence, we must trace instead a life backwards from the present to some construction of that past; although in some ways we are changed utterly in adolescence, we always project our future and past fighting.

that it is easy to document but hard to explain why young men are the most violent group within the human species. Just as marriage is based on the prohibition of incest, so the 'allowance' of war and warfare is dependent on the prohibition of murder. In what is only a seeming paradox, war would not be war if violence were not forbidden. Of course, war uses violence but to be productive of unconscious processes its legality rests on its prohibition. War itself, or war and peace as dialectical terms in which war emerges elsewhere,[20] is always present as one of the main ways by which humankind becomes social.

Survival of any sort brings with it the ecstasies of being alive. However, war's brotherhood makes ecstasy a centre-point – are there traces here of the toddler's excitement at the prospect of eradicating its new sibling? What is undoubtedly prominent is the thrill of the group whose necessity was, as Buxbaum argued, a noted feature after puberty. Steven Pinker quotes the Vietnam veteran and former US Marine, now well-known writer, William Broyles, who in his *Esquire* article 'Why men love war' (1984), wrote:

> The enduring emotion of war ... is comradeships. A comrade in war is a man you can trust with anything, because you trust him with your life ... war is the only utopian experience most of us ever have. Individual possessions and advantages count for nothing: *the group is everything*. What you have is shared with your friends. It isn't a particularly selective process, but a love that needs no reasons, that transcends race and personality and education – all those things that would make a difference in peace.
>
> (p. 56, my italics)

In fact, although most of the world can be rallied into the symbolic brotherhood of war, most do not belong to it. Through what we might here call the 'secondary' ideologies of religion, nationality and ethnicity, the excluded men can be temporarily incorporated into the military brotherhood, the 'vile' can 'gentle their condition', briefly they may share Broyles' utopia. Those who used to be referred to as 'cannon-fodder', Falstaff's erstwhile companions, Pistol, Nim, Bardolph, the Vietnam Vets and the rest, the wretched of the earth, are called out of poverty and immiseration to fight

---

20 Pointing out that war's monuments and weapons are cultural artefacts, Fernand Braudel, historian of the Mediterranean, has a general proposition which is crucial: 'Did the end of ... war mean peace? Not entirely, for *by some apparently general law*, warfare simply took on new forms, reappearing and spreading in this guise' (my italics). *The Mediterranean and the Mediterranean World in the Age of Philip II*, Volume II, trans. Siân Reynolds, Berkeley: University of California Press, 1995, p. 865. The way wars are fought is very various. It is then a 'general law' that although war is of course not all there is to society, nevertheless, so far war is coterminous with it. From the perspective of unconscious processes, legal warfare touches on traumatic origins in that it is compulsively repeated and never abandoned.

and once the battle is lost or won, it is to a peacetime of poverty and immiseration that the vast majority, the mass of humankind, dead, raped, mad, maimed or alive, oppressed will be returned. Why then do men 'go to their graves like beds'? (*Hamlet*, IV.4.54). As Broyles says: the comradeship or brotherhood of war 'transcends race, personality and education'. We need to listen again to what Pontalis made of fratriarchy.

A Commander today, as with Shakespeare's Henry V yesterday, can only conduct war if he creates a temporary brotherhood. But reciprocally, to date we have wars in order to renew regularly the gendered brotherhood of society – fraternity. Because warfare constructs human society, the prohibited violence between siblings in adolescence is sublimated, socialized and reconfigured in the brotherhood of warfare. Although warfare may be planned patriarchally, it is young men, banded and bonded together, who do the fighting. The social depends not only on those who are included but also on those who are formally excluded. Warfare it seems is gendered not just incidentally but as a constructor of a gender distinction within the social. While it is the eternal seriality of brothers that fight, it takes two, a pair to marry, but does marriage being assigned to women play the same role as the key to a gender distinction?

Siblings' love of 'the other as oneself' in infancy and childhood is given in puberty both a huge physical thrust and a new psychic dynamic. The brief sorties into 'being in love' are lateral relations; if the girl is more often the baby, then being loved as though one were the same person as the adoring toddler-lover has its compensations on which marriage bases its dreams. For the husband, making the wife the same as oneself makes the self safely bigger, 'a self king' as *Twelfth Night's* Orsino describes it. Sister–brother (actual or social) are in a paradoxical situation – their intensified incestuous desire will be subject to their own super-egoic prohibition at the same time as it must provide the psycho-physical basis for marriage in the 'in love' sorties of adolescence, the confusions about boys as with Winnicott's Sarah (Chapter 5).

There is nothing in the sex-differentials of biology that makes either sex less or more sexual than the other. Freud certainly describes the pre-marital adolescent girl and boy as both overwhelmed by the strength of their sexual drives. Yet in psychoanalytic theory, the working woman, that is to say, *every woman* is 'male' with a 'male' libido ('more masculine' as Freud puts it in 'Femininity') except, that is, for the wife whose work as a wife is declassified; whatever the rationalization, it is never counted. Excluded from the economy the housewife becomes what was her call-out if someone knocked at the door in Imperial China – 'no-one is at home'. The 'emptiness' of the 'annihilated' toddler repeated in adolescence for both genders (which Anna Freud describes) becomes for the adolescent girl, but not the boy, a preparation for the 'no-one' wife which masquerades as the only someone she can be – as the Duke in *Measure for Measure* says to Isabella: 'Why, you are nothing, then …neither maid, widow, nor wife?' (V.i.179–80). I found the same when researching the census in the UK in the early 1960s – there was simply no category for women except as daughter, wife or widow.

Above all, marriage is for the Oedipally 'sexually differentiated' mother and father who can properly only come *after* legal marriage. Marriage has to be already firmly in place for couples, in particular for the mother to be an acceptable parent. So the bisexual 'masculine' woman of the shared 'male' pre-Oedipus and the Oedipally 'sexually differentiated' mother are psychologically at odds with each other. And marriage cements the opposition: a non-married working woman versus a nobody wife and an ideal mother. This is the entirely societal division that Jacques Lacan and his followers would have us believe is original and integral to a divided psyche that defines and differentiates the woman *qua* woman – in herself: 'Her desire is to be. She participates in creation. But that is also how she is once more divided. It is the dividing of women, their suffering and their jouissance'.[21] This purports to tell us what a woman is and fails to address how she comes into being from a bisexual person as Freud rightly stipulated. Either unconsciously rooted social exclusion and/or pre-conscious and conscious 'allowances' and practices produce this Lacanian vista of a forever-and-a-day divided non-self in which one aspect is against the other as though it were set in stone as an original and essential definition. This division is intrinsic to women only as a condition of our oppression on the vertical family axis.

Psychoanalysis has firmly entrenched as a concept vertical 'sexual difference' and its allied notion of a permanent 'repudiation of femininity'. Neither pertain on the horizontal axis. 'Gender' as a social construct in distinction from or in relationship with 'sex' as a biological or possibly further constructed 'given' is now so widely used that a psychoanalytical specification can do it no harm and hopefully might lead to some hitherto under- or unexplored dimensions.[22] Psychoanalysis needs 'Gender' as a descriptor on the horizontal axis it neglects.

Something entirely new and absolutely different happens when a new baby is considered positively or negatively, when a child is a toddler. A younger child may know it is a sister or brother to its older siblings but as this involves neither trauma nor prohibition it will be descriptive not definitional. However, the actual or prospective addition has to be *a sister or a brother and cannot be neither nor both.* This is a categorical distinction of gender on the basis not of biological sex but of siblinghood. However strong or weak or non-existent a gender identity has been hitherto, it will have been based on *social interpretations* of biological sex and anatomy.

21  E. Lemoine-Luccioni, *The Dividing of Women or Women's Lot*, London: Free Association Books, 1987, p. 101.
22  Judith Butler now convincingly argues that the biological is also a construction as indeed in some sense it must be.

I propose that from now on 'gender' be used to describe all lateral social relationships which themselves emanate from siblings; this is a psychoanalytic use of the concept of gender. 'Gender' is meaningfully cognate with 'social sex' as its synonym in languages where the term cannot be used. This application of 'gender' matters because it marks the shift from automatic immersion in the existent social world into which we are conceived and born to the formation of the group that makes us participant in its construction and destruction. It is at this juncture that the sibling terms 'sister' and 'brother' are internalized as the gender which one is. There will be same sex or other sex pairs or a transgender position in the seriality of siblings on a horizontal axis. Seriality is in itself a position – as with a very gifted transgender boy described by Robert Stoller, who wanted to be his sister and argued that we are all different just as each snowflake is crystographically distinct. He was refusing 'sexual difference' and thus technically psychotic as is any small child, as in part we are all.

In order to use 'gender' as a concept, psychoanalytic practice and thinking has to address the primarily repressed gender *indifference* of the sibling trauma – a subjective 'gender' distinction does not yet feature here, just as 'sexual difference' does not feature before the castration complex. The unconscious (as well as conscious and pre-conscious) gender distinction only comes with the categorizations of 'sister' and 'brother'; all the defences such as 'splitting' that come into play are psychosocial expressions which refer to the sociology or biology of siblings. These can be same sex or other sex – that is not the issue. Pontalis' pairs of murderous brothers came from the same mother which Pontalis considered might be the determining problem. However, as was argued in Chapter 6 it is not the mother but dealing with the incest and murder taboo with someone who is sociologically or biologically proximate, or classified as such, that is at stake.

Lateral gender relations come into place with sisters and brothers negotiating incest and murder in relation to each other with the law of the mother; this is analogous to the advent of incest with the mother and murder of the father producing 'sexual difference' under the law of the father. There is nothing intrinsically oppressive about the social sibling relations which gender as a psychoanalytical category of analysis describes. Yet both 'gender' and 'sexual difference' are used more widely and loosely than the core prohibitions on incest and murder which psychoanalysis needs to specify. Nevertheless, something *is* missing in this specification: it is not possible to grasp the crucial contribution of the individual and social person to the construction of human sociality – nor therefore to oppression and being oppressed within its boundaries.

# Chapter 10

# Fratriarchy – Tomorrow, Today and Yesterday

Two-year-old girls as well as boys have tantrums. How is it that girls come to be unviolent and to receive murderous and sexual 'domestic' violence as a defining feature of their being women and commensurately boys perpetrate violence as a defining descriptor of their manhood? The answer does not have to do with children and their parents but, instead, with sisters and brothers and those who later come to stand for them as partners and enemies in the social world.

Some fifty years ago I presented the question of worldwide and world-long 'sexual difference' as a primal social construct under patriarchy. *Psychoanalysis and Feminism* (1974) turned out to be the culmination of an account of the psychology which I had found to be missing in my 'Women: the Longest Revolution' (1966).[1] That particular essay had hit the ground running, as the same year had set a marker for second-wave feminism with the foundation of NOW (the National Organization of Women) in New York. I was working in both the UK and the USA and was struck, indeed staggered, by American feminists' instant pillorying of Freud and psychoanalysis.

In the mid to late sixties, psychoanalysis did not feature in the emergent women's movement in England. But in the US a popular calendar presented a dart board of Freud's head with a dart through his eye: how vaginal frigidity had been made to trounce clitoral sexuality was a focus of the assault on psychoanalytic theories of sexuality. *De rigueur*, the forthcoming big-selling books would have a chapter blaming psychoanalysis for its role in patriarchy. Back home I went to the library to read a few essays by Freud and ended up reading all twenty-three volumes of his collected works. The effect was that after a few try-outs,[2] *Psychoanalysis and Feminism* was published in 1973/74 and was effectively a modest 'best-seller', translated into

---

1  'Women: The Longest Revolution', op. cit. and 'Reply to Q. Hoare', *New Left Review*, vol. 1, no. 41, pp. 81–3, 1967.

2  Juliet Mitchell: 'Why Freud?' *Shrew*, Dec. 1970; 'Mailer's Sex Ego, So the Revolution Called Again', *Modern Occasions*, vol. 1, no. 4, pp. 611–8, 1971; *Woman's Estate*. Pantheon

DOI: 10.4324/9781003347125-15

some eighteen languages. Wanting to know the material source of Freud's theories, I trained as a psychoanalyst and shifted from being a theoretician to a practitioner. Fifty years later this book on violence and fratriarchy is the sequel to that earlier analysis of sexuality and patriarchy.

*Psychoanalysis and Feminism* aimed to convince feminists that we must use psychoanalysis to understand how an oppressive *patriarchal* division of the sexes is embedded in everyone's unconscious processes. Now, reversing the book's audience, *Fratriarchy: The Sibling Trauma and the Law of the Mother* introduces to psychoanalysts my feminist thesis: the universal violence against women is initiated by the wish to eradicate a sibling who replaces the toddler as the baby. It suggests how, while psychosocially the brother remains older and dominant, the first sibling becomes a sister who becomes a wife or a sex-trafficked women who can be killed or raped. While this is partially unconscious, it is also a primal process of socialization along a horizontal axis. It underlies the *fratriarchal* dimension of the oppression of women.

Contemporary feminism has gratefully taken and intelligently used a great deal from psychoanalysis; although there are signs of this shifting, the exchange has not been reciprocal. It had been so with the shared interest in the mother by first-wave feminists and first-wave women psychoanalysts mentioned by Freud (Chapter 8). Here with the social individual in mind we can note the absence in psychoanalytic thinking of the feminist understandings of gender, of the sexed nature of oppression and with it the ego-syntonic nature of male hysteria, and of the need to politicize the private personal world in which the mother is idealized and exploited.

If we are to take seriously the place of the individual in the social, we need to include 'gender' as a category of analysis in our psychoanalytic clinical and theoretical thinking and thus make psychoanalysis useful to the study of gender – and, at least as importantly, vice-versa. On the vertical axis, 'sexual difference' embedded in the differentiating Oedipus complex of the girl provides a way of understanding the oppression of women. Even if of the still so far away, gender opens a vision out of this world-historical situation.

Oppression is omnipresent but, I suggest, as far as the oppression of women is concerned, its modality also differs on the horizontal from the vertical axis – differs, that is, from a psychoanalytical perspective when its context is *either* 'gender' *or* 'sexual difference'. Gender is a wider category of analysis than 'sexual difference'. It can manifest for all lateral relations as bisexuality, un-gender and the multiplicity of trans-gender, as the alternation of others and selves, and as pairing sisters within the framework of seriality or sisterhood. Above all, it is not limited to or co-extensive only with

Books USA 1971/2 and Penguin UK 'The Ideology of the Family and Psychoanalysis', *Modern Occasions*, pp. 49–65, 1972.

sexuality; when it implicates the Other, the significance of death predominates. So, with a psychoanalytic framework for the horizontal axis, we need to read together 'gender' and 'oppression' as – prospectively – conceptual not descriptive terms. What is offered here is only a résumé as we conclude with what could be a beginning.

## Gender and Oppression

'Oppression' applies to women in our generality – to rich and poor, to those of us who are individually highly privileged as well as to those who are abused, personally or collectively. Oppression is a material condition that also exists in the head and the heart; whatever the momentous improvements, the generic status of oppression persists. It is not a signifier of greater or lesser individual distress, it applies to the intrinsic – potentially and actually murderous – violence done to a recognizable collectivity as an in-built feature of the dominance of the status quo. As a technical term it has not as yet found its own defining features – although it is characterized by a covert violence from the dominating group which is often only perceived when it becomes overt – which it always does.

Many different peoples are 'oppressed'; local conditions feature within the unity of oppression. However enjoyable life may be for individual women, however many women 'dominate', they are definitionally oppressed as a collectivity in relation to the collectivity of men as the dominant group. Overwhelming worldwide division into wealth and poverty permeated by social class features in every oppressing and oppressed group. Many men may be hugely disadvantaged as individuals or members of another oppressed group. As large numbers of individual women are privileged, so many individual men do not dominate. This is about the 'generalized' social person and the individual within the social.

For the horizontal axis, the oppressed sister needs to join the mother who already features as adversely 'sexually different' and *outside* society in a vertical psychoanalytic account. Furthermore, Freud's theses suggest that marriage for a woman is both all-important and yet second best to gaining the father's desire, and motherhood is only satisfactory with a penis-bearing son. But for the lateral social sister, it is only in her vertical position as future mother that this applies. Because of the earlier taboo on lateral incest with the brother, her husband has to be the brother's friend rather than the reincarnated father of the vertical axis. The sister is not an Oedipal girl within the patriarchy where she is a daughter; however, something happens to her equal status with her brother under the Law of the Mother. It is for this sister in her lateral relations that we need a psychoanalytical perspective. As a sister in both her seriality – other sisters and sisterhood – and in her pairing, she is prohibited from committing incest and murder along with her sibling and, because of the prohibition, is thus *within* society – how and where can we locate her social 'oppression'?

## Simone de Beauvoir

In the days when she was protesting women's oppression but was not yet calling herself a feminist, Simone de Beauvoir ended *The Second Sex* with the hope that women could enter the fraternity. But could we? And if the sister could, would this end women's oppression? De Beauvoir had written: '[Woman] is defined and differentiated with reference to man and not he with reference to her; she is the incidental, the inessential as opposed to the essential'.[3] An all-important start had been made for an analysis women-men by de Beauvoir and at the same time by Frantz Fanon for the colonized–colonizer relationship. The theses of both presuppose that we take the essence of human relations as the play of co-creating 'self' and 'other' and that it is the abuse of this that characterizes oppression.

If one social group is regarded as always the Self and another social group with identical human characteristics is constituted always as Other, then we have a key aspect of the psychological structure of oppression. The divided self, which for Jacques Lacan defined the woman, defines the oppressed – 'selves' to themselves, 'other' to the oppressors. Self and Other as separate is a relationship of dominance. Although women and men's relationship to each other has looked various and has been experienced variously over the millennia, its core determinant of female *object*, 'Other', and male *subject*, 'Self', has always been the same.

De Beauvoir argued that women were unique in their oppression because there was no 'before' when they were un-oppressed. But this looks different both from an anthropological perspective and, if we recognize bisexuality and the mother's law, from the viewpoint of the horizontal axis. However, because of the dominance of the father's law the oppression of women does become seemingly eternal and all-embracing – such that, as mentioned previously, other oppressed groups become categorized as 'feminine' over and above their own specific oppressed history.

## Envy, Penis-Envy and the Oppression of Women

Where psychoanalysis needs the concept of oppression it has instead an analysis of the envy which is oppression's off-shoot. Melanie Klein made universal envy the immediate and innate direct expression of the death drive – Klein's is a major (and disputable) theory that can be used and taken

---

3   S. de Beauvoir, *The Second Sex* (1949), trans. H.M. Parshley, London: Jonathan Cape, 1953, p. 16.

somewhat differently. The oppression together with the envy which is its inevitable emotion will need its specificity (such as penis-envy) to be seen in the context of its universality, as it is in Klein's analysis. If women envy the penis, so too may Blacks or the Colonized envy white and colonial power. The problem for black people in their oppression is the self-superiority of white people; for the colonized, the self-certainty of the colonizers; and where women are concerned, the omnipresence of patriarchs. Slavery, which has been endemic for the greater part of human history, will have its envies somewhere and anywhere. Why envy and the death drive matter here is that Freud in a way that echoes popular conceptions increasingly made penis-envy a defining characteristic of women and one which becomes symbolic with the castration complex, whereupon a series of psychic equations culminate in the transposition, for the woman, of the penis into a baby. Freud suggests that penis-envy persists as effectively a definition of women to the extent that it is possibly unanalyzable.[4] Does 'oppression' turn the *generality* produced by the law of the mother into a *universality*?

That the oppressed (including and beyond women with our penis-envy) should be envious seems obvious – but what of those who are envied? Being envious is an unpleasant emotion to contend with, yet is being envied the condition that appears to avoid envy but is actually its other side? Taking the major characteristic of wealthy democracies to be the ever-widening canyon between the poor and the rich, are the rich hoping to avoid envy by being envied? There is plenty of evidence that the mega-rich are no happier than the mega-poor so could it be that it is universal envy which is in play here? Obviously, there are political, economic, demographic and other reasons for which the power is craved. However, the socio-psychological and emotional also feature; what would seem to be crucial is that wealth bestows immunity to the law enabling the mega-rich to act as they wish with impunity – a toddler's dream!

Even if excessive riches are bestowed beneficially there is the benefit of power for the giver and vulnerability for the receiver. As in our cultures we actively envy rather than fear the evil eye, what are the 'democratic', definitionally un-oppressed mega-rich up to? The epiphenomenon that confronts us in this ever-increasing divide between the poor and the rich is that the latter – perhaps unconsciously – know that their task of ensuring they will 'never-envy' is endless and therefore seems to demand ever-increasing wealth. For the enviable, the envious evil eye lurks around the corner – the victims of racism, colonialism, classism and sexism (suddenly

---

4   This is most obviously in the very late works where he is concerned with his legacy to psychoanalysis – for instance *The Outline of Psycho-Analysis* and *Analysis Terminable and Interminable*.

the castrating – rather than the castrated bitch), may be out to get those who may seem to be their oppressors.

Now at the time of writing in the pandemic of Covid-19, it is in particular women and children who face the severest immiseration because caring and being cared for are at a premium and women's unvalued work, both public and private, is simply too much. Apparently even in ordinary times Japanese women die in droves entirely because of overwork. Feminism is now a global politics. The origins of second-wave feminism began with a concept of oppression along with the fate of the colonized as argued by Fanon.[5] 'Oppression' in general had its earlier analysts, in particular in the theory built from the ground-up of poverty versus wealth by George Orwell.[6] If then, we first pursue penis-envy within this context, placing it in conjunction with oppression, and then envy becomes symptomatic more generally. This is where Klein's human-wide concept of envy comes in as an observation that relates it to the death drive.

## Actual Death and the Death Drive

The importance of Freud's 'death drive' is not only its fusion with the life drive to produce the aggression necessary to live or kill, for also at its core is the crucial 'return to the inorganic', to one's own death. From the moment of birth or conception the premature human being lives in the presence of its death – Winnicott claimed that what 'death' means to the baby is the mother's too-long absence; and an aspect of Pontalis understanding of the death drive is that a bodily enactment of an infantile experience of dying, an 'actual' neurosis when survived, is transformed into an internal psychic experience. However, for Freud it is only 'castration' that represents death. So what we have here is not the symbolic penis as a baby but the oppressor's violent fear that having his penis cut-off would be dying. The penis represents his present and future safety and survival only so long as he dominates. The oppressed can only envy what for the oppressor ensures he does not die.[7] And of course castration, like being murdered, does actually happen to

---

5   Today in the West, an alliance could be hoped for with Black Lives Matter.

6   George Orwell, whose thinking about 'oppression' is extremely pertinent, describes how when he worked as a colonialist in Burma, abuse of power was at his fingertips but also that the colonized oppressed oppressed those beneath. See Bernard Crick, 1980 *George Orwell: A Life*. Penguin Books.

7   See Elisabeth Bronfen: 'In respect of death, one could say, it names one thing ("I am the spectator/survivor of someone else's death, therefore I can tell myself there is no death for me") and means something else ("someone else is dead, therefore I know there is death")'; *Over Her Dead Body: Death, Femininity and the Aesthetic*, Manchester: Manchester University Press, 1992, p. xi. In short, representations *as* symptoms articulate unconscious knowledge and unconscious desires in a displaced, re-coded and translated manner.

oppressed people. Freud argued for the castration complex as death's representative because we have not died, though the issue, rather, is that we have 'died' but also in diverse ways that we have survived our death.

## Surviving and 'Survivors'

Pontalis noted that Freud was 'a survivor'. Those who more or less manage life have survived adequately; with 'biological' depression or deep melancholia, one cannot be sure: there can be too much death – the 'pure culture of the death instinct'[8] – for certainty. But between ordinary survival and being 'a survivor' on the horizontal axis, it would seem that dying intervenes again and the survivor such as Freud takes it on board – he has a body in fragments in his actual neurosis as Pontalis describes and, because he acknowledges, recognizes and uses it, he manages to come out the other side, as Pontalis perceives through the formulation of the concept of a death drive. There must be millions of such special survivors drowned in the Mediterranean Sea, incarcerated in the cages on the US–Mexican border, embedded in Central Africa and everywhere else in the world – but a few do succeed on their twelfth or thirteenth effort to survive the impossible. All peoples who are technically and horrendously 'oppressed' produce survivors who go through 'dying' as their brothers and sisters are murdered.[9] These special survivors will have known what it is to die, to want to give up and return to the peace, 'nirvana' or simply the nothingness of the inorganic. But they have fought against their own death drive – often for the sake of a child in their care. To repeat a refrain of this book – siblings simplify the issue. But

---

8  S. Freud, *The Ego and the Id* (1923), *SE XIX*, p. 53.
9  As this citation from Facebook illustrates: 'I need to drive my two-year-old to day-care tomorrow morning. To ensure we arrive alive, we won't take public transit (Oscar Grant). I removed all air fresheners from the vehicle and double-checked my registration status (Daunte Wright) and ensured my license plates were visible (Lt. Caron Nazario). I will be careful to follow all traffic rules (Philando Castille), signal every turn (Sandra Bland), keep the radio volume low (Jordan Davis) and won't stop at a fast food chain for a meal (Rayshard Brooks). I'm too afraid to pray (Rev. Clementa C. Pickney) so I just hope the car won't break down (Corey Jones). When my wife picks him up at the end of the day, I'll remind her not to dance (Elijah McClain), stop to play in a park (Tamir Rice), patronize the local convenience store for snacks (Trayvon Martin) or walk around the neighborhood (Mike Brown). Once they are home, we won't stand in our backyard (Stephon Clark), eat ice cream on the couch (Botham Jean) or play any video games (Atatiana Jefferson). After my wife and I tuck him into bed around 7:30 pm, neither of us will leave the house to go to Walmart (John Crawford) or to the gym (Tshyrand Oates) or on a jog (Ahmaud Arbery). We won't even walk to see the birds (Christian Cooper). We'll just sit and try not to breathe (George Floyd) and not to sleep (Breonna Taylor). These are things white people simply do not have to think about'. (24.4.21). One could also write this horrific and important history for domestically murdered women.

it is also more than this: life should be one of our aims and death should be another, or the other aim – a life and a death drive, in themselves separate but sometimes acting together. Surviving may change the quality of life or was it the quality of life that enabled the specialness of the survival?

## From Girl to Woman

When the girl enters puberty her bisexual self is flooded with the passions of incest and murder and their prohibition no less than for the boy as well as with the possibilities of reproduction, powerful genitality and the exciting and fearful bodily changes of secondary sexual characteristics – both boys and girls are alert to the self-sameness to each other within their difference. The girl will again be envious of the boy's invulnerability; the boy will dread its loss through castration. When the girl emerges into adulthood, she must care for her brother's brother who has become her husband and experience her exclusion from fighting as a perpetual fear of being the object of male violence – individually alone in the home and on the street, in the fields and marketplaces, and collectively in war's perpetual almost legalized raping.

Unlike under the Father's Law on the vertical, under the earlier Mother's Law we are analyzing the age-long and worldwide oppression of women *within society*. The mother's prohibition has allowed us, the sisters, into the construction of the social. Within society, reforms can be made: same-sex marriage and the quasi-official recognition of so-far oppressed trans-gender people are beneficiaries. The small child makes no distinction between same (homo) and other (hetero) relations or the enactment of bisexuality in a wider gender field. Despite the exclusion of the woman from society on the vertical axis, her inclusion within it on the horizontal indicates that oppression can be tackled within its social terms. But is this enough?

## 'The Personal Is the Political'

Feminism in the late 1960s produced the mantra: 'the personal is the political'. It emanated as a major and important protest against the equation of women with the family and the family with the private and the private as the virtually untouchable by the public and even by law and order. Making this personal world an equal aspect of the political world has made some headway in some cultures – but not enough. At the time of its formulation, I was a young university lecturer with slightly younger students, one of whom looked shell-shocked. Students at the time in the UK were not supposed to marry, but she was married and twice pregnant during the three years I knew her. She was being regularly raped and battered by her husband. Neighbours were not allowed to respond to her screams; the police whom she agreed to my contacting had no jurisdiction that allowed them to intervene or even enter the home – unless she was murdered – or as they put it, 'killed'. As the novelist, Elena Ferrante recalls: 'I grew up in a world where it seemed normal that men (fathers, brothers, boyfriends) had the right to hit you in order to correct you, *to teach you how to be a woman*, ultimately for your own good'[10] (my italics). The privacy of marriage and the family was sacrosanct. This still prevails in large parts of the world and in our own – although some laws have changed, the same response is still customary. Too often we personalize the political instead of politicizing the personal. And, unfortunately, without a horizontal axis psychoanalysis can feed into this dangerous mistake.

The human species is a violent one and seems to have simultaneously institutionalized as war and at the same time left raw as murder its instinctive aggression. As I ponder the winding down of this book the radio world service is announcing that more than sixty girls have been murdered as they left their school in Kabul, Afghanistan. Interviewed, the Afghani woman MP is saying that of course her personal life experiences produced her politics. The interviewer responds that if foreign troops were to go in against the Taliban then they would have to go into every country in the world to protect women's rights. That the personal is made the political gives breath to the struggle against violence in this – the longest revolution. Women are supposed not to be violent. This is why it is hard for them to be artists.[11] Not having access to our violence is as much a feature of our oppression as is the violence done against us.

## Denying Violence

Freud had hoped that what seemed like the unprecedented extremity of World War I would force its participants to call a halt to their *denial* of the horror and omnipresence of human violence; he felt that only when the denial of violence was rescinded could a route to pacifism be sought. The proposal of a 'death drive' was his contribution to stopping this denial; with this over-arching concept which could be explored people would have to acknowledge the presence of human murderousness. Immediately following World War I, he wrote on the social person[12] so prominent within war. The paternal Army and the fraternal Christian Church which he described are collectivities – however in both cases, patriarchal and fratriarchal, the framework of the explanation – theory and practice – was that of the family, not the social. It was this that Bion tried to put right with his study of group

---

10  E. Ferrante, *Frantumaglia*, op. cit., p. 349.
11  Artemesia Gentileschi had been raped by a family member – she painted Judith slaying Holofernes. Paula Rego contextualized paintings of personal and political abortions in Salazar's violent and lying patriarchal dictatorship.
12  S. Freud, *Group Psychology and the Analysis of the Ego*, op. cit., and see also the later *Civilization and Its Discontents* (1930), *SE* XXI, pp. 57–146.

psychology and Pontalis to fill in with an understanding of the supreme importance of death. In this book, the social is specified as the introduction
of a horizontal axis to match the vertical orientation of psychoanalysis and
thus take this social and this death drive still further.

My own *Psychoanalysis and Feminism* (1974) and its preludes in the latter
part of the sixties and early seventies urged a resistant Women's Movement
that Freud's theories were an analysis of, not a recommendation for, patriarchy. As such it could and should be used by feminism. We need now an
understanding of the contribution of feminism if we are to include the other
fifty-one per cent of the world's population into an analysis of unconscious
thinking. André Malraux wrote:

> I have experienced time and again, in humble or dazzling circumstances,
> those moments when the mystery of life appears to each one of us as it
> appears to almost every woman when she looks into a child's face and to
> almost every man when he looks into the face of someone dead.[13]

Was he correct to claim that men in their profundity contemplate dead men
while a woman's psycho-emotional depth has a live child at its source?

Lateral relations, a fully developed psychoanalytic portrait of the horizontal axis is mandatory in order to grasp the socio-psychological nature of
fratriarchy. To join the fratriarchy was what Simone de Beauvoir held out as
the hope for women – is it? Yes and no. While the symbolic world is patriarchal and holds dominance, does it trump the gender equality established
by the law of the mother? Or is it that largely, though neither uniquely nor
necessarily, brothers retain the stance of the murderous toddler and sisters
the position of the threatened but also cared for and caring baby? This possibility has raised its head here from time to time – but its fuller investigation
is for another study.

## Lateral Oppression

Wondering about Simone de Beauvoir's faith in fratriarchy was where my
intellectual and political interest in the position of women started at the
end of the 1950s as a mystified student in the privileged and rarefied social
class atmosphere of Oxford University where girls were one in twelve of the
student body. That there were gender problems seemed such an obvious but
unremarked consequence of a student body of privately educated 'public
school' young men, many of whom would become ruling politicians but
who – like Bion – had hardly seen a woman since being sent to an all-male

---

13 André Malraux, *Anti-Memoirs*, Harmondsworth: Penguin Books, 1967, p. 10.

boarding school at age eight or thereabouts. Adding the Mother's law which makes woman a citizen has been all-important; in addition to de Beauvoir's thesis of woman as the original and persistent Other is the further realization that the woman is also 'no-one' – which is both a curse and a blessing. To not exist as ourselves is impossible and outrageous, an act of oppression, but it also contributes to a profound survival and social strategy in which other peoples' existence as constituting a social entity can be as important as one's own isolation as an individual personality.

The action of the mother's law as an absolute prohibition ensures we are fifty-one per cent of the social human population – that is a finding of the horizontal axis and makes mandatory its contribution to our thinking. And of course, if we are in society, we can – and must – contribute to challenging its/our abuses and to changing it/them. The experience of oppression is one of created inferiority beneath constructed superiority and thus suggests verticality – but when we look laterally the picture changes. If the oppressed girl experiences penis-envy, what is commensurate with the soon to-be oppressing boy? I do not share Klein's thesis that envy is the death drive – but its importance as an organizing emotion seems undoubted. What happens with it on the horizontal axis?

## Fratriarchy

Although Freud mentions sisters or brothers frequently, there are no references to them in the index to the twenty-three volumes of Freud's *Collected Works* sibling 'avoidances', however, are noted. Sisters having to avoid their brothers is crucial. As well as this, the discussion of Goethe (Chapter 7) is a focal point for his general awareness of the sibling trauma, but it is *Totem and Taboo* which offers his clearest exposition of fratriarchy. The clans and tribespeople of *Totem and Taboo*, 'just like us' also have to turn the practical realities of death and life into cultural constructions and unconscious thinking and also have to survive them in their raw materiality. We can grasp this through the rare matriarchies and matrilineages that are still extant.

The Na of South-West China, richly described from scholarly research and prolonged participant observation by Cai Hua in *A Society Without A Father or a Husband*,[14] further demonstrate how, based on the crucial place of siblings, the extant past can help us to imagine a future. The Na as they call themselves, or more officially the Mosuo, make a gender distinction

---

14 Cai Hua, *A Society without Fathers or Husbands: The Na of China*, trans. A. Hustvedt, New York: Zone Books, 2001. I felt very excited when, finding this book on my shelves, I realized it had been sent to me by the author and that I had met the Na when I briefly visited China in 1982.

for the first time at age thirteen when the child becomes an adult. Prior to this they do not distinguish their children into girls and boys or differentiate into biological and social relations. The collective is a non-oppressive matriarchal organization. A father is a generalized social role rather than a biological designate. Sexual relations are never statutory but take place through the custom of 'a visit' whenever or wherever required. There is no marriage. The bonds of sisterhood as well as the responsibilities of the main mothers are strong. There is an unimportant horizontal gender distinction among adult collaterals but no vertical sexual difference. Importantly, the Mosuo suggest that crucial elements in Western patterns of relating would seem not to be hard-wired but rather very long term and customary. With this in mind, we can re-read Freud's 1913 contribution *Totem and Taboo* as a theoretical excursus into 'primitive' society different from, but analogous to the Na. Freud is reconstructing this from a twentieth-century viewpoint and finds these so-called 'savages' are 'just like us'.

The Mother's Law is not about symbolism or symbolic equations – that belongs to the Law of the Father. Through stories and narrative, rather, the mother and toddler realize that the infant has survived the sibling trauma – although the experience and fear of dying will come again and again, the toddler did not die. The resident storytellers of actual or imagined matriarchies tell of how death is survived – the story itself is an act of survival. The Na tell the tale of how their ancestors were not listening when they were offered the longevity of sixty years – so dogs obtained this sixty years and humans received the dog's allotted thirteen years. However, the dogs were willing to swap provided that with the exchange they were guaranteed three good meals a day. Thirteen 'dog' years is human puberty which became the most important occasion in Na existence – the hitherto completely undifferentiated and interchangeable females and males became gender distinct – and in a completely egalitarian way from now on they wore skirts or pants and became adults. *Totem and Taboo* tells a different story from comparable material.

### Re-reading *Totem and Taboo*

In Freud's mytho-anthropology, having slain the patriarch, the sons become predominantly brothers whose essential homosexual love for each other is sublimated into a fratriarchal social contract which, effectively as a side-issue, sees to it that in order to propagate their group they each must marry not their own but each other's sisters or these sisters' social equivalents. The sublimation of male homosexuality which produces the social contract needs a marriageable *sister* and nothing more.

What is important for us here is that, despite all the criticism it has received, *Totem and Taboo* (1913) is Freud's first overtly social text. In it he says that we have as much difficulty understanding the 'primitive' people who are its topic as we do understanding children, a thought that might cause surprise as the child seems to monopolize psychoanalytic attention. We know that the practice of 'infant observation' apart, it is the child in the adult, the baby in the child that is the object of psychoanalytic knowledge. But the observation seems more important than this frequently uttered truism. It rightly turns upside down, on its head, our common assumption that children are limited and simple: they are not. Psychoanalysis itself is extremely difficult because its struggle is to grasp something of the complex thinking of the child.[15]

Of use for our limited purposes here is that the complex, primitive people whom Freud is re-creating in this study function as a group according to kinship laws which are very much *not* those of the family but instead are of the wider social clan or tribe – comparable to Bion's social groups. As Freud reads both previous and contemporary anthropology and other scientific theses such as those of Darwin: manifold taboos are understood to be simply extensive and vastly elaborated prohibitions which are forcefully 'imposed (by some authority) from outside, and directed against the most powerful longings to which human beings are subject. The desire to violate [them] persist[s] in their unconscious...'.[16] The various and multiple taboos can be organized and reduced to two: once more the desire to kill and the desire for incest which are usefully elaborated here in all their variety by Freud.

There is the desire to kill first, the King or chieftain, second, the enemy, and third, the already dead who are also regarded as enemies – Macbeth must kill murdered Banquo's ghost who, together with his children, is his heir. In Shakespeare's *Measure for Measure*, Angelo must turn the condemned Claudio's apparent death into a certain murder to ensure Claudio cannot take revenge for his supposedly raped sister, Isabella. Freud selects the King as the kinship stand-in for a family's father, but for the horizontal axis it is the enemy, dead or alive, who matters most. Likewise, although in a complicated way incest with the mother and mother-in-law, as well as some aunts and cousins, is pre-historically taboo, it is the marriageable sister that is the focal concern of 'primitive' societies and of our lateral organizations. As every civil war highlights, brothers who are no longer brothers are instead enemies; those sisters who do not have to be avoided are instead wives.

Above all, what we must take away from *Totem and Taboo* is that, while Freud forgets that he is describing the social unconscious on the horizontal group axis, his interest and purpose nevertheless is that these primitive peoples whom he calls 'savages' are in their dealing with these universal processes, these desires and prohibitive taboos, *just like us*. What we have

---

15 This can be compared with Freud's irritation in the *New Introductory Lectures* with the public unawareness that scientific enquiry is never static or 'closed'.

16 S. Freud, *Totem and Taboo* (1913), *SE XIII*, pp. 34–5.

made unconscious for ourselves, in these clans and kin-groups will have been (or are) both unconscious and conscious rules and regulations. Thus, they are very helpful to think with. We have in a nutshell a starting point for the effect of the prohibition of the brother's desire for incest with the sister. Lovers and husbands are supposed to replace the all-desiring brother, but incest and murder lurk beneath the requirement.

'Wilt thou be made a man out of my vice? Is't not a kind of incest, to take life from thine own sister's shame'.[17] The sister Isabella and her abuser Angelo both know that for her to prostitute herself to Angelo in order to save her brother Claudio's life would be one of the many possible variants of incest; Isabella would be in her 'cousin' Julietta's place – 'Giv[ing] up to such sweet uncleanness [her] body/As she that he hath stained'.[18] As crucial and inter-linked is Angelo turning the legal hanging of this brother into his murder – 'That Angelo's a murderer, is't not strange?' Is this the scenario illustrated by Shakespeare's sonnets in which his male persona deeply loves a young man who in his turn will produce a child through a relationship with a woman? Thus, his homosexual desire for a younger man includes a vision of this lover's heterosexuality which is perhaps why commentators are never quite sure if the Shakespeare character loves a man or a woman. We might usefully continue to wonder about this problematic of primary homosexuality and secondary heterosexuality more generally; it comes up everywhere and may thus be the contribution of fraternity both in itself and as it underpins patriarchy.

Freud's anthropo-mythological account is a social story about the foundational moment of sociality. The range of avoidances with the sister are far and away the most prevalent of all the 'primitive' strictures; the rules and regulations for marriage which can only be with a sister or sister equivalent are beyond computation and of 'bewildering complexity' (p. 8). In a group situation the *brother's sexual desire for incest with the sister is so strong as to be almost unmanageable* and must be controlled. Finally, totems and taboos originally seem to pass through the female line – so that here in the *sister* of this primitive matriarchal *kin-group* may be a suggestion of the mother's law.

Where we can only have one mother whom we desire incestuously, a sister who, like her brother, is always plural even in polygamous practices, is singled out as a wife by the social arrangement and cut off from her other sisters. Thus, a division between the sister and the 'sistering' with other sisters is created which in turn informs the institutional sisterhood of nunneries, nursing – and feminism. In a fratriarchal as in a patriarchal society, in the larger struggle, it is sisterhood itself which has to be struggled for. In order to move forward we must turn back to the complex socializing child of to-day's horizontal axis; she is the heir to this neglected thinking.

17  Shakespeare, *Measure for Measure*. III.i.135–9.
18  Shakespeare, ibid. II.iv.54–6.

# Index

Note: Page numbers followed by "n" denote endnotes.